Jazz ————
———— Matters ————

The University of Arkansas Press

Fayetteville   London   1989

Jazz
Matters

Reflections on the Music
& Some of its Makers

By Doug Ramsey

With a Foreword by Gene Lees

Designer: Chiquita Babb
Typeface: Linotron 202 Sabon
Typesetter: G & S Typesetters, Inc.
Printer: Edwards Brothers, Inc.
Binder: Edwards Brothers, Inc.

The paper used in this publication meets the minimum
requirements of the American National Standard for
Permanence of Paper for Printed Library Materials
Z39.48-1984. ∞

Library of Congress Cataloging-in-Publication Data

Ramsey, Douglas K.
    Jazz matters.

    Includes index.
    1. Jazz music. 2. Jazz musicians. I. Title.
ML3507.R29 1989   781'.57   88-26165
ISBN 1-55728-060-6 (alk. paper)
ISBN 1-55728-061-4 (pbk. : alk. paper)

For Charlene

CONTENTS

FOREWORD

This introduction to a collection of essays by Doug Ramsey must, alas, begin with a lament. The volume contains between a third and half of his writings on jazz. Would that there were five more volumes to come from one of jazz's most perceptive judges and articulate chroniclers. There aren't.

The reason Ramsey has not written more in the field is that he has done it only and always as a labor of love, while pursuing a full-time career in another field. Doug is an outstanding television journalist. But the very career that has prevented him from writing more about American music imparts to his work in this field its distinctive qualities.

Most American writing on the subject has originated in New York City, with the bulk of other contributions coming from Chicago and Los Angeles. Doug brings another experience to the subject, and it imparts a freshness to his work. He is a true westerner, perhaps the first one to write significantly about jazz.

He was born in Choteau, Montana, October 3, 1934, a child of the Depression. His father did the various jobs necessary to survival, eventually making a good living in life insurance. The family moved to Wenatchee, Washington, when Doug was small, and he gives an impression of seeing himself as a product of that state.

He studied journalism at the University of Washington, and on graduating joined the *Seattle Times* as a police reporter and copy editor. That's where you really learn the trade. That's where you learn to get the facts right. That's where you learn to double check whether the fire was at 210 East Main Street or 210 West, and whether the owner of the building spells his name Green or Greene. That's where you learn to try to keep your opinions out of your writing, although the very act of choosing which facts to give the reader itself involves a personal judgment. It is where you learn the difference between a fact and an opinion. Facts go on the front page; opinions go on the editorial page. At least that's the way it's supposed to be. And good journalists strive to attain this ideal.

When Doug was faced with the choice of being drafted or joining one of the services, he chose the Marine Corps, was sent to officer's training, then shipped to Japan as a second lieutenant. At first he was an adjutant to a helicopter squadron, then he became the first Marine officer assigned to Armed Forces Radio. He spent two years in that position, and fell in love with broadcasting. When he came out of service he didn't even try to get a newspaper job. He went to work as a newswriter and broadcaster at radio station KIMA in Yakima, Washington. One day, as he was finishing a radio broadcast, he was told to get himself into the studio of the station's television division and replace someone who was unable to go on the air. His television career began.

From there he went to KYW-TV in Cleveland, where he wrote and produced documentaries, then he returned to the west as a TV reporter and anchorman in Portland. From there he went to New Orleans—a city with which he obviously feels a strong identity— where he was for five years principal anchorman at WDSU-TV, an NBC affiliate. He did a considerable amount of reporting for NBC during that period. He also was one of the original board members of the New Orleans Jazz Festival produced (at Doug's insistence) by Willis Conover and still remembered as one of the most intelligent festivals of jazz ever staged, possibly the best of all.

Then he went to WPIX-TV in New York, where he worked for three years as the station's principal anchorman. After that he covered Washington, the White House, and the United Nations as Chief Correspondent for UPI Television News. Then he was news director at television stations in San Antonio, New Orleans, and San Francisco.

Finally he went to his present job, Senior Vice President of the Foundation for American Communications, which is sponsored by various news organizations and foundations and devoted to improving news coverage of political, scientific, and economic issues. He now lives in Los Angeles. But the breadth of his viewpoint is the consequence of all those years in cities other than New York and Los Angeles; his writing about jazz in Texas, for example, offer us insights into the practice of the art in all that fly-over country that New York and Los Angeles people too often forget exists.

The skills of the journalist were not the only assets Doug brought to his writings on jazz. He has a keen technical insight into the music. Where did that come from?

Jazz musicians—some of them anyway—are prone to dispose of the awkward problem of reviews they don't like by sniffing that jazz critics are failed musicians.

Doug Ramsey and Dave Frishberg have in common that they both studied music and majored in journalism. Doug became a journalist, Dave became a musician. Nobody says that Dave Frishberg is a failed journalist. Paul Desmond studied creative writing at San Francisco State, never intending to become a musician. Nobody says that Paul was a failed writer.

Talent in one of the arts often and perhaps usually involves talent in two or more and perhaps all of them. Any number of writers and actors are enthusiastic "amateur" musicians. Anthony Burgess, known primarily as a novelist, is also a composer.

In one of the first essays of this collection, Doug makes fun of his alleged inadequacies as a musician, lending a superficial validation to that favorite dismissal of the critic by musicians. But it should be obvious that anyone who has ever struggled with a musical instrument is infinitely more able to appreciate the skills of its masters than someone who has never tried. And one does not turn to journalism because one has failed as a musician, no matter the self-congratulatory assumption of many musicians that no man in his right mind would do anything but make music. Journalism is a fascinating profession in itself, I sometimes think the most important profession of a free society, since democracy is premised on an informed electorate and the journalist is the man charged with informing it.

The ethical standards of the responsible journalist suffuse all the writing in this volume. And that is more unusual in jazz criticism than you might think. Much of the writing on jazz has been by people who were enthusiasts for the music first and writers second. Indeed, it was the passion for jazz that impelled its early champions to begin writing. And that is commendable: without them we would lack some of the information we do have about the music's history; unfortunately they lacked the disciplines of the historian and journalist, which is why much of it is in fact misinformation. Jazz has suffered from too much criticism and too little reporting.

Far too much writing on jazz has been by men whose primary if not sole interest was to impose their subjective responses to the music on the world as incontrovertible "facts" about the music, when these opinions were only facts about the writer. Their purpose has been to elevate the careers of those whose music they liked and to destroy those of musicians whose work they did not like. A decent and respectful curiosity fills Doug Ramsey's writing. When he expresses reservations about someone's work, he does so gently and reluctantly.

And he praises beautifully. This is the hardest thing to do in criticism. Any writer can make himself look clever by excoriation, which calls for witty analogies and comparisons, but a rare and sensitive gift goes into the writing of persuasive praise. It is a mark of Doug's ability that I found myself wanting to listen again to those familiar works and musicians he admires, and to seek out and explore the unfamiliar artists and records he praises. And Doug has a gift of imagery, rather like that of Whitney Balliett, to give impressions of music through words.

Finally, there is the tone of his writing. Like Doug, I have worked in television and radio, though not nearly as much. My career has been primarily in print and in songs, but years ago I worked for the radio division of a wire service. My job was to rewrite copy for radio stations. One night, as I was driving home from work, I heard a newscaster reading copy I had written. He stumbled over a phrase, and I realized immediately that it was my fault. The phrase might read well in print, but it did not come trippingly off the tongue. From that day on, I have written for the ear, not the eye, even when

I am writing for print. Since I learned that when we are reading silently the muscles in the throat move in subtle subvocalic simulations of the sounds, I have become convinced that writing that would be awkward in speech tends to also trip up the silent reader.

Doug writes for the ear. All his experience in radio and television is manifest in the tone of his writing, the sound of it, the lovely flow of one syllable into another. He says this is not conscious. But then, we chuckled a little about scripts you write for yourself and find, in the studio, are hard to read and require on-the-spot revision. You learn quickly not to make things difficult for yourself, and this habit of writing only what reads well aloud soon becomes intuitive, part of your working practice.

"The primary responsibility in writing about anything is to help people understand," Doug said.

That, above all, is what Doug Ramsey does.

—Gene Lees

Gene Lees is author of *The Modern Rhyming Dictionary: How to Write Lyrics; Singers and the Song; Meet Me at Jim and Andy's: Jazz Musicians in Their World;* and *The Will to Swing: A Biography of Oscar Peterson.* He is editor and publisher of *Jazzletter,* PO Box 240, Ojai, California 93023.

PREFACE

This book is a collection of articles, essays, and reviews written over the past thirty years. In many cases, introductory or following material has been added to supply biographical information and historical context. The book is not intended to be a history or an encyclopedia of jazz. Most of the major figures in the music are covered, even though there are not full-fledged essays on several important musicians; Duke Ellington, for an example, Count Basie for another.

Some understanding of the importance of Ellington's music and of his unique abilities as a leader is, I hope, provided in the piece about Clark Terry and in the section of Ellington reviews. Basie's crucial role in the development of jazz is dealt with in the Gene Ramey profile and in several discussions about Lester Young. The quintessential contributions of Young, Louis Armstrong, and Charlie Parker are currents that course through the book as they do through the music.

Recordings are mentioned with the most current catalogue titles and numbers available at the time of publication. However, it is in the nature of the record business that albums are unpredictably dropped, revived, remastered, pirated, and—in these days of cassettes, compact discs, and digital audio tape—assigned new formats. Compendium catalogues like Schwann's can be valuable in tracking down a desired recording; so can a knowledgeable record store, which, under the regime of chain outlets dedicated to quick turnover, is increasingly hard to find.

The book is intended to be helpful to readers new to jazz and interesting to those familiar with it. If it is, the author wants them to be aware of his indebtedness to the many musicians and colleagues who have shared their knowledge and insights. They include, for early ear training, formal and informal, Jack Brownlow, Don Lanphere, Bob Dyke, Johnny Wittwer, and the late Paul Neves; for long conversations or patient instruction, Dizzy Gillespie, Dave Brubeck, James Moody, Marian McPartland, Richard Allen, Al Belletto, Danny Barker, Ellis Marsalis, Eugene Wright, Chuck Mahaffay, Red Kelly, Gerry Mulligan, Clark Terry, Eddie Miller, Al Cohn, Barney Kessel, Nat Adderley, Joe Zawinul, Earl Turbinton, Willie Turbinton, Chuck Berlin, and Billy Taylor; also Paul Desmond, Cannonball Adderley, Zoot Sims, Woody Herman, Monk Hazel, Paul Barbarin, Allan Jaffe, Jack Teagarden, Sonny Stitt, Gene Ramey, Earl Hines, Budd Johnson, Blue Mitchell, and Larry Young, all, regrettably, gone; for encouragement and opportunities, Gene Lees, Dan Morgenstern, Willis Conover, Orrin Keepnews, A. Louis Read, Don Schlitten, John Snyder, the late Leopold Tyrmand, Ira Sabin, Greg Curtis, and the late Ralph J. Gleason. Special gratitude goes to Miller Williams of The University of Arkansas Press, without whose exhortations, patience, and guidance this book would never have been started or completed. To my family, heartfelt thanks for their forebearance.

Thanks are due and gladly offered for permission to reprint here the following reviews, notes, and articles from the sources shown.

"Art Farmer," *Notes on the Arts*/Smithsonian Institution, January/February, 1982.

"Art Pepper," *Radio Free Jazz**, September, 1976.

"Art Pepper's Last Chorus," *Texas Monthly*, September, 1982.

"Bass Hit," *Texas Monthly*, May, 1981.

"The Big Beboppers," *Texas Monthly*, May, 1976.

"Brother Ray: Ray Charles's Own Story," *Texas Monthly*, October, 1978.

"Bud Powell," RCA Bluebird note for compact disc remake, 1987.

"Cannonball Adderly," *What I Mean* (Milestone M-47053), 1979.

"Charles Lloyd," "Jazz Review" WDSU-FM New Orleans, February, 1968.

"Charles Mingus," *JazzTimes*, April, 1987.

"Chet Baker," *She Was Too Good to Me* (CTI 6050 S1), 1974, and *You Can't Go Home Again* (A&M/Horizon 25), 1977.

"Diz—or: On Creative Dignity," *Chronicles of Culture*, July/August, 1980.

"Don't Shoot the Critic; He's Doing His Best," Gene Lees' *Jazzletter*, May, 1986.

"Duke Ellington," *Texas Monthly*, June, 1978, March, 1984, and June, 1986.

"A Few of My Favorite Things," *Radio Free Jazz**, June, 1976.

"Four Tenor Saxophonists," *Texas Monthly*, March, 1981, and April, 1985.

"Frank Sinatra/Antonio Carlos Jobim," "Jazz Review" WDSU-FM New Orleans, June, 1967.

"Freddie Hubbard Live at Rosy's," *Radio Free Jazz**, February, 1979.

"Gene Ammons, "Jazz Review" WDSU-FM New Orleans, August, 1967.

"George Benson and Jack McDuff," *George Benson/Jack McDuff* (Prestige P-24072), 1977.

"George Russell," "Jazz Review" WDSU-FM New Orleans, September/October, 1966.

"Gerry Mulligan/Chet Baker: Carnegie Hall Concert," *Carnegie Hall Concert* (CTI 6054), 1974.

"An Hour with Clark Terry," *Radio Free Jazz**, June, 1978.

"John Coltrane," *Rain or Shine* (Prestige P-24094), 1980.

"John Handy," *Texas Monthly*, July, 1983.

"Keeping Time with the CLU and Other Thoughts," *Chronicles of Culture*, January/February, 1980.

"Lester Young," "Jazz Review" WDSU-FM New Orleans, August, 1966.

"Listener's Journal," *Radio Free Jazz**, July, 1976.

"Louis Armstrong: An American Genius," *Chronicles of Culture*, May, 1984.

"Love for Sale," *Texas Monthly*, January, 1980.

"Miles Davis," *Dig* (Prestige PJ24054), 1975.

"Modern Jazz Quartet/Paul Desmond," *down beat*, March, 1972.

"The Music," *Los Angeles Times, The Book Review*, March, 1987.

"New Orleans Jazz: A Family Album," *Tulane Review of Books*, 1969.

"New York Jazz Repertory Company," *Coda*, May, 1974.

"Ornette Coleman," "Jazz Review" WDSU-FM New Orleans, July, 1966.

"Phil Woods," *Musique du bois* (Muse 5037), and *Different Drummer*.

"Prince Albert," *Texas Monthly*, October, 1980.

"Remembering Desmond," *Radio Free Jazz**, 1977.

"Requiem for a Heavyweight," *Texas Monthly*, September, 1979.

"Riding on a Blue Note," *Chronicles of Culture*, February, 1983.

"Roswell Rudd," "Jazz Review" WDSU-FM New Orleans, December, 1966.

"Seeing Red," *Texas Monthly*, May, 1977.

"Stan Getz/Laurindo Almeida," "Jazz Review" WDSU-FM New Orleans, February, 1967.

"Stan Kenton: Artistry in Rhythm," and "The World of Count Basie," *Chronicles of Culture*, March/April, 1982.

"Stompin' by the Bayou," *Texas Monthly,* December, 1980.

"Take Five with Paul Desmond," *down beat,* October, 1962.

"Thelonious Monk," *Radio Free Jazz*,* April, 1977.

"Truth through the Art of Riff," *Chronicles of Culture,* November/December, 1979.

"Twenty-Fifth Anniversary Reunion," *25th Anniversary Reunion,* (A&M Horizon SP-714), 1976.

"Unabridged Webster," *Texas Monthly,* January, 1984.

"The Uses of Tradition," *Chronicles of Culture,* May, 1985.

"Wardell Gray," *Central Avenue* (Prestige P-24062), 1976.

"Woody Herman: 1963," Phillips, 1974.

"Woody Herman on Musicians, 'Civilians,' Recording Companies, Etc.," *Radio Free Jazz*,* April, 1976.

"Zoot Sims," *Texas Monthly,* September, 1985. *down beat,* January, 1970.

*Now *JazzTimes*

Jazz

Matters

When my family and I were living in New Orleans in the late 1970s, a friend asked my wife what career I would have pursued if I had not chosen journalism. My wife said she thought I might have been a jazz musician.

The friend's response typified how much Americans know about the music described to the point of cliché as America's only native art form. "Oh," she said, "I can't imagine Doug down at Preservation Hall with all those old men."

My wife's friend is a native New Orleanian, a sophisticated woman with a Ph.D. and a career. She is married to a medical doctor who is a respected educator and philosopher. She studied music for years and is an accomplished pianist. Both she and her husband are socially and culturally aware, yet her first and, it turned out, only accurate impression of jazz was of Preservation Hall, an admirable institution dedicated to the music as it was played during its infancy nearly six decades earlier.

That jazz had developed through several important stylistic periods, producing such masters as Lester Young, Teddy Wilson, Charlie Parker, Coleman Hawkins, Miles Davis, Bill Evans, and John Coltrane, escaped our friend. She had a vague familiarity with Duke Ellington and had heard of Woody Herman and Ella Fitzgerald ("Oh, is she a jazz singer?").

The lady would have known of Louis Armstrong, of course, and of Pete Fountain and Al Hirt. They are New Orleans celebrities. She would have been unaware of Ellis Marsalis, Al Belletto, Earl Turbinton, Al Hermann, James Black, June Gardner, Emily Remler, Johnny Vidacovich, James Rivers, and Red Tyler, a few of the superior jazz musicians active in New Orleans at the time.

People involved in or close to jazz perpetually tantalize themselves with the notion of widespread popular acceptance of the music they love. Just as the New Orleans woman did not know that jazz had developed into an art music, many musicians and aficionados fail to see that jazz has only a slightly stronger chance than chamber music of making it to the top of the popularity charts, or even of paying most of its players a comfortable wage.

For a few years in the 1930s and 1940s, when the big band phenomenon resulted in a congruence of jazz and popular music, jazz records sometimes became best sellers. That happened not because the music was jazz but because it was popular despite its being jazz. The high artistic quality of a hit like Erskine Hawkins's "Tuxedo Junction" or Charlie Barnet's "Cherokee" was coincidental. In succeeding decades when an anomaly like Stan Getz's "Desifinado" or Dave Brubeck's "Take Five" made the top-forty, there was a revival of the old hope, born during a few unreproduceable years of the swing era, that jazz could again be a part of mass culture.

It is understandably painful to jazz musicians to witness the enormous popularity of inferior music based on jazz, and to see many of its practitioners become wealthy. A talented musician working for union scale might feel despair to read in one day's newspaper that Bruce Springsteen, the rock star, earned an estimated $56 million in 1986–87, and in the next day's edition find Springsteen quoted, "Chuck (Berry) played in a lot of strange keys, like B-flat and E-flat," these "strange keys" actually being two of the least complicated. Like so much in life, commercial dominance by the slightly talented and musically ignorant is not fair. It may be time, however, as the brilliant alto saxophonist Phil Woods has suggested, for jazz players and listeners to accept the fact that their music is art music, that commerce is commerce, and that the more sophisticated and artistically complete jazz becomes, the less likely it is to be a wide commercial success.

Because of its enormous strength, vitality, and creative energy, jazz has from its beginning influenced trendy popular offshoots. Fusion, crossover, and the so-called New Age or earth music of the 1980s are only the latest manifestations of a tradition that goes back at least as far as the soupy sweet bands and chirpy pop songs of the 1920s. Indeed, the popular music of the past sixty years in virtually all of its forms, especially including rock, would not have existed had there been no jazz. This could fairly be called a mixed blessing.

Still, despite the occasional brief popular acclaim of a jazz artist, the mother lode of American music remains untapped by most Americans. It is that core music, developed by a handful of geniuses, with which this book is concerned.

A Common Language

1987

You don't need a degree in musicology to understand the language of jazz. It employs African rhythms and European harmonies; that's often said and true enough, although a considerable oversimplification. Jazz is based on the common language of music understood around the world.

The listener, whether musician or nonmusician, who is willing to spend the time and pay attention, can learn the idioms and vernacular of the language. It is simply a matter of absorption through exposure. My only caveat is this: in the learning process, don't waste your time listening to imitators and second-raters. Spend it with the masters, with Louis Armstrong, Charlie Parker, Lester Young, Duke Ellington, Count Basie, Teddy Wilson, Earl Hines, Roy Eldridge, Ben Webster, Bud Powell, Jack Teagarden, Coleman Hawkins, Dickie Wells, Fats Waller, Dizzy Gillespie, Thelonious Monk, Miles Davis, Bill Evans, John Coltrane, Red Allen, Art Tatum, Zoot Sims, Paul Desmond, Charlie Christian, Ornette Coleman, Hank Mobley, Milt Jackson, Django Reinhardt, Bob Brookmeyer, Cannonball Adderley, Art Farmer, James Moody. That's a partial list, but for someone unfamiliar with jazz it's a start.

Pure improvisation born of absolute inspiration, a solo created out of whole cloth, is likely to be as remarkable as it is rare. Most solos are combinations of inspiration and used parts. The creative process of improvisation is selective, and what is selected is influenced by a number of elements including the music's harmonic structure, the tempo, rhythmic qualities, the musician's fellow players, and his memory. His brain has a stockpile of musical knowledge, general and specific. The specifics include phrases from his own experience and that of others. They are pressed into service as quotations and worked into the new performance. Sometimes they are inserted piecemeal, sometimes merely alluded to.

The alto saxophonist Charlie Parker, possibly the most inventive of all jazzmen, was fond of interpolating into his solos, among other things, Louis Armstrong's famous introduction to "West End Blues," bits from Stravinsky's "Petrouchka," field hollers and gospel shouts, Alphonse Picou's classic clarinet solo from "High Society," snatches of popular songs, and phrases from Wagner's operas. He often incorporated quotes so ingeniously and with such a spirit of high hilarity that they are among the most exhilarating moments in music. Listen, for an example, to Parker's use of the opening notes of "Cocktails for Two" near the end of "Warming up a Riff" (Savoy 2201). His repetitions, modulations, and sardonic asides cause his collegue, Dizzy Gillespie, to erupt into a guffaw. The first-time listener is likely to do the same.

Like every art form, jazz has a fund of devices unique to it and universally employed by those who play it. Among the resources of the jazz tradition available to the player creating an improvised performance are rhythmic patterns, harmonic structures, material quoted from a variety of sources, and "head arrangements" evolved over time without being written. Mutual access to this community body of knowledge makes possible successful and enjoyable collaboration among jazzmen of different generations and stylistic persuasions who have never before played together. It is not unusual at jazz festivals and jam sessions for musicians in their sixties and seventies to be teamed with others in their teens or twenties. In the best of such circumstances, the age barrier immediately falls.

Maturity

1987

The young talent flowing out of New Orleans in the mid-1980s to freshen and strengthen the jazz mainstream could be credited in large part to one man, Ellis Marsalis. Marsalis not only fathered a pair of brilliant soloists in Wynton, a trumpeter, and Branford, a saxophonist; he taught his four sons and many other youngsters to play jazz. He taught them superlatively. For several years, the distinguished bandleader and patriarch of drummers, Art Blakey, virtually staffed his group with players developed in Marsalis's music school at the New Orleans Center for the Creative Arts.

Such musicians as saxophonist Donald Harrison, trumpeter Terence Blanchard, flutist Kent Jordan, bassist Reginald Veal, and pianist Harry Connick, Jr., learned their art from Marsalis at NOCCA. Marsalis is a first-rate pianist and a superb teacher. Like all good teachers, he has learned from his students, not music but a generational lesson of attitudes and expectations.

Marsalis was a member of the proud and iconoclastic generation of musicians of the late forties and early fifties, in love with bebop, disdainful of commercialism, unwilling to compromise musical principle for popular acceptance. Nonetheless, something of the attitudes of the twenties and thirties clung to those defiant young artists. If they no longer considered themselves primarily entertainers, they had inherited the conditioning of their predecessors in regard to pay and conditions. Black and white alike, jazz players had been trained by experience and tradition to accept low pay and humiliating treatment.

"We walked in with our heads down, went to the dingy little dressing room, took the bad pay. We figured that's how it had always been and how it would always be," Marsalis told me. "I've learned otherwise by watching my kids."

"A couple of times when Wynton's piano player has been out, I've played with his band for a couple of weeks. I've watched how their attitude toward the business of music affects their lives. These guys simply expect limousines, good hotels, and lots of money. And they get it. Now, I think that way too. When a club owner offers me too little money, I don't jive and shuffle and settle for it. I tell him what I expect. And I get it."

Wynton Marsalis is prodigiously talented. And he has not compromised artistically; that is a lesson he learned from his father. He and other members of his jazz generation are symbolic of a new self-respect and maturity. That is a lesson for their elders.

Don't Shoot the Critic,
He's Doing His Best

1986

If you heard me play the trumpet—and you never will—you would ponder the thin tone, lagging time, missed intervals, and wrong chord changes and be puzzled. Why? you would ask or, possibly, scream. Why does he make the attempt?

Let's admit the truth of an ancient suspicion frequently voiced by musicians. Most jazz critics are failed performers. Some have demonstrated their failure publicly and been laughed off the stand or, more likely, simply tolerated by real musicians; jazz players are among the most civil people and rarely show open contempt. Other critics are performers only in their living rooms or the closets of their minds and have never put their real or imagined musicianship to the test of combat. When a musician has been harshly handled by a critic, the conventional wisdom among musicians concludes, that jazz writer is a frustrated and bitter amateur who is driven by jealousy to try to tear holes in the achievements of the talented. Musicians say, altering a charge often made against teachers, those who can do; those who can't, become critics.

It has been years since I have inflicted on an audience other than my family my attempts at improvisation. One of the last public displays was a New Year's Eve gig with Don Lanphere at the Enchanted Gardens of the Chieftan Hotel in the heart of downtown Yakima, Washington. That was some years before Lanphere's Christian reformation, and about the only clear recollection either of us has of the evening is its conclusion. At dawn we stood calf deep in snow in an apple orchard playing "Auld Lang Syne." Some time later I took part in one of Les Lieber's "Jazz at Noon" pro/am events in the appropriately named Rough Rider Room of the Roosevelt Hotel in Manhattan. Zoot Sims was the guest star that day. Lanphere and Sims have the distinction of being the only two of the many Four Brothers thus afflicted.

Despite all of that embarrassment, I have always felt that if I had a few weeks to practice I could win an audition and play third trumpet for the Woody Herman Band. That's the solo chair, I believe.

I persist in picking up the horn and jamming with records, hamburger chops be damned. My current rhythm section of choice is Bill Goodwin, Hal Galper, and Steve Gilmore, on loan from Phil Woods by way of Jamey Aebersold's mail-order play-along emporium. I'll tell you this: I'm still fumbling through the bridge of "Chelsea Bridge," but those guys never complain when I have to go back over the transition from the five flats of the first sixteen bars to the four sharps of the bridge, or the bar change from $E7+9$ to A. Need I mention the D-flat$+4$ to $C7$ in the eighth bar of the bridge? Billy Strayhorn was a master of beauty, but a sadist. I'll tell you something else: Having humiliated myself repeatedly with that exercise, I stand more in awe than ever of Ben Webster.

When I start spinning out phrases of architectural logic; when I conceive of a quote to snuggle into a remote corner of a chord structure where it has no business fitting; when I ascend suddenly from a low G to a high F; when all of that inventiveness collapses in smouldering ruins, I appreciate Lester Young, Paul Demsond, and Ruby Braff. When I throw caution to the winds and blossom into a flurry of sixteenth notes, harmonics and halve-valve effects, doubling the double-time, and it sounds like a drunken bugler, Don Cherry begins to make sense. When, on the other hand, I put together a simple series of descending whole notes and the effect is of a first-year student laboring through Arbans, I see the genius of Harry Edison.

These excursions in masochism build character. I'm a better person because of them. And, I hope, a better listener and writer about music. So, friends, when a reviewer wounds you fairly or unfairly and you ask, "Oh, yeah, I wonder how well he plays?" the answer is probably that he plays badly. But give him the benefit of the doubt.

Maybe his trying to play at all has improved his hearing a little.

Keeping Time with the CLU
and Other Thoughts

1980

When you are sitting in the midst of a couple of thousand life insurance agents and their wives listening to the New York Jazz Repertory Company recreate Louis Armstrong, and the audience begins clapping time, and they do it on the correct beats (second and fourth), you begin to suspect that something may have gone right with American culture. Twenty-five years ago I sat in *Jazz at the Philharmonic* audiences composed largely of the jazz cognoscenti, and they invariably kept time [sic] on the first and third beats, a gross violation of hipness but one that was common in those days and, indeed, until recently.

Come to think of it, the mere fact of the New York Jazz Repertory Company or any other jazz band being engaged to provide entertainment for a conclave of insurance agents confirms that something in the collective unconscious has made average Americans feel the rhythmic essence of jazz, or at least has persuaded them to no longer regard jazz as a cultural embarrassment.

The site of this revelatory evening musicale was the Hyatt hotel in New Orleans, where the College of Life Underwriters was holding its annual national seminar. The concert was replete with ironies and coincidences. Here in New Orleans, possibly the birthplace of jazz, a band of New York musicians had been imported to pay tribute to America's Mozart, the New Orleanian who virtually created jazz as a soloist's art. Why bring a crew of New Yorkers, none of them with New Orleans origins, here to summon the spirit of Armstrong? A convenient booking for the CLU, perhaps, because of previous contact with the NYJRC or because Dick Hyman, the NYJRC leader, went after the business. Perhaps it was because the repertory company has in five years established a fine reputation with its skillful ensemble versions of Armstrong solos.

Nowhere in New Orleans, to my knowledge, is there a group of professional musicians that has shown an interest in preserving the letter of Armstrong's work. Whether or not there are musicians here interested in preserving the spirit of his work is the subject of debate among all levels and spectra of the jazz establishment in the city. And the city's own commitment to preserving its most famous son's memory is in doubt. The Armstrong Park project, on the site of the former Congo Square, languishes half finished under the administration of the first black mayor in New Orleans history.

At any rate, it would have been interesting to hear at the CLU affair a band from, say, Preservation Hall performing an Armstrong piece. The contrast with the slickness of the NYJRC would have been, at the least, stark. New Orleans players of approximately Armstrong's vintage are unlikely to demonstrate much fascination with the challenge of reading or memorizing someone else's solos, even those of the master. The spirit of independence that made Armstrong artistically possible is still abroad in the city, although not matched with his genius. It exists in younger musical generations as well, even among those not directly involved with jazz. The rock and soul performers who develop here, but must go elsewhere to flourish, are Armstrong inheritors. Listen closely to Dr. John, the Nevilles, the Meters, and you will find Louis in the phrasing.

Under the assumption that no one trumpet player can equal Armstrong, the NYJRC assigns his recreated solos to three. Played in unison, harmonized, and given group dynamics, the masterpieces, ironically, often take on less dimension rather than more, like butterflies pressed between plates of glass. But when Bernie Privin, Jimmy Maxwell, or Francis Williams steps forward for his own solo or to play obligatos behind Carrie Smith's evocation of Bessie Smith, the spirit of Louis fills the room, as if he were cheering his successors and scoffing at an arranger's attempt to capture his soul on paper. Nonetheless, Hyman's work is admirable. It has brought Armstrong's classic solos into the ken of people who otherwise would never have heard them, and it has recalled his blazing talent to those who might have begun to forget. Combined with film clips of Armstrong reminiscing and with snatches of his recordings, the NYJRC's program is a sort of portable museum, a musical Freedom Train dedicated to the glories of a major American artist. The insurance agents and their wives loved it, as they should have. But until recently, who would have dared to predict that they would sit still for it?

As the trumpet trio and Hyman, at the piano, were repeating the astounding 1928 improvisations of Armstrong and Earl Hines, not fifty yards away Hines was playing the first set of the evening in LeClub, the Hyatt's jazz room. At seventy-four, Hines is, if anything, an even more ferociously experimental creator than he was at twenty-three, when he and Armstrong blew the lid off the bottled-up possibilities of jazz soloing with "Weather Bird." Much of a Hines evening is devoted to paternally backing his sidemen and his protégé vocalist. He smiles engagingly, sings occasionally in a style composed of legato and gravel, and solos sparingly. He shows unflagging and apparently genuine interest in the efforts of his sidemen when they are soloing, urging them on and rewarding them with public praise, "Well done, young man, well done." It is fine entertainment and often more.

Then, Hines constructs a cathedral. It may happen during one of his stock items, possibly "St. Louis Blues" or "Rosetta," or it may come in a piece he hasn't touched in twenty years. Rummaging in the basement of the keyboard, applying rococo layers of chords in the middle and a lightning scattering of tenths on top, erecting arhythmic passages that somehow continue the beat, taking pauses that suggest a gliding eagle surveying possibilities, Hines is in full cry, eyes closed, head back, grimacing in intellectual strain and the ecstasy of creation. Possessed of a tone with the brilliance of polished metal and fingers with the speed of pistons, he indulges himself in the surprises he loves: runs, curlicues, doodads, pizzazz, castles in the air, tension, release, single and multiple explosions, harmonic excursions into unknown territory, feats of metric foolery. Conversation stops and the noisiest drunken life underwriter is compelled to listen. Other pianists look anxious; this is clearly impossible, and the impossibility has nothing to do with technique. That is why there has never been a successful Hines imitator. The imitation would have to go beyond notes. The most meticulously written transcription could not capture the joyous rage, the abandon, the whimsy.

Hines is of an era when jazzmen assumed that their obligation was to entertain. Talk of artistic matters makes him nervous and he appears not to understand when his music is discussed in terms of art. His club dates and concerts are designed to entertain, and they do. But at some point in nearly every Hines evening, he unveils his continuing artistic growth, all but unprecedented for a septuagenarian in jazz. Even Armstrong had stopped developing long before he reached his seventies. But Hines shows no sign of diminishing powers. No mere charming survivor, he can scare the hell out of you with his creativity. A giant is among us, still.

Hines died of a heart attack at his home in Oakland, California, on April 23, 1983. He was seventy-nine. He had been rehearsing a new band, an octet, which had been booked for a series of appearances beginning with a tour of the Caribbean.

Stompin' by the Bayou

1980

Having threaded his way through the cultural politics of Houston, in late September Lanny Steele produced the first annual Houston Jazz Festival. For the forty-five-year-old Texas Southern University music professor, jazz pianist, and entrepreneur, organizing the festival had been no cinch.

The music, as it turned out, was the easy part. Steele wanted the event to be free, as the Juneteenth Blues Festival in Houston has been since 1977. And he wanted it to be in Hermann Park's Miller Outdoor Theatre as is the blues festival, which his SUM Concerts organization also produces. Free concerts for the people in the people's city-owned theatre; why not? Well, because of the same kinds of problems Steele had encountered with the Juneteenth idea: the opera-oriented Miller board's proprietary feelings about "their" theatre, fear that jazz audiences (read "black") would cause disturbances, and difficulty in lining up funding.

But Steele went to work on the city and on corporations, wealthy citizens, the musicians' union, the Cultural Arts Council of Houston, the National Endowment for the Arts, and the Texas Commission on the Arts. Because of the enormous success of the blues festival (and the good behavior of its audiences) and because of his dogged persuasiveness, Steele brought all those elements together and got the somewhat reserved blessing of Mayor Jim McConn to boot.

The festival had an auspicious beginning despite a spate of hot, rainy weather that dampened all three nights of the event. Attendance was undoubtedly affected by the elements. The covered theatre was nearly full every night, but the hill that overlooks the Miller was too soggy for sitting.

Steele assembled an interesting blend of nationally known artists and Houston performers. I arrived on Friday, the second night of the festival, for a concert dedicated to the memory of Charlie Parker. Saxophonist Jimmy Ford, whose quintet a laggardly airline caused me to miss, reportedly played a first-rate set. I did catch Red Garland, the Dallas pianist who is one of Texas's most celebrated jazz artists, and the New York based sextet of Art Blakey.

In the fifties Garland preceded Bill Evans as pianist in the Miles Davis band generally conceded to have been Davis's best. Garland was a profound influence on the younger Evans. The Houston performance came just a few days after Evans's death, and Garland seemed to emphasize the elements of his own style that Evans had adapted. The most obvious of those effects is the use of a clearly struck single note in the right hand, sustained for several bars while the left hand continues to churn out accompanying chords. Evans's refinement of the device helped account for the celebrated floating feeling of his music: a masterful contrast of opposites, a fixed note heard against a backdrop of motion. Evans learned other things from Garland—certain voicings, a strong rhythmic approach to block chords, and the introduction of variety and momentary surprise into a solo by placing the beginning of a phrase so far behind the beat that it almost pushes the beat. All of this Garland wove into an "Autumn Leaves" solo so evocative that Evans's spirit filled the theater.

Decked out in a powder-blue jump suit, the white-bearded Garland received almost idolatrous ovations for every solo. He acknowledged them with delight, bowing low and beaming. Responding to cries of "play the blues," the quartet chose Thelonious Monk's "Straight, No Chaser." Garland built a passage of thundering, rolling tremolo, blurred it with an adjustment of the Yamaha electric piano, and brought the audience to its feet shouting. It was an uncharacteristic but undeniably successful bit of bravado.

Tenor saxophonist Marchel Ivery and drummer Walter Winn, Garland's more or less constant musical companions of the past few years, performed with their customary zeal. On "Straight, No Chaser," Ivery sent great growling, looping phrases into the moist air, ideas piling up like clay on a potter's wheel so that when the solo was completed it could almost be seen, whole and glistening. Winn is an artist whose painterly gifts of symmetry and color can be heard not only in his solos but in his accompaniments. Bassist James Gillyard is a valuable member of the rhythm section, but unless a bassist is an extraordinary soloist, a performance can be marred when he is assigned a solo on every tune. Garland, kindly leader that he is, lets everyone solo every time. The routine wears a bit thin.

The volcanic drummer Art Blakey is famous for recognizing and developing talented young musicians. Clifford Brown, Lee Morgan, Freddie Hubbard, Chuck Mangione, and Wayne Shorter are a few of the major soloists who matured in Blakey bands. The sextet he took to Houston has every indication of developing into one of his best units. It contains one player who seems certain to become a major jazzman, Wynton Marsalis, a nineteen-year-old trumpeter from New Orleans.

Marsalis's stunning technique embraces speed, absolute control, flawless pitch, and range to the top and bottom of the horn. His tone is fat and full and does not become pinched above high C. Those characteristics might describe many accomplished trumpeters being produced by universities. But Marsalis, who studied at Juilliard after leaving New Orleans, has something rare in a young jazz artist, a sense of tradition. His father, Ellis, is one of the most admired modern jazz pianists and music educators in New Orleans. Since Wynton was a baby, the family home has seethed with quality music of all idioms.

At the festival Marsalis's "My Funny Valentine" began as a cadenza that was a tour de force by itself. Then, in a duet with pianist Jimmy Williams, the trumpeter shifted into a faster tempo and played a solo replete with sixteenth and thirty-second notes, slurs, growls, half-valve effects reminiscent of the great Ellington cornetist Rex Stewart, and an allusion to the classic 1928 Louis Armstrong

introduction to "West End Blues." The solo, like virtually all of
Marsalis's work at the concert, had humor—not comedy, but a wry,
good-natured refusal to take itself too seriously. That attribute, together with the ability to conceive beautiful ideas and the virtuosity
to execute them, puts Marsalis into a select company of jazz players. If he maintains his sense of balance, and if the barracudas of the
music business don't try to capitalize on his artistry, Marsalis may
take off on a remarkable career as a creative musician.

Blakey's rhythm section is one of his best in recent years, with
particular rapport between pianist Williams and bassist Charles
Fambrough. No matter how demanding and complicated the figures he executes, Blakey maintains such an elemental, irresistible
beat that his drumming serves as a life force in jazz. When Blakey
solos, the other band members gather around him, watching and
listening intently and smiling broadly. In fact, the musicians so obviously appreciated one another that their good humor and enthusiasm radiated from the stage to the audience, which received the
Blakey sextet with a standing ovation after the first number, "Lift
Every Voice and Sing," and was on its feet often during the one-
and-a-half-hour set.

Alto saxophonist Bobby Watson and tenor saxophonist Billy
Pierce are Marsalis's companions in the Blakey front line. Watson's
Kansas City origins are on full display in his spacious, joyous,
jumping solos. Charlie Parker could be heard whenever Watson
played, but this talented young man also incorporated post-Parker
developments into his work. He shows every sign of becoming a
truly distinctive soloist. Pierce is a more subdued improviser. His
solos in the Wayne Shorter manner were solid and often interesting,
but without the exuberance of his companions' work.

The Saturday of the festival was Arnett Cobb Day in Houston by
proclamation of the mayor. The sixty-two-year-old tenor saxophonist, injured in a car wreck long ago, made his way onto the
stage with a pair of canes and used a stool to support himself between numbers, but Cobb's four pieces with the Milt Larkin All
Stars disclosed a huge sound and a vigorous style undiminished
since his work with Lionel Hampton in the early forties. Third ward

Councilman Anthony Hall presented Cobb with the mayoral proclamation. The saxophonist also received a portrait of himself by
Charles Ford. Cobb was given a standing ovation, then had to leave
for his gig at a nightclub. Life goes on.

The big band led by Larkin, who is seventy but looks fifty, had
an interesting mixture of young and no-so-young musicians, black
and white. Larkin's vocals on "Time after Time" and the bluesy
"Barmaid" were attractive, if a bit shaky in spots, and his valve
trombone solo on his old theme song, "I Love You," was mostly
inaudible. Strangely, even the younger members of the audience
seemed to know his hits from the forties. Larkin's loose conducting
style was eccentric but effective. The finest solo moments in the
Larkin set came from Jimmy Ford (whose ability to play like Charlie
Parker is almost eerie), pianist Lanny Steele, and tenor saxophonist
Larry Slezak. Slezak requires something less than a bar and a half in
any solo to begin generating gutbucket excitement redolent of the
R&B tenor bands of the forties and fifties. He is not subtle. He is
enormously entertaining.

Slezak was also featured in the Houston Jazz Society big band led
by Kit Reid. On a Bill Holman composition called "Ticker," he
took on avant-garde coloration but suffered no loss of his testicular
attributes. Fellow tenorist Johnny Gonzales was excellent in Frank
Foster's arrangement of John Coltrane's dreamlike "Naima," and
he roared through Don Menza's "Groove Blues" with a gritty tone
and a headlong swing reminiscent of Menza's own tenor work.

The HJS section work was polished and precise, and when the
band backed singer Horace Grigsby its dynamics were carefully
controlled to complement his smooth baritone. Grigsby, though a
pleasant vocalist, fools around with lyrics. When he tinkered with
Ira Gershwin's words the meter generally suffered. He redeemed
himself somewhat with a gently swinging "Like Someone in Love."

Longtime Houston bandleader and teacher Conrad Johnson's
Flight 80 big band sounded under-rehearsed, particularly on an intriguing Johnson composition called "Northdom" which had some
of the impressionistic qualities of the Boyd Raeburn band. I would
like to hear it after more woodshedding. Trumpeter Jeep Smith's

"All of Me" solo contained a series of Louis Armstrong phrases that were not merely tacked on but worked into the fabric of the solo.

To these ears, Johnson's only alto saxophone solo of the evening was the most original and personal statement of the set. It came in his composition, "That Woman," which opened with an ensemble quote from "Over the Rainbow" that led into a sort of neo-Gershwin interlude by pianist Marsha Frazier, who managed to incorporate some free touches in the manner and spirit of Cecil Taylor. Johnson's alto solo was the southwest blues in the tradition of Louis Jordan and Buster Smith—stompin'. It was a lovely moment.

Singer Mickey Moseley was featured with Flight 80. Although she had some problems with keys and forgot a few lyrics, her swing, good humor, and fine coloratura carried the occasion. Moseley is a hometown favorite, and the crowd loved her. The Flight 80 and Houston Jazz Society performances were both marred by the regrettable and widespread practice of leaders talking over the music, usually to credit soloists. Why can't they wait until the piece is done? Milt Larkin, bless his heart, usually did.

Houston has given the world a number of fine jazz musicians, among them Arnett Cobb, Jimmy Ford, Milt Larkin, Harold Land, Eddie Vinson, Billy Harper, Hubert Laws, the Crusaders, and Ernestine Anderson. No fewer than five members of the current Duke Ellington Orchestra are recent graduates of Lanny Steele's TSU Jazz Ensemble. And yet, says Steele, "Jazz in Houston is still something of an oddity. Maybe it's because the audience here is used to that club atmosphere; the audience wants a drink in its hand."

Nonetheless, at the first Houston festival most hands were kept busy applauding.

No prescience was required for the above evaluation of Wynton Marsalis on the threshold of his meteoric career. He was, clearly, about to take off. In the next four years he did manage to evade the barracudas of the music business. He subdued a major producer famous for diluting the music of talented artists, insisting on and get-

ting control of his own record dates. In addition to a number of excellent jazz albums, Marsalis brilliantly recorded classical works for trumpet. He won jazz popularity polls and professional honors. He achieved financial success. Having made such early artistic and worldly gains, having spoken less than humbly about his music, not having fought his way up through poverty or narcotics addiction, not having presented himself as an oppressed victim of racism, Marsalis was a logical target for critics who place pain, suffering, struggle, and failure above musical evidence. The following piece in part addresses that phenomenon.

The Uses of Tradition

1985

Jazz is biding its time. It is in a period of consolidation and reflection that began as the 1970s wound down. It may be that the search for roots and basic values presaged, as movements in jazz often have, a change in the society at large. The Reagan years were not far off.

The jazz tradition is not being challenged or extended; it is being absorbed and examined. In a period like this, critics watch for a messiah. When a brilliant young musician like trumpeter Wynton Marsalis appears, the outriders send back a signal that the next major innovator is about to reveal himself. No one wants to be caught napping, as most critics were in 1958 at the advent of Ornette Coleman. Marsalis tries to protect himself. He says, plaintively, that he is not the next *anyone*, that he is just trying to play his music and develop his abilities. But he is so spectacularly talented that he is held to account, made to feel obliged to lead jazz forward. His failure to find the promised land, after a professional career of four years, opens him to attack by last year's adulators.

His admirable album *Hot House Flowers* (Columbia FC 39530) is pilloried by critics. It is a collection of ballads, exquisitely played by Wynton and his saxophonist brother, Branford. Both are accomplished soloists well within the jazz tradition of the past two decades. Both have enormous promise, but neither is a stylistic trailblazer. Arrangers Robert Freedman and Marsalis have given the pieces settings that are unconventional and subtle, so subtle that they elude *down beat,* which calls them "forced, coaxed . . . lackluster . . . turgid." *Down beat*'s reviewer derisively uses the phrase "easy listening." Marsalis's playing, which is disciplined, controlled, and humorously good natured, is described as uninspired. *High Fidelity,* referring to Marsalis as a "trumpet-playing machine," says the music is boring. These are serious mis-hearings of a successful venture. Marsalis has committed the sin of unfulfilled expectation; he is not Louis Armstrong, Lester Young, Charlie Parker, or Ornette Coleman. He is being punished for winning awards and making money.

Tenor saxophonist John Coltrane, the last and most influential of the great iconoclastic innovators, has been dead since 1968. Alto saxophonist Ornette Coleman is alive, but the elements of his revolutionary work have long since been absorbed into the mainstream. Coleman's latest departure was the application of his "harmolodic" concept to a fusion of jazz and rock. It was dry academic theory compared with the upheaval caused by his passionate, disturbing music of the late fifties and early sixties. That music was, in many ways, a premonition of the coming decade of political change, racial furor, and Vietnam.

Coleman's first album, *Something Else* (OJC 163), has just been reissued in Fantasy's admirable Original Jazz Classics program. When it was released in 1958 on the Contemporary label, many critics found it easy to dismiss; amateurish, they said. To others, it was impenetrable, even frightening. Only a few found Coleman's music important and prophetic. Ears conditioned by developments of the intervening years are likely to hear the Coleman quintet's 1958 music as bebop yearning to be free. That is precisely what it was, down to the classic bop instrumentation of alto saxophone, trumpet, piano, bass, and drums, and to the use of recognizable harmonic patterns. This record is still the best place to begin for anyone wishing to understand Coleman's music; it has a traditional frame of reference. Within a year the piano would be gone and so would most of the familiar harmonic guideposts. Coleman would be off germinating musical change, the Johnny Appleseed of free jazz.

Wynton Marsalis is only the most celebrated of a number of young jazz players who have begun to mature in the past five years and are functioning within the traditional framework. Also concerned with the jazz tradition are musicians who were profoundly influenced by the new freedom brought to jazz in the late fifties and early sixties by Coltrane, Coleman, Miles Davis, Bill Evans, and a few others.

Symbolizing the inward turn taken by many avant-gardists in the last decade was the saxophonist Archie Shepp, one of the most celebrated of the angry young "New Thing" musicians of the 1960s. His music, like Coleman's and much of Coltrane's, abandoned the conventions of harmony and rhythm. Around 1977, Shepp began reexamining his roots. The result was a series of albums exploring the blues, gospel, and bebop (Steeplechase 1079, 1139, and 1149). His playing, although hardly conventional, adhered to traditional rules. He was not alone. Dozens of his colleagues from the leading edge of jazz experimentation "rediscovered" standard songs, conventional harmonic patterns, and the charms of recognizable melodies.

The attractiveness of such values may account, in large part, for the success of reissue programs like Fantasy's. The Original Jazz Classics program now includes upwards of two hundred albums recorded in the fifties and sixties on the Fantasy, Prestige, Riverside, Milestone, and Contemporary labels. Those companies' artists included such influential musicians as Thelonious Monk, Miles Davis, John Coltrane, Dave Brubeck, Bill Evans, and Benny Carter.

Carter's *Jazz Giant* (OJC–167), recorded in 1957 and 1958, is one of the alto saxophone and trumpet master's greatest sessions. If only for Carter's elegant statements and the billowing tenor saxophone solos of Ben Webster, it would be a classic. But it also comprises some of Carter's finest writing and an illustrious support team of trombonist Frank Rosolino, drummer Shelly Manne, guitarist Barney Kessel, and pianists Andre Previn and Jimmy Rowles. Carter's trumpet solo on "I'm Coming, Virginia" emphasizes both his lyric expressiveness on the instrument and the unfortunate fact that he plays it so rarely.

Apart from the OJC program, Fantasy has brought forth a massive, intelligently conceived and beautifully produced Bill Evans collection, *Bill Evans: The Complete Riverside Recordings* (Riverside R-018). Its eighteen LPs contain, in sequence, everything but snippets and outright rejected attempts that the late pianist recorded for the company from 1956 to 1963, when he left to join Verve. It is not simply a collectible for the Evans completist; it is a compelling, sometimes stark, view into the creative processes of a major artist. Seventeen solo pieces from 1963, never before issued, reveal Evans in deep introspection. Among them, "All the Things You Are" is one of the most stunning developments of an improvisational sequence ever captured in a studio. It illuminates Evans's importance as one who helped expand the jazz tradition by working from within it, and it gives us a glimpse into an astonishingly fertile and complex musical personality.

A company much smaller than Fantasy, Mosaic, is also responding to the groundswell of demand for the collected works of historically important jazz artists. Acclaimed for earlier releases of music by Thelonious Monk, Gerry Mulligan, John Hardee, Albert Ammons, and others, Mosaic offers *The Complete Blue Note and Pacific Jazz Recordings of Clifford Brown* (Mosaic MR 5-104) and *The Complete Pacific Jazz Small Group Recordings of Art Pepper* (Mosaic MR 3-105).

Brown was killed in an auto wreck in 1956, but in a few years as a professional, he left a legacy of recordings that is still a dominant factor in jazz. Some of the finest were made for the Blue Note label, and they are all here, including several previously unissued masters. The collection also contains the celebrated Pacific Jazz ensemble date with its exuberant Brown solos and its carefully crafted arrangements by Jack Montrose.

Art Pepper was an alto saxophonist of the bebop era who developed out of, or despite, the looming shadow of Charlie Parker. His playing had a mellowness owing a great deal to Benny Carter, one of his early mentors. It also had astringency and daring that in some ways took him beyond Parker. The Mosaic recordings capture him in the mid-1950s when he had worked out the developmental problems of his youth and established tonal qualities and personal uses of rhythmic values that made him a distinctive stylist. In more than half the music on these three LPs, Pepper is in partnership with trumpeter Chet Baker, and a particularly fruitful partnership it was. Both men deserved more respect than they received nearly thirty years ago. Their music was of lasting value and both went on, despite daunting personal problems, to make important contributions well into the 1980s, as Baker still does.

Pepper, who died in 1982, recorded copiously in his final years. Much of the recording took place during an engagement at the Los Angeles club called Maiden Voyage. *Art Pepper Quartet* (Galaxy GXY 5151) is the third album to emerge from that experience. Pepper's playing incorporates some of the New Jazz freedom he admired in Coltrane and Coleman, a growling ferocity that could quickly turn to lyricism and a self-deprecating humor that reflected the confidence and relative peace he found only near the end of his life. His performance of "What's New?" represents all of those elements plus the remarkable rapport between Pepper and George Cables, the pianist he often called his favorite.

The "rebirth" of jazz tradition in the seventies was welcomed by listeners and critics. Some of the avant-gardists even found the audiences that had eluded them before their born-again jazz conversions. There has been a parallel trend, a reaction to the adventurism and experimentation of the sixties and seventies. It is the development of a body of music that is a retreat not only from the forthrightness of jazz but from the tyranny of commercial rock. This music, personified by the pianist George Winston and his fellow musicians of the Windham Hill label, is soft, dreamy, unaggressive, and nonelectronic. Windham Hill's most recent sampler (WH-6-1035) sums up the approach. The music incorporates some of the rhythmic and improvisational aspects of jazz, but in safe and undisturbing ways. Sometimes called New Age music, it has been described as a Yuppie Muzak and it may be to the Reagan era what Mantovani was to the Eisenhower years. This music is marketed and promoted as jazz.

So is a bewildering array of styles generally categorized as fusion, which melds jazz elements with funk, rock, country, classical, Latin

American, and even Balinese music. Confusingly, many of the artists offering fusion have reputations as jazz musicians, and their fusion efforts are sold as jazz. Some of them are Herbie Hancock,
George Benson, Quincy Jones, Sadao Watanabe, Earl Klugh, the
Crusaders, and Stanley Clarke.

Hancock continues to function part of the time as a modern
mainstream jazz musician through his "V.S.O.P." bands devoted to
preserving the style and spirit of the Miles Davis quintet of twenty
years ago. He is also the proprietor of a fusion group that has
scored enormous pop successes, including the ubiquitous "Rockit."
Benson, a luminescent jazz guitarist, is all but totally immersed in
his career as a pop singer. Jones, one of the greatest jazz arrangers,
occasionally makes an album of near-jazz, but is primarily occupied
with producing hit records, including those of Michael Jackson.

Prince Albert/Don Albert

1980

Beaming at the unexpected recognition, trumpeter Don Albert stepped out of the audience at the 1977 San Antonio Jazz Festival. The master of ceremonies had called him forward to introduce him as one of Texas's jazz pioneers. It is doubtful, though, whether the emcee or many members of the young audience knew that Albert's courageous leaps across the barriers of prejudice in South Texas three decades earlier had helped create the climate that made possible the evening's racial mix of musicians.

Don Albert Dominique—he dropped his last name early in his career—was born of black and French Creole stock in New Orleans in 1908. He died last spring in San Antonio. In the twenties he was in the middle of the pack of young New Orleans trumpeters; in the thirties he had led his own swing band across the United States; and by 1940 he had settled permanently in San Antonio, the city that has been his base of operations for a decade. He was always a popular figure in South Texas, but he made an indelible mark on the Alamo City when he took over the Keyhole, a nightclub on Poplar Street. Even though Albert could have passed for white, he simply and stubbornly insisted on having black, white, and brown musicians and audiences in his club. He held out against enraged establishmentarians even in the face of harassing raids, threats to close down the Keyhole, and promises that he would have to play his trumpet without benefit of teeth.

With Albert as the trailblazer, musicians in San Antonio made a modest but visible dent in the city's hard shell of racism long before the activism of the sixties and the political consciousness-raising of the seventies. He booked hot black bands like King Kolax and Louis Jordan as main attractions and encouraged mixed jam sessions after hours. The Keyhole's Sunday afternoon sessions are remembered by dozens of San Antonio bebop musicians, many of them Mexican-American, as their only opportunities to learn the music firsthand.

New Orleans master banjoist and guitarist Danny Barker, Albert's childhood friend and early musical companion, recalls an incident that reflects the seriousness of some San Antonians' objections to his activities: "Some of Don's family looked even whiter than him. His sister Pauline, beautiful girl, looked absolutely white, and she went to San Antonio to be with Don and his family. Some of those rednecks decided there was a white woman messing around with black men. One day in New Orleans my family saw a big black car with Texas plates pull up in front of the house. Three or four big cowboy-looking guys came over and asked about Don's family across the street, wanted to know if they were colored. How about the one called Pauline, they wanted to know. My folks said yes, she certainly was. The guys got back in the car and left, back to Texas, I guess."

As a soloist Don Albert was no Louis Armstrong, but he had confidence, the ability to lead, and a showman's flair. "He was out of the Louis tradition," Barker says. "He loved Armstrong's style and did a good job with it. And he used Louis's pieces of business too—wiped his lips and mopped his brow with a big white handkerchief."

Barker thinks Albert was a better jazz soloist than his New Orleans cohorts give him credit for. Among his contemporaries, Kid Howard, Alvin Alcorn, and Ernie Cagnalotti might have had cause to sweat a little when Albert was having a good night. "Don always had a beautiful sound, and he could play," Barker says. "But he never worked in that straight Dixie style. Maybe that's what the guys didn't like."

In the late twenties Albert showed up in San Antonio as a member of the Troy Floyd outfit, one of the best of the many territory bands in the Southwest. His trumpet style had been forged in the New Orleans tradition, but now his playing took on the spaciousness of spirit that was and is the hallmark of so many Texas jazzmen. With Floyd, Albert grew into an admired musician whose reputation traveled beyond the band's stomping grounds. Little of his playing from the twenties was recorded, but his glowing tone and orderly conception are the keys to the success of Floyd's "Dreamland Blues," recorded for Okeh in 1929 and a collector's item today. Albert's solo on the piece was nearly matched by that of a colleague who went on to greater recognition than Albert, the explosive tenor saxophonist Herschel Evans.

In 1929 Albert formed his own band, a cooperative of mostly New Orleans players, and competed with Floyd until his mentor bowed under the weight of the Depression and disbanded in 1932. The band was called Don Albert and His Ten Pals, and later, as more musicians were added, it evolved into Don Albert and His Music, America's Greatest Swing Band. It never achieved the national reputation that the Bennie Moten organization did after Count Basie assumed leadership or the financial success of Alphonse Trent, another of the great territory bands. But its impact on other musicians has lasted to this day. The celebrated trumpeter and flugelhornist Clark Terry adopted Albert as an idol and role model. Slender, good looking, self-assured to the point of occasional arrogance, Albert looked and acted like the young musician's vision of a bandleader.

"I was a kid learning trumpet when Don was a star," Terry recalls. "He was one of the most respected bandleaders and businessmen. Aside from Duke Ellington and Jimmie Lunceford, there wasn't a more highly thought of black dude around. Good trumpet player, too. That band he had in the late thirties was a perfectionist's band. The cats still talk about it."

Albert and his ten-plus pals traveled to most of the forty-eight states as well as to Canada and Mexico. Their life on the road epitomized existence in the Swing Era for all but the most successful white bands. Herb Hall, who now lives in the hill country town of

Boerne, led the Albert reed section from 1929 to 1937 and again from 1938 to 1940. He recalls the routine: "Usually when we finished we had to get right on the bus and head for the next town. The roads were bad in Texas then, and often the next job was a hundred and fifty miles or more away, so we had to get rolling. We played every little village and hamlet, mostly one-nighters. And of course we played strictly for dancing. There were no concerts in those days. Once in a while in a big city there was an opportunity for a jam session if we were laying over. We traveled all over the South and up into the Midwest. I remember Omaha and South Bend and all parts of Florida, and we went up into New York and Massachusetts."

Fortunately, a demand for the Albert band in San Antonio made for long stretches of steady work at two clubs, Shadowland and the Chicken Plantation. They sometimes played at one of the clubs for as long as eighteen months before succumbing to the call of the road.

"It was always a groovy band, always a swinging band," Hall says. "The arrangers did things in the Ellington vein, or like (Jimmie) Lunceford or Moten. Everything was polished and very well played. The soloists were good, and the band was always, always danceable."

The engagements at Shadowland provided Albert's biggest audiences by way of broadcasts over KTSA, which was heard all over the South. His fan mail came from as far away as Florida. People liked what they heard and clamored for more, but the band recorded little. A few tracks on bootleg albums are all that survive.

My last encounter with Albert followed one of the concerts at the 1977 San Antonio Jazz Festival. I was seated at a kitchen table with Clark Terry and pianist Billy Taylor in the home of Jo Long, one of the festival's organizers, listening to Albert's expansive recollections of the triumphs, frustrations, and frights connected with integrating a South Texas nightclub in the forties. Terry, taking it in with the same wonder he must have felt as a boy listening to Albert's band on the road in St. Louis, took advantage of a pause to murmur, "The cat's really somethin', you know."

Clark Terry

Clark Terry's career as trumpeter and flugelhornist has included significant associations with Count Basie and Duke Ellington, the most important big band leaders in jazz. A prodigiously gifted musician who early in his career combined the finest attributes of earlier swing era players like Rex Stewart with the dazzling techniques of Dizzy Gillespie, Terry developed a unique and instantly identifiable solo style.

Through the 1950s he was a mainstay soloist with Ellington, who relied on Terry for some of the most colorful interpretations in the band's repertoire. After he left Ellington in 1959, he toured Europe with a remarkable orchestra led by Quincy Jones, then spent twelve years as a member of the NBC staff orchestra. Through his exposure on "The Tonight Show," on which he was frequently featured as an instrumentalist and occasionally as a singer, Terry became one of the best known jazz musicians in the country. In 1964, his fame increased with the unexpected success of "Mumbles," a track from an album he made with pianist Oscar Peterson in which Terry vocalized the blues in a hilarious incoherent fashion that fell somewhere between speech and scat singing.

His combo recordings with valve trombonist Bob Brookmeyer are some of the finest small band albums of the 1960s. Since 1972, when "The Tonight Show" moved from New York to Los Angeles, Terry has led his own group and been in great demand as a featured artist in clubs, concerts, and festivals.

An Hour with Clark Terry

1978

Just before his recent European tour for the State Department, trumpeter and flugelhornist Clark Terry was the month-long featured artist at LeClub, the Hyatt Regency's contribution to the New Orleans music scene. With the science fiction bulk of the Super Dome looming through the mist outside his hotel room window, we talked for an hour about New Orleans, jazz festivals, trumpet players, Duke Ellington, and the philosophy of this fifty-seven-year-old phenomenon who looks ten years younger.

Terry's ties to the city have been more spiritual than personal, but his admiration for a New Orleans hero led almost a decade ago to one of the most important gestures of his life. A few blocks from the Super Dome a monument to Louis Armstrong is nearing completion. It might very well not have been built without Terry's inspiration.

New Orleans's Armstrong Park has been a project of the administration of former mayor Moon Landrieu, who deserves full credit for paying tangible tribute to the city's greatest artist. But impetus for the idea came in 1969 on a bus ride during the second New Orleans Jazzfest. As a musicians' tour was passing Jane Alley, Armstrong's birthplace, Terry deplored the fact that while New Orleans seemed to have statues of half the Latin American presidents in history, there were none of the city's most famous son. Then and there, he started a fund to commission a statue. His first dollar was symbolic. His organizing ability and leadership were much more. Nine years later, that statue is on the verge of becoming the centerpiece of an entire park dedicated to Armstrong's memory. The park's completion slowed in the six-month transition period between Landrieu's administration and that of Mayor Ernest Morial. But assuming Morial, the city's first black mayor, gets behind the project,

Armstrong Park should be the New Orleans equivalent of Copenhagen's celebrated Tivoli Gardens and open by 1980.*

Even before young Clark Terry became a professional in his native St. Louis, he was an admirer of Armstrong. But his most direct influences were home town players, including Shorty Baker, who became a mainstay of the Duke Ellington band. Baker was just one of a pool of gifted St. Louis brass artists.

"There were a couple of dozen excellent players, guys like Charlie Creth, Dewey Jackson, Levi Madison, Crack Stanley, Buzz Woods, Baby James, George Hudson, Sleepy Tomlin. Sleepy's one of the cats responsible for making me really study and work hard to develop a sound. He used to put me on, used to call me 'Fuzzy' because of my beginner's tone. 'Hey, Fuzzy,' he'd say, 'Howya doin', Fuzzy, someday you'll get it, Fuzzy, heh heh heh heh.' I used to cry, I'd get so mad at him. I said I'll show that S.O.B. one of these days. Every time I'd practice, I'd think about Sleepy Tomlin calling me 'Fuzzy' and eventually I wasn't fuzzy any more."

Terry himself was to provide inspiration for young St. Louis musicians. There's a famous story about the time an aspiring trumpet player tried to get Terry to explain some of the mysteries of jazz.

"I was working with Benny Reed, the peg-legged piano player, at a May Day celebration in Carbondale, Illinois. In those days, they still had the dances where they wound the flags and streamers around the May pole. We were the professional band doing the jazz gig, and the high school band from East St. Louis was there too. This kid from the school band kept trying to get my advice, but I was interested in the attentions of a young lady and I fluffed him off. Several months later I walked into a jam session and heard someone playing fantastic trumpet. It was the same little cat, and he turned out to be named Miles Davis."

The two became close friends. In later years when Davis became a jazz star of the 1950s, Terry was one of the few influences he

---

* Armstrong Park was formally dedicated on April 15, 1980, by Landrieu (then U.S. Secretary of Housing and Urban Development), Morial, and Armstrong's wife Lucille.

would acknowledge. During his formative early period, Terry says, Davis's tone was nothing like the smooth sound for which he became famous.

"He always wanted to use a big wavy vibrato. He was crazy about Harry James. His teacher, a friend of mine named Buchanan, thought Miles had a lot of talent, but that vibrato worried him. He told me, 'He'll be all right as soon as I get through rappin' his knuckles about that shakin' he's doin'. I tell him to stop shakin', man, he's gonna shake enough when he gets old. And Buchanan intimidated Miles to the point where he started getting that straight, pure tone. He owes it to Buchanan, that beautiful sound he got.'"

Terry may have been a professional at the time of the Carbondale encounter, but he wasn't getting rich in anything but experience in the early forties. His pay as one of the two horns in the Benny Reed band was seven dollars a week, plus tips. Room and board was a dollar and a half a week. And in Reed's band, the leader made getting fed a challenge.

"In order to get breakfast at the boardinghouse before all the food was eaten up by Benny, we'd hide his leg. We'd hear him upstairs bouncing around on his one good leg yelling, 'All right, which one of you sonsabitches got my leg' . . . boom, boom, boom. And after we were half stuffed, we'd get his leg for him. It was kinda dirty, but if we didn't do that, we'd starve, because Benny would scoff it all down."

Terry worked in a succession of small bands around the Midwest, including Dollar Bill and His Small Change.

"His motto was, 'I'm Dollar Bill from Bunker Hill, I Never Worked and Never Will.' And he was always telling us, 'I'm Dollar Bill. You just remember, you're only one of the pennies.' During that time I also worked with Fate Marable. He was an old man then, but he was still leading bands on those Mississippi steamers. He used to get a big kick out of playing tunes in weird keys. You'd go on this gig and you'd be accustomed to playing something in F, he'd play it in F-sharp and laugh through the whole tune while you struggled. It was good training."

Marable's sense of the unusual extended to non-musical matters and may have given rise to a colorful addition to the language. Terry says the river boats were equipped with axes to be used in the event it became necessary to chop an exit from a flaming cabin or passageway. Marable used the implement instead of a pink slip.

"Whenever Fate would get ready to make a change in the band, he'd tell the rest of us to come early. Then, when the cat he was going to fire would come at the regular time, he'd find an ax on his chair. I've never heard any other explanation of the term, so it seems logical that's where it came from. Cat got the ax."

Terry never got the ax from Marable or from any of the other famous leaders for whom he worked. After a stint in a Navy band during World War II, he played with Lionel Hampton, George Hudson, Eddie "Cleanhead" Vinson, Charlie Ventura, Count Basie, and Duke Ellington, the association that made him one of the best known soloists in jazz. With Ellington, Terry blossomed. Duke's genius for recognizing and capitalizing on the characteristics of his sidemen has rarely had more startling results than in the case of Clark Terry.

Ellington sensed in Terry something of the New Orleans tradition. When Ellington was preparing "A Drum Is a Woman," his suite in which New Orleans plays a large part, he chose Terry to portray Buddy Bolden. Bolden's style is entirely legendary; no recordings of him are known to exist. Terry recalls protesting the assignment.

"I told him, 'Maestro, I don't know anything about Buddy Bolden. I wouldn't know how to start.' Duke said, "Oh, sure, you're Buddy Bolden. He was just like you. He was suave. He had a good tone, he bent notes, he was big with diminishes, he loved the ladies, and when he blew a note in New Orleans, he'd break glass across the river in Algiers. Come on, you can do it.' I told him I'd try, and I blew some phrases, and he said, "That's it, that's Buddy Bolden, that's it, sweetie." That's how Maestro was. He could get out of you anything he wanted. And he made you believe you could do it. I suppose that's why they used to say the band was his instrument. The Buddy Bolden thing is on the record, and Duke was satisfied. So as far as I'm concerned, it was Buddy Bolden."

That 1969 New Orleans Jazz Festival was the last before the event became part of a pre-packaged road show. Remembered by Terry and most people connected with it as one of the great artistic successes among jazz festivals, it set Terry to thinking about the excesses and failures of festivals today.

"That was a *jazz* festival," he says. "Now, it's reached the point where they put a bunch of people on second base in the biggest ball park in town and drive them to the bandstand in those cars that take pitchers to the mound. And the person sitting up in the bleachers, all he can say is, 'I was there last night, man, and it was a gas.' At least they told him it was. It's unfair to call some of the packages they put together jazz festivals. There are enough people to support jazz, maybe not enough to fill up a ball park. But it's been proved that anything that's packaged and marketed properly can be sold in this country. It has to be thought out, produced, and presented with the right players and with a lot of cooperation from both ends. A lot of the fault lies with the middle men. But we're very fortunate in some instances with the Norman Granzes, Paul Lentzes and Willis Conovers. In some instances, we're not so fortunate."

This prompted a question about the New York Newport festival. "I have mixed emotions about Newport," he said. "It's a big, big money-making proposition, and I think some of the acts presented are not jazz. George Wein is a very enterprising man who's done an awful lot for jazz. But I think there could be some improvement there. I love George, he's a good friend of mine, but nobody's perfect."

Over the years, Terry has been featured in several festivals and concerts produced by Willis Conover, including the 1969 New Orleans Festival and the seventieth birthday party for Duke Ellington at the White House the same year. Conover is now inactive in the production of public jazz events because of his Voice of America duties and publishing ventures. But the musical purity and sophisticated production of his concerts and festivals set standards that are rarely met today.

"Willis is the most beautiful cat, man; I love him. I know he doesn't have the time, but I really wish he'd produce a festival again.

Willis knows how to present people who may not be household names but have been into jazz all their lives and play well, the kind of people who should represent jazz. He knows how to put these kinds of people together and present them in a way that the audiences react to. It's a way of producing that is smooth and professional, but the musicians never feel boxed in, rushed, or restricted. Willis knows people on both ends, the powers that be and the musicians who do their thing in a way that can be respected."

Terry thinks the habits and behavior of jazz players must be considered as important as musicianship by those who hire them to play.

"You like to think that when you send somebody to represent you, you're not going to have to worry about his decorum, his appearance, his habits. Those things are very important, and I think too quickly overlooked because a cat can play. I try to teach young musicians I'm involved with in the colleges and universities to steer clear of pitfalls. It's hard enough to master your craft, to be on time, to politic and tend to business. But when you get on stage with a fifth of whiskey in your gut or something in your arm, or you tell off your audience, it's bad for the profession. Maybe I'm too old-fashioned, but I think things are hard enough without great musicians who play well but won't take care of themselves. They endanger the perpetuation of our craft."

Typically, Terry wouldn't mention names because he doesn't want to cast stones. But he says, foxily, "They know who they are."

The day we talked, Terry had just heard for the first time tapes of the concert played by the all-star band at Ellington's White House birthday party. He was enthused. Among his colleagues in the band were J. J. Johnson and Urbie Green, trombones; Gerry Mulligan and Paul Desmond, saxophones; Jim Hall, guitar; Milt Hinton, bass; Louis Bellson, drums; Hank Jones, piano; and Bill Berry, trumpet.

"I don't understand why that music isn't released on record," he says.

"When you get together a bunch of guys like that, beautiful musicians who were so happy to be playing together, everybody should have a chance to hear it.* I was so busy playing, I don't really remember all the festivities. But I do remember Nixon sitting in the front row with his wife. When we did 'Squeeze Me,' I got out the plunger mute—the plumber's friend—and he was nudging his wife, pointing at it and saying, 'Look at that, look, it's a toilet plunger, look at it.' I guess he hadn't seen a whole lot of jazz bands."

Terry was asked for brief comments on other trumpet players.

On Art Farmer: "Fantastic."

Shorty Baker: "Just the most fantastic tone. A fun guy with a beautiful heart. He played that way."

Jack Sheldon: "Beautiful. I like Jack. He's a good buddy of mine, and I think he plays just fantastically."

Cat Anderson: "Phenomenal player. He and Maynard Ferguson are both masters of the art of playing high notes. You might have a ball player who can hit doubles, and steal, and get on base all the time. But there's nothing more thrilling than a cat who can step up to the plate and knock the ball out of the park. Cat and Maynard are home run hitters."

Chet Baker: "Next."

Sam Noto: "Very good player, but [I] don't hear too much of him."

Willie Cook: "Love him. He went to Europe with me on my last trip and he's going on the next one. Great player. It was a joy to be in the Ellington trumpet section with him, Cat, and Ray Nance."

Richard Williams: "A great little player. I love the way he plays. That has nothing to do with our personal differences."

Doug Mettome: "He was a beautiful trumpeter. I'll never forget one day he and his wife came to the Apollo Theater not long before he died. Doug was very sick at the time, had no money, and they wouldn't let him in backstage. I gave him and Cissy a little money to go around front and see the show. I still hear from his family in Salt Lake. I always respected him as a great all-around trumpet player,

---

*As of 1988, the music still has not been released.

great lead, great soloist. Anybody who can get along with Benny Goodman can't be all bad."

Terry insisted on mentioning some others he admires; Freddie Hubbard, Roy Eldridge, Blue Mitchell, Benny Bailey, the late Lennie Johnson and, of course, Dizzy Gillespie.

"Birks is the sweetest cat in the world. He's got the biggest heart. And I wouldn't advise anybody to try to catch him on a weak day and jam him into a corner. Don't do it. He's poison. That cat is mean. He's forgotten more about trumpet than the average cat will ever learn. But Birks is often taken for granted because he's always coming on with comedy. People remember him more for his gyrations than they do for his trumpet. But he's an incredible player.

"And we can't possibly talk about trumpet players without talking about Bobby Hackett. Bobby, Dizzy, and I were in Japan together and it was quite noticeable that the three of us loved each other so much. He thought Dizzy was the most phenomenal trumpet player around. All through the tour, we kept buying one another gifts. Bobby had the mark of a master craftsman. He could stay involved with his own thing and still show his great respect and love for the person with whom he was participating. And that's how it is when Dizzy and I are performing together. Neither of us is trying to carve the other, but to complement and do our thing."

Terry ended the afternoon with a sort of credo.

"I find that I can't play anymore with somebody on the bandstand I feel doesn't dig me or whom I don't particularly dig. I go to great lengths to seek out people I love."

Art Farmer

Never widely known outside of jazz and most unlikely to lust after pop music status, the trumpeter and flugelhornist Art Farmer has had a career pattern closely resembling that of a classical soloist like trumpeter Maurice Andre or pianist Richard Goode, players uncompromisingly dedicated to the highest musical values who are deeply respected by their peers and by knowledgeable listeners, and whose talents keep them in demand. His musicianship, flexibility, and open-mindedness have led to playing situations ranging from big bands through mainstream combos to adventures that helped expand the frontiers of jazz.

Farmer was born in Council Bluffs, Iowa, in 1928, but grew up in Phoenix, Arizona, where he and his twin brother Addison developed their early musical skills. (Addison, an accomplished bassist who worked frequently with Art, died in 1963 of a cerebral aneurism.) Entranced by jazz, the brothers moved to Los Angeles in 1945 when they were sixteen, with a promise to their mother that they would finish high school there. Farmer worked with the big bands of Horace Henderson, Floyd Ray, and Jimmy Mundy and then, upon earning his diploma, made his way to the East Coast with Johnny Otis. In New York in 1947 and 1948 he played in Jay McShann's band, among others, and formally studied the trumpet. Back in Los Angeles in 1948, he worked with Benny Carter, Wardell Gray, Dexter Gordon, Gerald Wilson, and others in the rich Central Avenue musical environment.

In 1952 Farmer joined Lionel Hampton's big band, with which he toured Europe. Establishing New York as his base in 1953, he became one of the most sought-after trumpeters of the fifties, recording copiously and working steadily in his own bands and those

of a variety of other leaders. He won the down beat *critics poll in
1958. Late the next year, he and tenor saxophonist Benny Golson
founded The Jazztet, a seven-piece band that thrived until 1963,
when Golson began to concentrate heavily on composing and
Farmer went on to establish a superb quartet. Twenty years later
the two were to revive The Jazztet for recordings and occasional
live appearances.*

*Faced with a deteriorating jazz scene in New York, Farmer in
1968 moved to Vienna, where he became a member of the house
band of the Austrian Broadcasting System under an arrangement
that gave him time to tour, record, and maintain his career as a jazz
artist. In the late 1980s he was spending about half of his time in the
United States.*

1982

During a 1963 "Jazz Casual" telecast, the late journalist and critic
Ralph Gleason asked Art Farmer why he had switched from trumpet
to flugelhorn. Farmer offered a typically direct and practical answer.

"Because the sound is a little warmer," he told Gleason. "Playing
in small clubs with small groups, I find that I can play this horn
without using mutes. When you use mutes you run into bad P.A.
systems and can get messed up."

It is difficult to conceive of Farmer ever playing a shrill note. Like
his long-time colleague, guitarist Jim Hall, Farmer performs with
such gentleness and ease that his virtuosity and harmonic wizardry
are often overlooked or taken for granted. His solos have always
been marked by restraint and a reluctance to fill all available space.

Much of his eloquence stems from a sense of power held in reserve. For Farmer has the ability to play with blistering speed,
covering all imaginable harmonic possibilities, and to swing irre-
sistibly at a dynamic level that rules out any trace of exhibitionism

or volume for the sake of volume. Though he is the least overtly spectacular of major jazz brass soloists, the logic of his constructions and his uses of dynamics, silence, pitch, humor, and harmonic daring combine to form music of presence, music that commands attention.

Even on some of Farmer's first recordings in the early 1950s it was clear that he was a first-rank soloist in the making. By 1956 Farmer's work showed a combination of incisiveness and lyricism that added elegance and style to the bands of leaders as disparate as George Russell, Gerry Mulligan, and Horace Silver. Such versatility has long been a matter of inconvenience for writers who need categories like "hard bop" or "cool."

Shortly thereafter, Farmer became one of the few contemporaries of John Coltrane who absorbed, understood, and had the technical and artistic gifts to put to personal use the Coltrane innovations of the "Giant Steps" period of the early 1960s. He is virtually the only trumpeter who did so. Many players were swamped by the Coltrane influence. Farmer integrated it into his style and his lyrical range grew because of it.

At about the same time, he took up the flugelhorn, that lovely and demanding instrument. When he added the new horn, and eventually set the trumpet aside, the lovely muted work he had done on trumpet was lost. But the change of instruments accented what critic Richard B. Hadlock called Farmer's "soft edge," the quality that allowed listeners to accept his masterfully played but audacious ideas, passages they would reject as too far out if performed by most other players. He had found the voice that would carry all the impact of his remarkable invention and plumb all the depths of his feeling. And, happily, in a recent collaboration with Jim Hall, Farmer's Harmon mute materialized again after more than fifteen years.

Farmer is a great melodist. He loves and observes the melodies of the songs he plays. They are often surpassed by the melodies he creates. I have rarely heard a Farmer solo sound like the product of reflex processes. In times of flagging inspiration, or in uncongenial circumstances, even the most inventive players fall back on a sort of

universal phrase book. But in a recent jazz festival jam session
(hardly his preferred context), the clarity and beauty of Farmer's
solos remained in memory long after the dissipation of scene-
stealing clichés generated by most of the other players. That is
artistry.

Unlike his contemporary, Art Farmer, Miles Davis obviously does have a driving desire to be a pop music superstar. What's more, he knows how to become one and has proved it with his phenomenally loud and colorful rock bands of the second half of the 1980s. The careful and patient listener can detect, in the storm of DX-7s, ring modulators, phase shifters, megawatt amplification, and relentless percussion, that Davis's trumpet can still be lyrical and moving. Many of the most ardent admirers of the jazz artistry of the first thirty-five years of Davis's career have concluded that such moments are too few and far between to justify enduring the onslaught. But he has identified and captivated a new audience weaned on rock and roll.

And so, in his tireless campaign to always be in the vanguard, Davis in his sixties has managed, without appearing ridiculous, to be au courant to people forty years his junior. His music, however, is blazing no trails, as it did in several of his earlier bands. It has, in fact, regressed.

Born in 1928 to affluent parents in East St. Louis, Davis was an accomplished trumpeter by the age of sixteen. Sent to study at Juilliard in New York in 1945, he looked up Charlie "Bird" Parker, whom he had met when Bird passed through St. Louis with Billy Eckstine's band. At nineteen, he was working on 52nd Street with Parker, Coleman Hawkins, and other leading jazz figures. He toured with Benny Carter and with Eckstine. In the late forties he led bands at the Royal Roost and recorded with one of them, a nine-piece group of unusual instrumentation playing brilliant arrangements by Gil Evans, John Lewis, and Gerry Mulligan. Although it worked rarely and briefly, through its recordings the band even-

tually became one of the most universally admired and influential units in jazz history. Later labeled the "Birth of the Cool" band, it employed a lighter sound than predominated in bebop and was an incubator of ideas that greatly influenced music in the 1950s and after.

Through the early fifties, Davis worked in an assortment of small band contexts, honing a trumpet style that had already become one of the most hauntingly personal sounds in all of jazz. In the second half of that decade he led a superb quintet, then a sextet that not only embodied the essence of many of the best aspects of jazz, but through the ingenious use of modes and scales led the way into a new kind of freedom in music. Further, in the latter part of the fifties Davis renewed his association with Gil Evans. Against the stunning backdrops of Evans's orchestrations in their collaborations on the albums Miles Ahead, Porgy and Bess *and* Sketches of Spain, *Davis fashioned imperishable solos, some of the most enduring statements in jazz.*

In the 1960s, Davis's celebrated sidemen . . . John Coltrane, Cannonball Adderley, and Bill Evans . . . had all long since become successful leaders. From 1963 to 1968, his band consisted of another collection of budding stars, saxophonist Wayne Shorter, pianist Herbie Hancock, bassist Ron Carter, and drummer Tony Williams. Davis soon virtually abandoned standard songs and concentrated on original material, opening up increasingly to aspects of the free jazz of the sixties and frequently having Hancock play electric piano. With this group, particularly in the visceral interplay between Davis and the remarkable young Williams, the trumpeter did some of his hottest and most emotionally direct playing. By the end of the decade, he had replaced Hancock, Carter, and Williams with Chick Corea, Dave Holland, and Jack DeJohnette and recorded In a Silent Way *and* Bitches Brew, *albums that included guests like electric pianist Joe Zawinul and jazz/rock guitarist John McLaughlin. Davis was moving steadily toward rock, a tendency that became pronounced in 1970–72.*

Inactive during much of the rest of the 1970s because of serious auto accident injuries, Davis organized a new band in the early

1980s. It was even more basically a rock outfit, although it often included interesting jazz or jazz-oriented players like guitarist John Scofield and saxophonists Branford Marsalis and Kenny Garrett. Against charges of pandering, Davis has been defended by such admirers as Quincy Jones, who claims that Miles's "range," and his "scope,"* are demonstrated by his long excursion into a pop music area where the audience is made up primarily of teenagers or those with teenage tastes. Harsher critics, recalling the gloriously adult music made by Davis in earlier incarnations, disagree.

1975

Jazz is where you find it. The Polish novelist and essayist Leopold Tyrmand, who spent much of World War II as a forced laborer in Germany, tells of hearing the music of Benny Goodman from a hand-cranked phonograph in a rowboat in the middle of a river. The phonograph was operated by a Nazi soldier afraid of being thought an American spy or sympathizer if he listened openly. With difficulty, Tyrmand talked his way into the soldier's confidence, and a strangely matched pair of fans spent a Sunday afternoon spelling one another at the oars and illicitly digging Benny.

Under considerably less dramatic circumstances, records have brought jazz to millions of listeners and millions of listeners to jazz. Who knows how many admirers of Miles Davis discovered him by chance in the listening booths of records stores in little towns?

Remember listening booths?

Remember little towns?

Wenatchee, Washington, the Apple Capital of the World and the Buckle of the Power Belt of the Great Northwest, is a far cry from

---

*Quoted in *The Encylopedia of Jazz in the Seventies,* by Leonard Feather and Ira Gitler, Horizon Press, 1976.

The Apple, in every conceivable way. That's where I first heard
Miles, not quite by chance. My hometown's most celebrated jazz
musician is Don Lanphere, who achieved some prominence in the
late forties as a bop tenor saxophonist. Lanphere recorded with Fats
Navarro ("Stop," "Go," "Infatuation," "Wailing Wall") and Duke
Jordan ("Spider's Webb," "Strike up the Band"). He also worked
off and on with Woody Herman. Between gigs he returned to
Wenatchee to help out in his father's music store, take dance jobs,
teach and play occasional concerts in Seattle, Spokane, and Yakima.

The musician who worked most closely with Lanphere and, indeed, taught him a great deal, was Jack Brownlow, a pianist of uncanny harmonic inventiveness and unique touch. After his service
time in Claude Thornhill's Navy band, Brownlow worked briefly
with Lester Young, Lucky Thompson, and Wingy Manone around
Los Angeles. He followed Dodo Marmarosa as Manone's pianist. Wingy, no more sure of names than he was of bop musicians,
used to yell at Brownlow, "Man, you're weirder than that Bobo
Barbarosa."

But in the very early fifties, Brownlow and Lanphere were around
and influencing the musical climate of our little town to the point
where, for example, I can recall members of the trombone section
of the Wenatchee High School band arguing the relative merits of
J. J. Johnson and Bill Harris. That was a short and most unusual
period in the cultural history of the apple country. As an aspiring
trumpeter and fledgling jazz listener, I gravitated toward Brownlow
and Lanphere and began learning much more about music in my
spare time with them than I was picking up in the brass section of
the marching band.

My Muggsy Spanier and Ink Spots records began to be displaced
by Nat Cole, Lester Young, Dizzy Gillespie, Bud Powell, Charlie
Parker. With Parker, on the Savoy and Dial 78s, came a trumpet
sound that was to become a part of the music in my head. I didn't
really understand what was being played on those bop records, but
the sound Miles Davis produced—that personal, intimate, almost
speechlike sound—went past all technical considerations of harmony and rhythm directly to my emotions. Miles was an incom-

pletely formed soloist; I hear that now. But Bird must have chosen
him for reasons other than mere potential. The human qualities in
Davis's playing, the visions of beauty and loneliness, contrasted
with Parker's ecstatic, mercurial expressions and made Miles an
ideal foil for Bird. And with Parker, he built on his natural gift for
harmonic innovation. Davis's absorption of harmonic theory was
remarkable after he arrived in New York from East St. Louis in
1945 and began to play with Bird. He studied at Juilliard, but one
suspects he studied harder on the bandstand. And by the time he
recorded the *Birth of the Cool* sides with a ten-piece band in 1949
and 1950 he was, at twenty-three, a master of subtle harmonic
expression.

Lanphere, who knew Miles, saw to it that I listened to those first
Birth of the Cool 78s in a booth at Belmont Radio & Music. (For a
time there was an inspirational sign in the Belmont window: "Teach
your kid to blow a horn, and he'll never blow a safe.") Later, Don
introduced me to "Morpheus," "Down," "Whispering," and "Blue
Room" in an evening of first hearings that also included Ravel's
"Daphnis et Chloe." Heavy session, full of revelations, one of them
Sonny Rollins, another lifelong addiction.

Today's youngsters are more likely to arrive at Miles by way of
Sly Stone or Mahavishnu than through Bird. But they are into his
music. And that music, electronic, amplified, modal, has resulted in
many listeners who were ardent fans through the fifties and sixties
turning their backs on Miles (that's a switch). Davis is unconcerned
about leaving fans behind. He knows there are so many ahead.

A fantasy: Miles has just concluded one of his electronic extrava-
ganzas at Avery Fisher Hall. The packed house is roaring for an encore. Miles unplugs his battery of amplifiers—reducing by a third
Consolidated Edison's income for that week—and motions to the
wings. The Greek chorus of percussionists and guitarists who provide the current Davis atmosphere fade away and here come Al
Cohn and Zoot Sims, John Lewis, Kenny Clarke, and, from God
knows where, Sonny Truitt and Leonard Gaskin. They play "Tasty
Pudding," "Willie the Wailer," "Floppy," and "For Adults Only."

The audience, ears ringing from the earlier onslaught of decibels,

hypnotized by the evening's succession of two-chord patterns, is at
first puzzled by this quaint acoustic ensemble playing changes. But
feet tap. Earlobes dip. Smiles emerge. There is whistling, stomping,
a standing ovation. The rock press acclaims Davis as a daring innovator who seems to be able to get away with any musical experiment, no matter how far out. The *Rolling Stone* reviewer proclaims
Miles the "Maria Muldaur of the trumpet," capable of reaching
into history and recreating styles long forgotten.

Fantasy, indeed. Miles Davis does not look back, is not governed
by nostalgia. Miles's turf, as Ralph Gleason perceived, is always
contemporary music. Critics fuss and fume because Davis won't
recreate the past, won't go back to 1953, 1963, 1973, won't jam at
Newport with Dexter Gordon and Art Blakey. Miles smiles. He
knows something we don't. He knows it may be twenty years before
we know he knew. But he's not telling; he's playing. Gleason once
tried to get Miles to suggest what he'd like brought out about his
music in some liner notes. No liner notes, Miles said.

"There's nothing to say about the music," he told Ralph. "Don't
write about the music. The music speaks for itself."

And on another occasion: "Critics write whole columns and
pages of big words and still ain't saying nothing. If you have spent
half your life getting to know your business and the other cats in it,
and what they are doing, then you know whether a critic knows
what he's talking about. Most of the time they don't. I pay no attention to what the critics say about me, the good or the bad. The
toughest critic I got, and the only one I worry about, is myself. My
music has to get past me and I'm too vain to play anything I think
is bad."

We may assume that, critics to the contrary, Miles does not think
what he is playing in his two-chord megawatt milieu of the mid-
seventies is bad. He's never been wrong before. For more than
twenty-five years, Davis has demonstrated what critic Dan Morgenstern has called his "amazing capacity for change and self-renewal,"
and has led the way in jazz. Now, he is a major force, quite possibly
the major force in contemporary popular music. To anyone who
knows Miles even slightly, it is unreasonable to believe that he has

abandoned his flinty artistic integrity to achieve his immense popular success. His image as a personality is often negative and may well be calculated; he is a master of the put-on. A long interview in *down beat*'s special Miles Davis issue consisted almost entirely of Miles's special brand of scatological shuckin', which became more outrageous as the awestruck interviewer continued to lap it up. But it would be out of character for Miles to be cynical about his music.

And yet. And yet, try as I will to get into his new thing, knowing that Miles will always be ahead, my fantasy intrudes. When it does, praising Thomas Edison I get down my early Miles albums. The ten-inch versions are worn practically white. Bless Prestige for reissuing this music every several years. Bless Miles for being too vain to play anything he thinks is bad. Oh, he has played sloppily. He plays sloppily on these records, here and there. The tone fuzzes occasionally, the attack fails. But his taste is flawless, his emotional commitment total, his time perfect; he has one of the finest senses of swing in jazz. His warmth, inventiveness, and humor are burningly personal. And his assimilation of the history of his music is unsurpassed. Eldridge, Armstrong, and Gillespie populate his choruses, but subtly. On "Dig" the outright use of one of Dizzy's most celebrated licks is unusual for Miles.

There are also intimations of things to come in these performances. "Bluing," for an example, contains solo phrases that evolved into parts of the ensemble sections of Davis's 1954 "Walkin'," one of the most influential recordings of his career. This October 1951 session provides fascinating early glimpses of saxophonists Sonny Rollins and Jackie McLean, Parker disciples still under Bird's wing but developing rapidly. McLean has deprecated his work of the period. That is understandable in light of the polish and dash of his later achievements. But the fire the nineteen-year-old displayed in his first recording session was impressive. And Sonny, typical reed trouble of the period notwithstanding, shows the thematic and melodic creativity which later in the decade led to a masterpiece like "Blue Seven."

Benny Green was a stablemate of Miles through the early fifties for club dates and occasional record sessions. He was and is one of the few bop trombonists not heavily in debt to J. J. Johnson, and his relaxed, good natured solo on "Whispering" is a charming introduction to his work for those encountering this strangely neglected player for the first time.

Because of his omnipresence in jazz for nearly thirty years, John Lewis's spare, sophisticated, yet earthy piano work is unfamiliar to very few. If you've heard the Modern Jazz Quartet, you've heard John. At least as conscious of the jazz heritage as is Davis, Lewis has absorbed the lessons of the piano masters and distilled from them one of the most economical and consistently meaningful of styles. Naturally, since he leans toward economy and understatement, he leans toward Count Basie. The introduction to "Whispering" is essence of Basie. "Whispering," of course, is a popular song based on the harmonic changes of Dizzy Gillespie's jazz standard "Groovin' High." Or something like that.

At the time of these recordings, Lewis and Percy Heath were on the verge of forming the MJQ with Milt Jackson and Kenny Clarke. Percy was on the verge of becoming a major bassist. Art Blakey and Roy Haynes were veteran drummers, even in 1951. Kenny Clarke was the first bebop drummer and in many essential ways the best. Bassist Tommy Potter and pianist Walter Bishop, Jr., were members of Charlie Parker's rhythm section. Bird was a studio guest the day of the "Conception" date.

The "Tasty Pudding" session of February 1953 has occupied a special place in my affections since its original release on a ten-inch LP. The combination of Al Cohn and Zoot Sims with Miles was felicitous. Al's tunes and arranging for the date remain among his finest work. Considering Cohn's track record, that is high praise for products of his comparatively early years. The pieces have, as Mark Gardner commented for an earlier reissue of this music, "flow, wit, poignancy, swing, and good taste in equal proportion." Miles plays with a marvelous lilt throughout this session. It's always a pleasure to hear him sounding so joyous during a period when his life was not particularly happy. I've always thought this was the album that should have been called *Miles Smiles*. Fantasies aside, it is unlikely that we'll ever again hear Miles with Al and Zoot, so these sides are valuable and moving documents of a time when such encounters were regarded as natural.

More than a decade after the earliest of these recordings, my first opportunity to hear Miles Davis live came when I was in New York for a week and he was playing the Jazz Gallery in Greenwich Village. In the interim he had, to quote Colman Andrews, "sent his demons roundly back to hell;" recorded the milestone "Walkin'" session; formed the quintet with John Coltrane, Red Garland, Paul Chambers, and Philly Joe Jones; been "rediscovered" at the 1955 Newport Jazz Festival; reorganized his combo into the mind-blowing sextet with Coltrane, Cannonball Adderley, Bill Evans, Chambers, and Jones; collaborated triumphantly with Gil Evans; masterminded the *Kind of Blue* date, possibly the most influential record session of the past twenty years; and become a household name.

At the Gallery, Chambers and Jones were still abroad. Wynton Kelly was the pianist. Tenor saxophonist Hank Mobley and trombonist J. J. Johnson were the other horns. Teddy Wilson's trio was appearing opposite the Davis band.

Aside from the distinct recollection that Miles, Philly Joe, and J. J. played superbly that night, two memories of the evening survive. Between sets, Miles sat at a table in front of and slightly to the right of the piano and listened to Wilson intently and with great enjoyment. During a later break, he came to the bar and took a stool next to mine. I had heard all those stories about Davis's surliness and wasn't about to get him riled up by coming on like the hick fan I was. But he initiated a conversation and for maybe twenty minutes we made small talk, little of it about music. The freezing weather came up, as I recall, the New York newspaper strike, foreign cars, and Teddy Wilson. There was no handshake, no exchange of names. Then, as Miles got up to return to the stand, he asked where I was from. No place he'd ever heard of, I said, Wenatchee, Washington. He paused a moment, then said:

"Say hello to Don Lanphere."

Don was pleased.

John Coltrane

The pervasively influential saxophonist John Coltrane was born in Hamlet, North Carolina, in 1926. He learned the essentials of music from his father when he was growing up in Philadelphia, later studying formally with teachers and informally in the unusually active jazz community of that city. Coltrane worked in the 1940s with the rhythm and blues band of singer and saxophonist Eddie "Cleanhead" Vinson and with one of Dizzy Gillespie's combos. In the early 1950s he was with Earl Bostic and Johnny Hodges.

In 1955, Coltrane was hired by Miles Davis to be the other horn in what would turn out to be the most important small band of the decade. His ability improved and his style developed markedly during his years with Davis. He became a master saxophonist. By the time he left Davis in 1960 to form his own group, Coltrane was one of the best known, most influential, and most controversial figures in jazz. Accused by some critics of packing his solos with mindless runs, he was hailed by others as a liberator of jazz from the conventions of the past. During the next seven years, Coltrane moved steadily away from the mainstream playing of his so-called "middle period" of the Davis years, becoming one of the major figures of the free jazz movement of the sixties. Beginning with his album Giant Steps, *and his playing on Davis's* Kind of Blue, *both recorded in 1959, Coltrane in effect directed the approach of an entire new generation of saxophonists and the musical thinking of young musicians everywhere. His influence was so powerful that it also affected the styles of countless established saxophonists, causing many of them to allow their own musical personalities to be dominated by Coltrane's, in some cases permanently.*

By 1965 he was a cult idol to young jazz artists and rock musi-

*cians. Coltrane took his music increasingly into an area of religious
expression and spiritualism that had been coherently and movingly
explored in the album* A Love Supreme. *Percussion instruments began to dominate his performances, and he took up a kind of chant-
ing. By the time of his death in 1967, Coltrane had surrounded himself with musicians not near the quality of the members of his
famous quartet, pianist McCoy Tyner, bassist Jimmy Garrison, and
drummer Elvin Jones, all of whom had left. His music had become
impenetrable and puzzling.*

The following essay evaluates Coltrane's style and influence.

1980

To listen to John Coltrane's recordings of late 1957 and early 1958
is to hear an old friend speak. The metaphor is not quixotically
offered. To one degree or another, all of the master horn soloists
in jazz have approximated the inflections of speech. Allusions to
the phenomenon are frequent in the way musicians refer to and
comment about one another's playing: "Tell your story, man," "I
hear you talking," "Cat's sayin' something," "Cat ain't got nothing
to say." From the gruff trombone announcements of Tricky Sam
Nanton to the ironic asides of Eric Dolphy's alto saxophone, speechlike phrasing is an important component of the styles of many jazzmen who can be easily identified by their playing.

Coltrane's tenor saxophone had a vocal quality. The most striking aspect of his playing was his incredibly human sound, and
during the period of searching and growth represented by the recordings at hand, he sustained an effusion of warmth and humanity.
The densely packed improvisation of his "sheets of sound" period
was not far off; you can find hints of its development in places in
these recordings, notably on "Little Melonae."

When these records were made, Coltrane was between two engagements with Miles Davis, during both of which he developed prodigiously. In the summer of 1957 and on into the fall, he worked with Thelonious Monk. It was one of the most stimulating events of Coltrane's career, a six-month association which he later credited with accelerating his development. Their long engagement at the Five Spot Cafe in New York and the few recordings they made together are part of the jazz lore of the fifites. 'Trane emerged from the Monk experience more sophisticated harmonically and with a confidence also rooted in increased rhythmic assurance.

As he told *down beat* in 1960, "Working with Monk brought me close to a musical architect of the highest order. I felt I learned from him in every way—through the senses, theoretically, technically. I would talk to Monk about musical problems and he would sit at the piano and show me the answers by playing them. I could watch him play and find out the things I wanted to know. Also, I could see a lot of things I didn't know at all."

Coltrane was never a player of less than extraordinary intensity. But after Monk the intensity took on a palpably Monkish quality that had to do with improvising on the theme as much as on the harmonic changes, a method used before Monk adopted it, but never more personally. That approach is part of what Coltrane appropriated during his time with Monk, and his use of it helps account for the atmosphere of adventure in his solos. It was a technique that would meld seamlessly with the method of improvisation on modal and scalar material that Miles Davis was to perfect in 1959, during Coltrane's second Davis excursion.

But in early 1958, Coltrane's primary legacy from the Monk relationship seemed to have been a crackling, almost swaggering, authority. He moves headlong through his material at any tempo with none of the groping one often sensed in the early days of the Davis quintet. Hear his breathtaking choruses on the ripsnorting versions of "Lover" and the only slightly slower "Rise 'n Shine" and the ebullient, conversational Coltrane of "If There Is Someone Lovelier Than You." On the latter, Coltrane the phrasemaker re-enters after the bass solo with eight bars of distilled beauty capped by a little whoop of joy, a simulation of verbal expression that was one of his most appealing devices.

Knowing the chronology of the Monk-Coltrane alliance, one can hear a difference in Coltrane's playing over the eight months covered by these recordings. In August, 1957, he was more or less in the middle of the Five Spot experience. By March of 1958 the job with Monk had ended and he had had several months to absorb and practice what he had learned. Even when one is making comparisons among material that is in jazz's basic form, the blues, the increased complexity of Coltrane's harmonic explorations is apparent in the later work. His March 1958 performance of "By the Numbers" has harmonic leaps more daring than anything attempted on either take of the August 1957 blues variously titled "Slowtrane" and "Trane's Slow Blues." It should be noted, however, that the modulations of his first chorus and his doubletiming on the second in "Slowtrane" are superior examples of his more "conventional" playing.

Now that Coltrane's technical and stylistic innovations have been absorbed into the general musical language, even the casual jazz listener can respond to the warmly human qualities in his work. But in "Lover" and "Rise 'n Shine" there are passages of sixteenth notes ripped off with such speed and precision that it is not at all difficult to understand why Coltrane's playing seemed formidable not only to saxophonists but to listeners coming to it for the first time.

During his last years, in the quest for what he described as a "universal sound," Coltrane abandoned the standard song in favor of settings that untied him from the harmonic structures and rhythms of 32-, 16-, and 12-bar forms. Considering the bounds-breaking energy and rush of ideas to be heard on this album and others of the period, perhaps it was inevitable that Trane would have to go outside the song form. But it was the very struggle against the limitations of the pieces he played that created the tension which helps make the work of his middle period so compelling. That is less true of ballads than of the middle- and up-tempo performances, but even on "I See Your Face before Me," relaxed as it is, there is urgency in Coltrane's transition from the melody to the second chorus as he begins to explore the harmonic possibilities of the song.

I had been so captivated by Coltrane's work of the fifties and early sixties that when he went beyond his *Giant Steps* period into what seemed to me some arena of musical voodoo, I was mystified and sometimes indignant about the direction his work was taking. Then, after he died and I was preparing a series of radio programs dealing with his music, I engaged in a massive listening project that took me past *Giant Steps* into *A Love Supreme* and beyond. As I listened, I became more intrigued, and more awed by his dedication, his huge talent, and the increasingly obvious fact that he knew precisely what he was doing. I was struck then, for the first time, by the notion that Coltrane might have been more than a surpassingly moving player, that he might have been one of the handful of geniuses that jazz music has produced. Certainly, I do not think everything he recorded during his "free" period was of value. Unquestionably, some of his sidemen of the final years did not deserve to be in his company.

But as I immersed myself in the music of his mid-sixties recordings it occured to me that Coltrane may have been achieving in jazz something very like the music of the great Brazilian composer Heitor Villa-Lobos. The comparison goes beyond the fact that some of Coltrane's later compositions sound as if they could have been written by Villa-Lobos and beyond the similiarity in tone of Coltrane's horn to the saxophones in many of the Brazilian's works (Coltrane had the most magnificently "legitimate" tone of any modern jazz saxophonist). It extends to the controlled savagery and the peaceful fulfillment which exist simultaneously in the music of both men, and to the synthesis of native folk elements with modern techniques and theories.

In Villa-Lobos's case, the combination was of traditional Brazilian tunes and rhythms with so-called "classical" music. Listen to his "Nonetto" and "Quator" for mixtures of samba, folksong, primitive rhythms, and Ravel-like impressionism blended into some of the most fascinating, moving, and original music of the twentieth century.

Coltrane's bag was even more mixed. Certainly it contained a number of less recognizable elements, including the influence of Arabic scales, Indian modal improvisation, the mystique of free playing that guided the new jazz of the 1960s, the blues tradition and real scholarship into the complex mysteries of African rhythms.

All of that was woven through Coltrane's music and absorbed into its foundation.

It is music of grandeur, passion, and occasional frenzy. It has conviction, assurance, inner peace, religious fervor, and a nationalism that transcends the Black Nationalism attributed to Coltrane's music by LeRoi Jones and others with racial, social, or ideological axes to grind. It may be that Coltrane's work, in its time and way, will prove to be worthy of inclusion with Duke Ellington's, Charlie Parker's, Lester Young's, Coleman Hawkins's, and Louis Armstrong's, that it will be to America what Villa-Lobos's music is to Brazil.

For a complex variety of reasons, few of them musical, a legendary John Coltrane was created in the years immediately after his death in 1967. The legend persists, and it exists alongside the music as if on a separate plane. Coltrane the legend is a divinely inspired mystic who ultimately transcended music to deliver to the world a spiritual message of love and salvation. The legend comes complete with an appropriately mystical name for Coltrane, *Ohnedaruth*, evoking the mists, incense, and chants of some great Zen beyond, from which Trane is sending back vibrations.

I have been in the pads of youngsters who have constructed little shrines not unlike those of Japanese or Italian working class homes. But the centerpiece is not a lithograph of Buddha or Jesus. It is a print of the cover photograph from Coltrane's album *A Love Supreme*. In the late sixties and early seventies, the time of flower children, Haight-Ashbury, Vietnam, and burgeoning drug use, Coltrane became a convenient object of the search for heroes. And his early death seemed to qualify him, among those in need of martyrs, for the company of Dr. King, Malcolm X, and Robert Kennedy.

The legend came with disciples, many of them saxophonists who took as their starting point in music the area of freedom from the conventions of harmony and rhythm in which Coltrane was working with varying degrees of success in his final years. These musicians, without the thorough musical knowledge, craftsmanship, and heritage of their idol, thrashed about in imitation of the style of his free period. Some have worked through the overwhelming influence of Coltrane to find means of original expression within his legacy. Others continue flailing and have attracted substantial audiences of people who believe that if music is sufficiently agonized to be *called* New and Revolutionary and Free, it is.

To the young people who worship Trane as a burning prophet, I commend his playing in this collection for its humor and humanity; to the instrumentalists who concentrate on his freedom, for its discipline; to the audiences in search of agony, for its lyricism and calm beauty.

When these sessions were recorded, Coltrane had reached a stage of artistic development that most musicians never attain. He was about to rejoin Miles Davis in that incredible sextet that included Cannonball Adderley, Bill Evans, Philly Joe Jones, and Paul Chambers. The influence of Davis's concept exemplified in the *Kind of Blue* album was to provide Coltrane a point of departure that took him on to "Giant Steps" and "My Favorite Things." Then came the quartet with Elvin Jones, McCoy Tyner, and Jimmy Garrison which ultimately produced *A Love Supreme* and helped propel Coltrane into the search for further revelation that he was on when he died.

My only conversation with Coltrane took place in 1963 when he was appearing with his quartet at a Cleveland jazz club called Leo's Casino. I was the Cleveland correspondent for *down beat* and I was assigned to interview him.

"Why?" asked Coltrane on the telephone.

I allowed that he must be tired of interviews.

"Shouldn't I be?" he asked. "I can't explain anything. It's all in the music. Come to the club and hear the music."

It's all in the music. And it's like hearing an old friend speak.

Cannonball Adderley

Alto and soprano saxophonist Julian "Cannonball" Adderley was one of the most expansive soloists in jazz and one of the most convivial and popular members of the musical community. Born in 1928 into a musical family in Tampa, Florida, Adderley was an active jazz musician by his mid-teens. Following high school and college in Tallahasee, he became a high school band director in Fort Lauderdale. His Army career, from 1950 to 1953, was largely spent leading jazz groups, then he returned to his teaching post. Visiting New York in 1955, he played a few tunes with established musicians at a famous jazz club, stunned them and the audience with the maturity and force of his work, and became famous virtually overnight. In those days it was unusual, as it would be now, for a fully formed and distinctive soloist, unheralded and unknown, to materialize in the jazz center of the world ready and qualified to perform with the household names of the profession.

Within weeks, Adderley had a recording contract. Early the following year, he and his brother Nat, a cornetist, began working steadily with their own band. In late 1957, Adderley joined Miles Davis for two years, then he and Nat reformed their group. It became one of the most successful small bands of the 1960s and 1970s. The Adderleys managed the not inconsiderable accomplishment of appealing to the popular taste for simple, funky, blues-based music while getting their audiences to also accept sophisticated, complex jazz that often bordered on the avant-garde. Adderley died following a massive stroke in 1975, at the age of forty-seven.

Innocence and Beyond

1979

> Piping down the valleys wild,
> Piping songs of pleasant glee,
> On a cloud I saw a child,
> And he laughing said to me:
>
> "Pipe a song about a Lamb!"
> So I piped with a merry chear.
> "Piper, pipe that song again";
> So I piped: he wept to hear.
>
> —William Blake
> *Songs of Innocence*

"I sounded so innocent."

Cannonball Adderley was listening to the youthful Cannonball who had rolled onto the New York jazz turf from Fort Lauderdale in 1955. The occasion was one of his many visits to the studios of WDSU in the late 1960s. The Adderley quintet played New Orleans frequently in those days. Julian, his brother Nat, and pianist Joe Zawinul seemed to enjoy being on the "Jazz Review" program to listen, reminisce, philosophize, or just shuck and jive.

"I'm not saying it was good," Cannon clarified. "But it was innocent."

His playing on those early Mercury and Savoy albums was remarkably free of artifice. The sound and the style were open and guileless. Adderley's solos were largely without the darker components of tone and harmony that would make his later work often more interesting than in 1955 and 1956, but rarely more joyous. Which is not to say that his earlier playing was mere happy mindlessness. He was a listener, had been since the age of four, and he knew more about the fine points of the great soloists' styles than any other musician I have ever talked with. That knowledge and love of the jazz tradition were always apparent in his work.

Charlie Parker died in March of 1955. A successor seemed to be needed, and Sonny Stitt was in the process of being elected or appointed when Cannonball exploded into view in a blaze of publicity. In the jazz milieu, a blaze of publicity is a mention in *down beat,* a press release, three whispered conversations at Jim and Andy's, and an argument in front of the Club Baron. At any rate, the word got around: Cannonball was the New Bird. Or Sonny and Cannonball were fighting it out for the title. It must have occurred to someone that Bird was Bird and there could never be a New Bird. But whoever that someone was, he kept quiet about it. Cannon, a bit disturbed, a bit overwhelmed by all the Bird talk and by the instant stardom, nonetheless kept his balance and began carving out a remarkable career.

In 1959 he talked about the New Bird phenomenon in an interview with critic Ira Gitler in *Jazz Review* (the quarterly publication, not the radio program).

" . . . Most people think I'm kidding when I say that Bird wasn't a major influence on me as a saxophone player 'cause I never heard any of his records until 1946, '47, you see, and by that time I'd been playing saxophone for a long time. My first influences were Johnny Hodges, Benny Carter, the little I'd heard of him, and Jimmy Dorsey. But the tenor players used to be more effective to me and those men were all giants—Ben Webster, Chu Berry, Coleman Hawkins, Lester Young, Don Byas, and a guy with Andy Kirk who was really a bitch, Dick Wilson.

"The only thing that is a drag about it is I knew I had a lot of my qualities before I ever heard Bird but people will say 'Oh, anyone can say that.' And what can you do about it? I never consciously tried to do anything that Bird has done. I never tried to do a Bird-ism directly as a professional musician."

Webster, Berry, Byas, Hawkins. Young Julian heard them all, studied them all. And I mean *young* Julian. Here's what he said on "Jazz Review" (the radio program, not the quarterly) in 1967.

"I've been a jazz enthusiast since I was four years old. My dad was a trumpet player, and back in Tampa, where I was born, he used to take me to City Auditorium to see various bands which are no longer in existence, the old Earl Hines big band, Mills Blue Rhythm, the Fletcher Henderson band. Man, it was a great day for me. When I heard Fletcher Henderson, Coleman Hawkins was in the band. I think he was the most interesting looking jazz musician I've ever seen in my life. He just looked so authoritative. I kept looking at him. I never did look at Fletcher. I said, 'Well, that's what I want to do when I grow up.' I think I knew then."

Hawkins was a figure of influence and inspiration for Cannonball during the forty-three years of his life that followed the City Auditorium revelation. He never tired of hearing Hawkins or talking about him. Cannon's analysis of Hawk's harmonic dominance in the late 1930s was typical of his keen appreciation for the major developments in jazz.

"I have a funny chronological way of thinking about these things. When Hawk came back from Europe he seemed to make everybody chord-conscious. Before, guys were playing straightaway blues and 'I Got Rhythm' pattern things. If they played solos, they would play the obvious melodic material from the chord structure of the tune without really going inside it. But Coleman Hawkins came back and all of a sudden everybody was substituting harmonies and embellishing the chords. Very interesting. Don Byas was already trying to do things on his own, without the new Coleman Hawkins influence. He was trying to do things with chords, but not with the same imagination and facility that Coleman was. Suddenly Don got some new respect because people had thought he was weird. But now the master said, 'This is the way it is supposed to be done.'"

Cannonball shot into national recognition at the age of twenty-seven, after his famous jam session with Oscar Pettiford at the Cafe Bohemia, and managed to keep his sense of proportion and sense of humor while around him there were choruses of New Bird calls and all those record dates and all that instant fame. He and Nat formed a quintet, which was on the road for a couple of years. Then the brothers decided to stop living on instant fame and try to earn more money by going their separate ways. Julian later admitted that he accepted Miles Davis's offer to join the Davis quintet primarily because it would help in his commercial development. He told Ira Gitler: "I wanted to get the benefit of Miles's exposure rather than Miles's musical thing . . . it was a commercial move but I noticed that Miles could do some things naturally that I had difficulty doing, and so we started finding out why, and it was easy, you know, more or less."

With Davis, Adderley began to alter his conception. Miles often leads in strange and reticient ways. But he was never reluctant to tell his sidemen when he didn't like their playing. He told Cannonball he played too many notes, that when a note is played it should mean something. And Cannon, ever open, curious, receptive, listened more and more carefully to Davis's playing and to his criticisms. Miles's economy and his harmonic subtlety began to make themselves known in Adderley's playing. After John Coltrane was added to the band, Cannon's harmonic development accelerated through exposure to one of the most restlessly creative soloists in the history of jazz. The saxophonists rubbed together and threw off sparks. For a stunning instance of the way Coltrane influenced Adderley, consult their solos on "Two Bass Hit" (Columbia CS-9428).

A month or so after Coltrane died in 1967, Cannonball told me on the air, "It's still very hard for me to talk about him, except to say I learned more from him than from anybody."

By the time of the epochal *Kind of Blue* session in 1959, the innocence in Julian's solos had not been deflowered, but it had been tempered with deep insights into the possibilities of chords, with the wisdom that leads to a realization that one note can simultaneously serve more than one chord, with the knowledge that a pause may make a point more effectively than a trill. Cannonball became a more conservative player in the sense that he learned to hold something in reserve, but a more daring one in his harmonic aspects.

During the Davis experience, Adderley came to intimately know and respect the work of pianists Bill Evans and Wynton Kelly, whom he chose to accompany and co-star with him in the 1961 recording dates represented in the album at hand. The modal makeup of "Know What I Mean?" reflects the style of the Davis band during the latter days of Evans's and Addlerley's membership in it.

In October of 1959, having resumed his role as a leader, Cannonball (with Nat, Bobby Timmons, Louis Hayes, and Sam Jones) recorded a live album at the Jazz Workshop in San Francisco. It included a funky little ditty by Timmons called "This Here," which became an enormous hit by jazz standards. Lightning struck again in 1967, this time in the form of Joe Zawinul's "Mercy, Mercy, Mercy." Following both successes, Cannonball was subjected to the standard abuse of jazz artists who win public acceptance; he was called a sellout. Show me a solvent jazz band and I'll show you a band accused of selling out. The hail of sour grapes bounced right off Julian. About the success of "Mercy, Mercy, Mercy" he had this to say:

"It has given us an opportunity to play for more people. It gives us a chance to play other things. We get the 'Mercy' audience and expose them to everything that we do. We find that people by and large will listen if you tell them, 'This is something new, something a little different.'"

And Cannonball was always adept at softening up his audience with the funk tunes, sambas, and pretty ballads and then getting them to not only sit still for but thoroughly enjoy such abstractions as Zawinul's "Rumplestiltskin" or "Painted Desert." He helped open the public ear to the more difficult music of the free jazz practitioners of the sixties and seventies. He was acutely aware, for an example, of Ornette Coleman's musicianship and importance.

"Ornette is a dear friend of mine," he told me. "He is a kind of messiah in a way. I don't mean that he has that much influence on individuals, but he has so much on jazz philosophies. People don't emulate him the way they emulated Charlie Parker or Lester Young—copying phrases—so much as to pay some tribute to his influence in regard to taking liberties with things and saying, 'Well, you don't have to play just the exact chord.' Maybe you don't want to play a chord at all. Maybe you want to play tonality for a bar, let's be atonal for one bar, or frightening, or whatever. He's opened the musician's mind and that's a much more important thing than getting to the public, as far as jazz is concerned. There are people who can carry a message to the public and there are people who cannot communicate with the general public, and this is true in all art. Most of the people who really do something important for any art medium never get recognized until it's too late. But their influence is felt when they're here, by other artists who understand what they're trying to do. Ornette's force is being felt by George Russell, by Miles Davis, people who can carry what he does to the public and get greater acceptance on the basis of what they do than Ornette can. He is probably the most sincere jazz musician I've ever encountered."

As in all matters, Adderley was engagingly honest about Coleman the bandleader.

"I enjoy listening to him play. I don't like his band so much. I think his judgment regarding musicians rivals that of another dear friend of mine, Dizzy Gillespie. I've always wondered how guys can be so great and have other great guys with them and have some spots that are so glaringly weak. You just have to say, 'Well, are they serious?' Dizzy is that type and Ornette has some of the same problems. I think he initially came to New York with a great band, Billy Higgins, Charlie Haden, and Don Cherry. They had a sound identity. Everybody played well. He has since had some questionable musicians performing with him. And sometimes Ornette himself makes me nervous. He'll pick up the trumpet or the violin and it's very hard for me to believe that he's serious. But he is."

Julian's lack of preconceptions about the worth of individual players make him see the value of some performers not regarded as great by the jazz establishment. And he could hear historical connections that seemed to elude most of us.

"Charlie Barnet was one of the first guys I thought was unique. I can tell you step-wise how the alto players got to me. The first one I knew played alto was Jimmy Dorsey. Then Johnny Hodges and Benny Carter and Willie Smith. Then when I first heard Charlie Parker I heard something different, really different. There were some guys who were trying to sound like Charlie Parker. Then I began to notice Charlie Barnet for the first time, even though he'd been on the scene. He was saying an awful lot of different things. He was peculiarly original from the outset. He played only like himself. And not just on alto. Here's a guy whose tenor playing was far more influential than people realize. A great number of rock and roll players utilize Charlie Barnet devices. The so-called 'chicken' tenor sax playing of King Curtis and Boots Randolph—direct quotations from Charlie Barnet thirty years ago."

Adderley was equally perceptive in reevaluating his own positions on musical matters. I once asked him how his notorious 1957 blanket castigation of West Coast jazz sounded to him in 1969.

"I had the voice of a young, overgregarious, intrusive person," he said. "Actually, I wasn't in a position to evaluate West Coast jazz. But in all honesty I must say that most of the ultra-relaxed things that were happening then are still unimpressive to me. I think that West Coast jazz, sort of like avant-garde jazz, has allowed a lot of charlatans to exist who had no business being around. By the time it all settled down, you found that the great jazz musicians, the Chet Bakers and Gerry Mulligans and so forth, survived it all anyhow because they had a lot to say. And I survived my youthful foolishness."

The radio programs with Cannonball are fresh in my mind; every couple of years I listen to the tapes. There are other memories that remain strong because of special circumstances or simply the force of Julian's persona. One of his favorite restaurants in New Orleans was Vaucresson, a little place on Bourbon Street that specialized in a kind of Creole soul food, nicely spiced and very rich. It was just down the street from Al Hirt's, in those days a jazz club with a name policy, where the quintet played at least twice a year.

After the gig, or sometimes between sets, Cannon and the band would install themselves at the largest table in the place, inevitably to be joined by fans, friends, family, and assorted French Quarter regulars. The enduring image is of Cannonball surrounded by people, simultaneously laughing, expounding, questioning, and consuming, inevitably taking time for just one more dish.

"Yes, Mama," he'd tell the proprietress, "I think there's room for the bread pudding."

In his final years, Cannonball was able to indulge in some cherished musical projects, including the impressive *Big Man* (Fantasy F-79006), a John Henry dramatization he had hoped to mount as a

Broadway production. His success did not make him complacent but offered opportunities to broaden his range as a performer and leader. Unfortunately, one dream never materialized. It demonstrated the scope of his imagination.

"I would like to make a record," he said one night, "with Stan Getz, Harry Carney, the Beatles, and Laurindo Almeida. I have the whole concept in my mind. They don't have to do anything differently from what they do now, but I have spots for all these cats to play."

And you know what? If he had been given the time, Cannonball would have pulled it off.

With the perspective of history, bebop is seen to have been much less a revolution than a stage in the evolution of jazz. But, because of the circumstances that attended its development, this new and more complex form seemed to burst into existence. Its impact on American, and eventually world, music cannot be overstated. The influence of bop is universal; many of its harmonic devices and much of its musical vocabulary heard in the mid-1940s as bold or outrageous have been absorbed into the general language of music. Movie and television scores, arrangements for popular singers, the music piped into dentists' offices, country music, modern classical music (particularly that of the so-called minimalists), even high school and college marching bands, all reflect the departures made by a handful of young American black musicians nearly half a century ago.

The Big Beboppers

1976

Dizzy Gillespie is the quintessential bop trumpeter. He began developing his style, which grew out of Roy Eldridge's, while playing in Cab Calloway's orchestra in the early forties. But Calloway was unimpressed. The Hi De Ho man responded to Gillespie's fiery, iconoclastic, humorous solos with an ultimatum: "I don't want you playing that Chinese music on my band."

Tommy Dorsey was so upset about bebop that he attacked Gillespie and alto saxophonist Charlie Parker as "musical Communists," an excessive bit of nastiness, even for Dorsey.

Bop, which evolved naturally and inevitably from the styles that preceded it, seemed to spring forth full blown. There are a number of stories about how it came to be called bebop, but they all amount to the same thing; those two little words sound like a simple musical phrase of the kind that often appeared in solos. There developed a tradition of verbalizing the sounds of the new music that led to tune titles like "Oop Bop Sh'bam" and "Ool Ya Coo" and ultimately to the name which, for better or worse, was attached to the style.

Bebop demanded harmonic sophistication, depending as it did on substitute chords, inverted chords, and unconventional intervals. It also continued the work begun by Louis Armstrong, and carried dramatically forward by the tenor saxophonist Lester Young, of eliminating the concept of the bar line as a barrier in building an improvised solo. Young was not intimidated by the arbitrary time divisions that had limited most jazz soloists to rather choppy and often disconnected phrases. Riding on the smooth 4/4 beat of the Count Basie rhythm section, Young glided and swooped through his solo statements. Before Young, even the greatest soloists tended to explode their way through the bar lines. Lester leaped across them with grace and power, the Nijinsky of the Swing Era. Charlie Parker was profoundly influenced by Young, knew his every recorded solo by heart and continued to develop the rhythmic freedom Young pioneered.

Experimentation and development were taking place in a number of important bands and in jam sessions from 1941 to 1945. But the advent of this harmonically and rhythmically daring music was camouflaged from general notice by a global disaster, World War II, and a domestic annoyance, a ban on all recording imposed by James Petrillo, president of the American Federation of Musicians. The ban, which lasted more than a year during one of the most vital stages of the idiom's growth, kept the Earl Hines band effectively under wraps when it was a veritable bop incubator. Parker and Gillespie, the Romulus and Remus of bop, were the Hines band's horn stars. Budd Johnson, jazz's Leonardo, was its principal catalyst. Among them, they helped nurture the bop revolution.

Except to the few who heard it in live performance, the Hines band was a secret. Millions of the young American men who might have seized upon bop as their music were kept out of touch with developments. When they returned from the war in 1945, the evolution was so far along that the new music was almost completely strange to them. Considering the compressed development of jazz, it was for them something like going to bed when Haydn's symphonies were the most advanced music and awakening to Stravinsky's "Rite of Spring."

Nonetheless, bop had enchanted most musicians who were more forward-thinking than Calloway and Dorsey, and by the late forties it had become a pervasive influence not only in jazz but also in American popular music at large. As early as 1946, as Ira Gitler points out in his *Jazz Masters of the Forties* (Macmillan), "The influence of bop could be heard in the most commercial dance bands." Well, possbily not in the music of Guy Lombardo.

At any rate, the torrent of the bop revolution has long since merged with the mainstream and, at least subliminally, bop is a part of all of our lives. You hear echoes and reflections of Charlie Parker in the most mundane supermarket Muzak, in television and radio commercial jingles, in rock music, even in elements of progressive country music. The influence is so omnipresent among musicians that, like the bass player I once knew who was convinced that Stravinsky had stolen one of his licks, they don't necessarily understand where the inspiration comes from. It's simply in the air, a part of the musical atmosphere.

But there is a specific and rapidly growing new interest in bop itself, the real thing, the hard core, uncompromising, fountainhead music of Parker and Gillespie and their contemporaries and spiritual descendants. A series of concerts by the New York Jazz Repertory Company tracing Parker's musical development was so well received that it went on the road to Europe. Parker has been dead since 1955, but Gillespie is flourishing and playing more creatively than ever, if not always as spectacularly as in the forties and fifties. The brilliant pianist Bud Powell is gone, but his closest and most accomplished disciple, Barry Harris, is one of the busiest artists on the concert and recording circuit. Phil Woods, a virtuoso alto saxophonist in the Parker tradition, is a perennial poll winner. And Parker himself is gloriously back on the record shelves in some of his most important work.

Through dedicated and tireless effort by British critic Tony Williams, all of the available Parker material recorded for Dial in 1946 and 1947 has been assembled in six volumes and reissued on the Spotlite label. After an engagement at Billy Berg's club in Hollywood in 1945, during which Californians were hostile to the new music that was being enthusiastically received in the East, the twenty-five-year-old Parker stayed in Los Angeles. Needing money to support his increasingly problematical drug habit, he signed a contract with Ross Russell's struggling young company and in a twenty-month period made a superb series of recordings for Dial. They are presented in chronological order on Spotlite, with complete and accurate personnel listings and recording dates, and with helpful liner notes by Williams.

The series includes thirty-nine pieces, but there are as many as four takes on some of the tunes, affording a fascinating acquaintance with Parker's ability to spontaneously create fresh and thoroughly original solos. There is stunning evidence of Parker's endless creative resources in the eleven takes of three blues pieces he recorded with pianist Erroll Garner in February 1947. Each of his solos on "Dark Shadows," "Cool Blues," and "Bird's Nest" is based on the twelve-bar blues format, but each is as different from the others as one Beethoven string quartet from another. Garner may not have been the ideal accompanist for Parker, but he was not an incompatible one, and the session resulted in remarkable music. The four takes of "Relaxin' at Camarillo" provide another insight into Bird's kaleidoscopic blues vision.

Because of his narcotics addiction, this was an often confused and painful period of Parker's life. But on the recordings he achieves purity of a kind realized by very few musicians in history, and by only a handful of jazz artists. Even in his worst moments during the "Lover Man" session of July 1946, when he required physical support so that he could solo, his playing has an imperial, desolate beauty.

The musicians heard with Parker on the Dial sides include Gillespie (who Parker once referred to as "the other half of my heartbeat"); trumpeter Miles Davis, who began as a stylistic son of Gillespie but rapidly evolved into a unique musician; the vastly under-acclaimed tenor saxophonist Lucky Thompson; the admired and influential tenor artist Wardell Gray; pianists Dodo Marmarosa and Duke Jordan; and the explosive, provocative drummer Max Roach. Each of them has his moments of inspiration, grandeur, and fire on these recordings. Parker has virtually nothing but such moments; he was a musician of almost incredible consistency. This music is as essential to any serious jazz collection as the 1928 Louis Armstrong small band recordings or the 1941 Duke Ellington sides.

There is comparatively little of Gillespie and Parker together on the Dial albums. In fact, the two did not record together as frequently as one might suppose, given their co-equal status as founders of bop. But they did take part in one of the most unusual and most important sessions of the swing-to-bop transition. It was held in June 1945 in New York under the leadership of the veteran vibraphonist Red Norvo. Norvo, aware of the winds of change blowing through jazz, engaged Parker and Gillespie to join tenor saxophonist Flip Phillips (then a star of Woody Herman's First Herd), the elegant and harmonically sophisticated pianist Teddy Wilson, and Slam Stewart, the humming-bowing bassist. Drummers J. C. Heard and Specs Powell alternated from tune to tune.

The contrast between the established styles of Norvo, Wilson, and Phillips and the Sturm und Drang of the young boppers resulted in fascinating music full of tempestuous peaks and relatively calm valleys. The peaks, solos by Bird and Diz, are monumental.

Unimpeded by a rhythm section that would have seemed inappropriate for their kind of music, the two did some of their most devastating playing that day on "Slam Slam Blues," Parker producing one of the most memorable blues solos of a career packed with great blues solos. Spotlite has reissued the original Comet recordings and included alternate takes, many of which have solos at least the equals of the previously released versions.

Parker died twenty-one years ago after thirty-four years that included every conceivable kind of personal excess. Gillespie, a man of equally incendiary talent but more stable personal habits, had thrived over the past two decades. His playing in the seventies often recalls the fire of his youth. But it is now more consistently interesting from a purely musical standpoint in terms of what he plays, as opposed to how he plays it. His choices of notes are more considered and the notes themselves are more carefully placed than in the days when he was likely to bedazzle rather than move the listener. All of that is hardly to suggest that Gillespie today is a trumpeter of diminished capability. On several recent Pablo albums he demonstrates quite clearly that he is as likely as ever to burst into cascades of ascending and descending phrases, flurries of sixteenth notes at ridiculously fast tempos, and prestidigitatorial half-valve tricks.

But there is a more deeply thoughtful and tender Gillespie these days, and he can be heard in ballads like "What's New" on the *Dizzy Gillespie Big 7* album (Pablo 2310-749) recorded at last year's Montreux Jazz Festival. There are plenty of double-time passages and cliff-hanging demonstrations that prove it's quite likely he is still the greatest trumpet player alive. But Gillespie plays some phrases with respect for the eloquence of silence and with a low dynamic profile that can make the listener sit up and take notice just as surely as one of his wild-bull-of-the-pampas sorties.

Among the players who joined Gillespie in the Big 7 was Milt Jackson, the original and best bop vibes player, a graduate of the great Gillespie big band of the forties. For twenty-two years Jackson was in the Modern Jazz Quartet, where he occasionally felt constrained by the dignified ambience. Now he says he is interested only in "straight ahead jazz or bebop or whatever you want to call it." And whatever you want to call it, that's what he plays on this album; ringing, rolling joyful choruses of pure bop, Jackson pushing the beat ever so slightly. No compromises, no concessions.

The pianist on many of the Parker Dial recordings, Dodo Marmarosa, ignited briefly in the mid-forties. He and Bud Powell were the most admired pianists in the bop movement. Marmarosa recorded independently for Dial in a series of trio dates that were lavishly praised by critics and greatly admired by musicians, especially pianists. Spotlite has reissued many of them in a collection that again makes available the work of this gifted artist whose instability and lack of confidence drove him into self-imposed exile in Pittsburgh in the late forties. Little has been heard of him on record since, and what he has recorded since 1950 has been disappointing. But in 1947 he was technically awesome, fleet, melodically and harmonically inventive, and he imbued his work with an engaging kind of nonagressive but insistent swing. This recording includes originals, alternate takes, test pressings and a pair of solos taken from Armed Forces Radio Service broadcasts.

Bud Powell, as incandescent as Marmarosa, had a longer and much more influential career. He took the formidable technique of Art Tatum and the harmonic wisdom of Teddy Wilson into the bop era and added to them his own wild but classically disciplined imagination. Even toward the end of his life, half mad, cared for by his wife as if a child, Powell on a given evening could electrify an audience with the brilliance of his improvising. He had an enormous impact on every jazz pianist of his time, from George Shearing to Herbie Hancock. But there is no pianist more faithful to the spirit of Powell's style than Barry Harris.

In *Barry Harris Plays Tadd Dameron* (Xanadu 113) he honors one of the great bop composers and arrangers with beautifully conceived performances of eight of Dameron's pieces, including the classic "If You Could See Me Now." For the occasion, Harris adds recognizable touches of Dameron's own piano style. But he is first, last, and always a Powell man. Although he never slavishly copies Powell, Harris works so perfectly in Bud's idiom that at times it's difficult to remember that you're not listening to the master.

Another pianist drawing heavily on the Powell legacy is a blind

Catalonian Spaniard named Tete Montoliu. Long a respected accompanist and soloist in Europe, Montoliu is acquiring a reputation in this country. His "Catalonian Fire" (Steeplechase 1017) is
directly in the bop tradition. There are hints of the influence of
some of the younger free jazz pianists in Montoliu's playing, but
Powell's spirit hovers over this session like a benevolent genie. It is
possible that the spirit winces occasionally at Montoliu's repetitive-
ness; certain key phrases pop up more often than is entirely excus-
able. But he is unquestionably a stimulating, even an exciting pianist. Montoliu is in impeccable company with bassist Niels-Henning
Orsted Pedersen and drummer Albert Heath.

That Charlie Parker spawned a generation of alto saxophonists
who lived only to memorize and execute his every phrase is a com-
monplace, a cliché of the jazz writing trade. It also happens to
be true, just as it is true that a few of the disciples who did not give
up in frustration had the intelligence, taste, and ability to develop
their own ways of speaking Bird's language. One of the most impressive of those survivors is Phil Woods. Nowhere is he more
impressive that in *Musique Du Bois* (Muse 5037), a quartet album
in which Woods soars over the perfect rhythm section of Jaki Byard,
Richard Davis, and Alan Dawson with a freedom that makes one
wonder if this is what Parker would sound like today.*

Two alto players who have hewn somewhat closer to the letter of
Parker's example are Sonny Stitt and Sonny Criss. Stitt operates his
own stable of clichés, but he falls back on them in such a charming
manner that I find it impossible to be disturbed except when he is at
his most mechanical. There are such automatic moments on his recently issued "Night Work" (Black Lion 307), recorded in 1967.
There are other moments in which Stitt plays inventively. His companions are Howard McGhee, one of the first and finest bop trumpeters, and a rhythm section composed of pianist Walter Bishop,
bassist Tommy Potter, and drummer Kenny Clarke. Bishop and
Potter are former Parker sidemen. Clarke is the founding father of
bop drumming. McGhee was with Parker on the famous "Lover
Man" session on Dial. Unfortunately, on "Night Work" he was suf-

*The making of this album is described on pages 191–200.

fering from problems of intonation and execution. He fares considerable better, in fact splendidly, on his own "Shades of Blue" (Black Lion 306), recorded in 1961 and just released in the United States for the first time.

On his "Mellow" (Muse 5067), recorded in 1975, Stitt's playing lacks its usual edge despite a dream rhythm section of Barry Harris, bassist Richard Davis, and drummer Roy Haynes. Fellow saxophonist Jimmy Heath shares the front line with Stitt and steals the album with his thoughtful and forcefully expressed solos on tenor and soprano saxophones and flute. Stitt coasts along on the rhythm section. Heath takes advantage of its inspirational power.

Criss has what may well be the best album of his career in *Saturday Morning* (Xanadu 105) and at least an honorable mention in *Crisscraft* (Muse 5068). *Saturday Morning* has Harris on piano, with bassist Leroy Vinnegar and drummer Lenny McBrowne. Having been away from recording for six years or so, Criss had stored up considerable creative energy. What critic Mark Gardner has called his "piercing, passionate sound" is particularly moving on "Angel Eyes." *Crisscraft* hasn't quite the emotional thrust of *Saturday Morning* but it is a far above average album and I can recommend it, if for nothing more than a beautiful version of Benny Carter's "Blues In My Heart."

Criss died in 1979, Stitt in 1982. As this is written at the end of 1988, Harris is teaching and, when he performs publicly, playing beautifully. Woods has developed one of the most formidable quintets in jazz and his work is as forceful, uncompromising, and compelling as ever. Milt Jackson is with the reconstituted Modern Jazz Quartet, but also recording and making club and concert appearances with his own groups. Gillespie, at seventy, enchants and astounds audiences with his inventiveness. His band includes musicians less than half his age, and they are challenged not only by his musical wisdom and technique but also by his showmanship and stamina.

Bud Powell

1987

Virtually from the moment his playing became generally known, Bud Powell was the most important pianist in modern jazz. Founded on classical technique, driven by inspired imagination and demonic energy, his work profoundly influenced his contemporaries and the subsequent course of jazz piano.

Powell was born in New York City in 1924, the son of a pianist father. He began playing at the age of six and until he was thirteen rigorously studied the classics, including Bach, Beethoven, Chopin, and Liszt. As a teenager armed with formidable technique, he encountered jazz and became interested in Billy Kyle and, inevitably, Art Tatum, whose status among pianists was described by Fats Waller when he introduced Tatum to a night club audience as "God." Powell dropped out of high school at fifteen and began working professionally. He was initiated by fellow pianist Thelonious Monk, four years his senior, into the developing modern jazz scene at Minton's in Harlem. By 1943, when he made his first records with Cootie Williams, there were hints of a new, personal style in the idiom that came to be called bebop. The influence of Tatum, Earl Hines, and Teddy Wilson could be heard. Later in his career it became obvious in Powell's harmonies that the early exposure to Monk had also had its effect.

As early as 1945, Powell began suffering the mental illnesses that

frequently derailed his life, making his musical achievements inconsistent and his brilliance sporadic. But through the 1940s and much
of the early fifties, he performed at a level of energy and inspiration
no other pianist could match. Occasionally through the years until
his death in 1966, the old incandescence flashed briefly. Even when
the uncanny rush of his creative ideas was interrupted and the flame
of his almost superhuman energy had lowered, Powell's sound . . .
the way he touched the piano, the way he voiced chords . . . was
intact.

Powell is heard in pianists like Hank Jones and George Shearing,
who in the 1940s changed their styles after hearing him. He was the
core inspiration of Bill Evans, who used Powell's approach as a
point of departure for his own innovations. Directly or indirectly,
every jazz pianist who developed after the mid-forties is in debt to
Bud Powell, not only for demonstrating the Olympian heights to
which they could aspire but for performing an act of liberation.

Before Powell, even pianists as modern as Teddy Wilson and Nat
Cole were still committed, to a considerable degree, to a foursquare
rhythmic chording function of the left hand. Wilson, Cole, and
others including Billy Kyle, Clyde Hart, and Count Basie, had already de-emphasized the stride left hand in accompanying other
players. Powell relied, even more than the swing pianists, on the
string bassist to provide single note bass lines. He reduced his left
hand function to the occasional feeding of chords, as much for
punchy rhythmic emphasis as for harmonic guidance. The method
was employed behind horn soloists and as accompaniment to his
own right hand in solos. It allowed greater buoyancy because the
left hand was no longer anchored by the old 4/4 requirement. And
it left the soloist with greater freedom of choice in constructing his
improvisation because the left hand was no longer pre-empting the
lion's share of notes in every chord.

There is a famous story about Tatum, encountering Powell at
Birdland, accusing the younger man of being a right-handed pianist.
According to Ira Gitler in *Jazz Masters of the Forties*, Tatum said,
"You've got no left hand. Look, I've got a rhythm section in my left
hand." The following night, with Tatum again in the audience,

Powell set a breakneck tempo and played "Sometimes I'm Happy" with his left hand only. Tatum complimented him, which left Powell overjoyed at the praise from his idol.

Few pianists have had the technical ability and speed to adapt elements of Art Tatum's style, particularly his complex arpeggios. Few have understood Thelonious Monk thoroughly enough to sensibly incorporate into their own playing Monk's eccentric harmonies, quirky phrasing, and broken whole-note runs. Powell intuitively grasped both Tatum and Monk, in many ways the polar opposites of jazz piano, and melded those disparate legacies into his artistry. Earl Hines's voicings and Teddy Wilson's elegant runs also figure in Powell's style. But none of his heroes, including Tatum, achieved the headlong emotional rush that Powell, at his peak, maintained while observing logic and order in the development of his material.

No one would argue that the 1956 and 1957 RCA Victor sessions in this collection (*Time Was*, RCA Bluebird CD 6367-2-RB) represent Powell at that peak. Some of the tracks have the detachment of a lounge performer, however interesting the harmonies and attractive the touch. Others, particularly some of his original compositions and the bop standards "Salt Peanuts," "Shawnuff," and "Swedish Pastry" have sustained periods of Powell's incomparable concentration and psychic energy. The intensity grows through the final pieces of the October 5 session and into the February 11 date as if something had rekindled Powell's interest.

As in the recorded works of such artists as Charlie Parker, Art Tatum, and Lester Young, there are no unimportant Bud Powell albums, simply because he was Bud Powell. If this one contained nothing but the fascinating way he voices the melodies of "Coscrane" and "Jump City," or the variety of his approaches to the blues in "Blues For Bessie," "Another Dozen," and "Birdland Blues," it would be an item needed by any Powell student and enjoyed by any listener. I might add that the way Powell is supported by George Duvivier and Art Taylor provides bassists and drummers a valuable lesson in the strength of subtlety and simplicity.

It is always instructive to study even the lesser works of the masters.

Wardell Gray

1976

Benny Goodman was ambivalent about bebop. He was not ambivalent about Wardell Gray.

"If Wardell Gray plays bop, it's great. Because he's wonderful," Goodman said in 1949. For a year or so, the King of Swing fronted a band that included young second-generation beboppers like trumpeters Nick Travis and Doug Mettome, drummer Sonny Igoe, trombonist Eddie Bert and, on one memorable recording session, the luminous trumpeter Fats Navarro.

The organization's personality was as split as Benny's feelings about bop. It couldn't decide whether it was to continue the great Goodman swing tradition or hop aboard the bop bandwagon that was transporting from one era to another Woody Herman, Charlie Barnet, Dizzy Gillespie, Boyd Raeburn, Claude Thornhill and, in his less grandiose periods, Stan Kenton. There was discussion of engaging Tadd Dameron and Gerry Mulligan to write arrangements for the Goodman "bop" band. Chico O'Farrill got the assignment. There were some good, if fairly restrained, charts. Benny never got the hang of bop's rhythmic complexities. Besides, business was not notably good, and in late 1949, he shucked the entire bop venture, returning to a small band format and sidemen more in tune with his thinking.

But Gray made a splash with the big band and the Goodman sextet. As a *down beat* reviewer wrote in an otherwise lukewarm assessment of one of the band's concerts, "The star of the evening from the applause standpoint was tenor star Wardell Gray."

It may have been Gray's musically expressed love for Lester Young that led Benny, a charter member of the Pres Admiration Society, to hire Wardell and feature him so extensively. Lester's influence did account for a great deal of Gray's musical makeup, but Don Byas and Charlie Parker also had their stylistic effects. And some have remarked that in Gray's ballad performances can be heard the example of his frequent employer Benny Carter.

The few records the Goodman sorta-bop band made for Capitol, and the NBC air checks captured during its stint at a Virginia Beach resort, make it quite clear that Gray was indeed playing superbly with Benny, as he did in any setting. Gray was one of those natural tenormen, like Zoot Sims and James Moody, whose expression was honest, straightforward, basically happy and, apparently, totally without artifice.

With the possible exception of Dexter Gordon, he was the ideal tenor companion for Charlie Parker. Gray and Gordon were the most formidable and exciting two-tenor team of the late 1940s. Their celebrated "The Chase" is still the standard by which tandem tenor performances are judged.

Wardell Gray was born in Oklahoma City in 1921, but his family moved to Detroit when he was a child. He studied clarinet, laying the technical foundation for saxophone, and took up the alto some time in the late 1930s. Not a great deal is known about his early years in music. Pianist Hank Jones recalls having heard Gray with Benny Carew's Detroit band; the teenaged Lucky Thompson was another member of the saxophone section. In 1943 Gray joined Earl Hines's big band, playing alto and clarinet and soon switching to tenor, as had Charlie Parker, who left the band shortly before Gray arrived. Later Parker and Gray were to cross paths in the Dial studios in some of the most important recording sessions of the forties. After two years with Hines, Gray settled in Los Angeles when Central Avenue was the West Coast headquarters of the burgeoning bop revolution. It was the California version of New York's 52nd Street.

In 1945, young musicians burning with the bop message con-
verged in Los Angeles, many of them fresh out of the service. The
brilliant trumpeter Howard McGhee stayed in L.A. when his boss,
Coleman Hawkins, returned to New York after an engagement
on the Coast. There was no shortage of sympathetic players for
McGhee to jam with. Many of them were homegrown Angelinos,
including saxophonists Sonny Criss, Teddy Edwards, and Buddy
Collette, drummer Roy Porter, bassist Charles Mingus, and Hampton Hawes, still two years away from high school graduation and
already impressing veterans with his incandescent piano choruses.
Pianist Dodo Marmarosa, tenor saxophonist Herbie Steward, and
guitarist Barney Kessel blew into Los Angeles as members of Artie
Shaw's band. Boyd Raeburn's iconoclastic, slightly crazy bop band
showed up bearing saxophonists Frank Socolow, Hal McKusick,
and Serge Chaloff, arranger/pianist George Handy, and trombonist
Earl Swope. Trumpeter Art Farmer and his twin brother Addison,
the bassist, were attracted from Phoenix by the explosion of the
new music. An idol of the young boppers, Lester Young, settled in
Los Angeles, his psychologically torturous Army experience behind
him but still doing its disturbing work.

Clubs like the Brown Bomber, the Bird in the Basket, Papa
Lovejoy's, the Downbeat, the Last Word, the Jungle Room, and
who knows how many afterhours joints, were providing at least in-
termittent employment for the boppers, and virtually unlimited
jamming opportunities.

Late in 1945, Dizzy Gillespie took his sextet to Billy Berg's Club
in Hollywood. The band included Charlie Parker, and now the Los
Angeles scene was replete with the founding fathers of bebop (aged
twenty-eight and twenty-five), the inspirational fountainheads of
the new music. After a spectacularly successful opening, business
fell off drastically; the California public simply wasn't ready for
bop, no matter how enthusiastically its acknowledged masters were
received by Los Angeles musicians. Gillespie returned to New York,
but Bird stayed behind, illuminating the jam session circuit, recording some of his most profound solos and reaching an all-time low in
compiling his impressive lifetime average of narcotics strikeouts.

His famous recording, "Relaxin' at Camarillo," celebrates the state correctional treatment center where he recovered from a drug-induced total collapse. It would be unfair to say that every bop musician in L.A. was on drugs, but not grossly unfair. And the example of Bird's superhuman ability to ingest and inject every type and combination of destructive chemical substance had something to do with the high rate of addiction among young musicians. As Hampton Hawes points out in his chillingly honest autobiography, *Raise up off Me* (Coward, McCann and Geoghegan), the reasoning was that if they approximated Parker's state of narcotic euphoria, "they might get closer to the source of his fire." That sort of idolatry and self-deception led to many destroyed lives and many premature deaths and ultimately became a source of extreme pain and sadness to Parker.

But, Hawes recalls, Wardell Gray was not among the horse rustlers. Hawes says everybody . . . everybody . . . he knew, except Gray, was on heroin. After Bird, the skinny tenor man from the Billy Eckstine band was the musician most admired and respected by the younger players. He spoke quietly and articulately, admired the philosophy of Jean-Paul Sartre and the politics of Henry Wallace, boosted the NAACP and advised the fledgling jazzmen on music and life, particularly in regard to the futility of messing with drugs.

Gray's playing was not as startling, as daring, as Parker's. Both came out of Lester Young, but Bird took Lester's pioneering work in rhythmic freedom a step (or two, or three) further, fragmenting time, turning it around and inside out, sometimes seeming to break it apart. Gray was always superbly relaxed, his lines comfortable and rounded, even at the fast tempos of which he was a master. Little wonder that when Count Basie, whose band had provided the rhythmic nest in which Young matured, needed a saxophonist he called on Gray twice, for his big band in the late forties and again when Basie put together a small group to go to Las Vegas in 1950. Also with the Basie small band was the young trumpeter Clark Terry, who was involved with Gray in some electrifying Los Angeles jam sessions.

During the period he was with Goodman, Gray recorded his famous "Twisted" session, using Charlie Parker's 1949 rhythm section of pianist Al Haig, bassist Tommy Potter, and drummer Roy Haynes. "Twisted" is that most basic of jazz vehicles, a B-flat blues. Gray's solo on the originally issued take was gripping in its symetrically lyrical simplicity, and it was a favorite record of musicians long before it was converted into one of the most popular jazz novelty items ever made. Three years after Gray made "Twisted," Annie Ross added lyrics to fit Gray's solo, and her tale of a nutty psychoanalyst became something of a jukebox smash. Thus once removed, Gray's solo was made familiar to a great many people who had never heard the original or heard of him. Or of jazz, for that matter. Years later, two additional takes of "Twisted" were issued for the first time. Comparison among the three is a glimpse inside the creative process of a major soloist. There is little melodic resemblance of one solo to the other two. Gray, like Parker, was capable of creating fresh and original statements each time he blew his horn. In the Gray discography, there is remarkably little repetition of ideas.

Gray's East Coast adventures included not only the Goodman and Basie bands, but jobs with Sonny Stitt and the spirited small band that Tadd Dameron kept busy on 52nd Street. Recordings from the period demonstrate not only how well Gray fit into any context but also his remarkable consistency as a creative musician. In 1951, he returned to California to free-lance, occasionally ranging as far as Chicago. In Los Angeles, where some of the young Central Avenue boppers of 1945 had matured into impressive players, Gray formed groups of his own. One of the best included Art Farmer and gave the young trumpeter his first record date. Such other increasingly prominent players as Hampton Hawes and drummer Lawrence Marable also worked with Gray.

Still free-lancing, Gray joined his old mentor Benny Carter for an engagement in Las Vegas. The occasion was the opening in December 1955 of the plush Moulin Rouge. Two days after the debut performance, Gray's body was found in the Nevada desert, the neck broken. There has been speculation for two decades about how he died. Newspaper reports said the cause was an overdose of heroin and that the body had been thrown from an automobile. Hampton Hawes's description of Gray as a dedicated non-user may not disprove but certainly contradicts the drug theory. Others who knew Gray well swear that he was murdered, possibly for nonpayment of gambling debts. Given the climate of prejudice in Las Vegas at the time, the possibility of racial violence cannot be ruled out. There is no record of an autopsy. Whatever the circumstances of Gray's death, it was a shameful loss for music.

Always an inspirational player, Gray was a jazzman whose pure musicianship made him universally admired. Whenever he played, he was instinctively tasteful, inventive, uncompromising, and noncommercial. Having gone through a couple of decades in jazz when last year's music often sounds experimental, quaint, and farfetched, we can be grateful that there is preserved on records the perenially fresh and undated improvisation of Wardell Gray.

Seeing Red / Red Garland

1977

Between chords, puffs on his cigarette, and sips of his drink—all of which seem to be executed simultaneously—Red Garland offers his fellow musicians declarations of encouragement and appreciation. A strategic cymbal splash from Walter Winn, and Garland twists around to bathe the drummer in beatific smiles. A pungent quote from tenor saxophonist Marchel Ivery, and the pianist whoops, "All right, my man!" He sits, hands folded, chuckling approval during Charles Scott's bass solos. Young trumpeter Chuck Willis receives appreciative murmurs. Garland is back at work and loving it.

The Recovery Room: an appropriate place for a comeback. The bandstand in the little club on Cedar Springs Road in Dallas is a sort of shrine to Charlie Parker, with paintings of Bird on the cinder block walls and a border of white doves on the ceiling curtain that marks the stand's perimeter. The music is in the Parker tradition, and Garland is clearly delighted to be playing bebop again.

Garland was part of the most admired rhythm section in jazz as Miles Davis's anchorman in the late fifties. He has been a stylistic influence on hundreds of pianists. Since his mother's death in 1965, he has spent most of his time in Dallas. There were a few trips for club appearances in Los Angeles and New York, and there was a recording session for a German label. But to the international jazz constituency he acquired during and after his four years with Davis,

Garland has been among the missing. There were rumors that he was dead, ill, retired, drying out, despondent, or working for the post office. Dallas music insiders knew he could occasionally be heard at the Rounders, Wellington's, Arandas, and the Texas Magic Asylum. But in the spring of 1975 Garland dropped out altogether. "Let's just call it a vacation," he says. "After the Texas Magic Asylum folded, I didn't know whether to go to New York or go back out to the Rounders. The record royalties were coming in, so I did nothing. I watched television for eighteen months. Sitting around idle. There were nights I said, 'Damn, I sure would like to go and jam someplace,' and I thought about the Recovery Room, but I said, 'Well, I'll just take a little more time.'"

One of Garland's most passionate fans, Jeanie Donnelly, operates the Recovery Room with her husband Bill. She was determined to end Garland's vacation. A diminutive woman full of good-natured intensity and with a musician's ear for the idiosyncrasies and surprises of jazz solos, Mrs. Donnelly knows not only what she likes but also why she likes it, and that endears her to jazz players.

"She should be a musician, she's got such big ears," Garland says. "One day in September, Jeanie sent a friend by to see if I was doing anything. I wasn't, of course. She asked how I'd like to play at the Recovery Room. I said when, and she said tomorrow night, and I've been here ever since. It was that easy."

The room can't hold both a grand piano and enough tables to pay the freight, so Garland operates a spinet, which in his honor is kept in tune, a departure from the jazz club norm. A former professional boxer who once took on Sugar Ray Robinson, Red smilingly punches out block chord accompaniments to Ivery's expansive tenor saxophone solos. Those locked chords are a Garland hallmark. Melding the chords with extremely fast single-note lines and the irresistible pulse that underlies everything he plays, he created one of the most warmly compelling keyboard styles in jazz. Garland generates the hard-edged excitement developed by bop pianists like Bud Powell and George Wallington, yet retains the smooth, swinging melodic flow native to so many jazzmen from the Southwest. The late critic Ralph J. Gleason said in a *down beat* review in 1958,

"He has brought back some long-absent elements to jazz piano, made them acceptable to the ultra-modernists, and proved over again the sublime virtue of swing and a solid, deep groove."

When Garland returned to the keyboard he made a painful discovery. "After laying off for a year and a half, I was out of shape. For the first week I sat up there and played like this," he says, holding his hands in playing position and grimacing. "All my fingertips were sore, and the nails were broken down in the quick. I soaked them in warm salt water, but it didn't help. You can lose your chops, just like a trumpet man." But he didn't know that; there had been no other layoffs since he first learned to play the piano.

Red was born William Garland in Dallas on May 13, 1923. His father, William Sr., was an elevator operator at the First National Bank. "None of my family played," Garland recalls. "My dad used to say, "William, we're not musical. It must be something you were meant to do."

Garland's first instrument was the clarinet. He learned alto saxophone under Buster Smith, a great Texas saxophonist who was a profound influence on the young Charlie Parker. Smith was a stickler for reading music, and that ability served the eighteen-year-old Garland well when he was presented with an opportunity to learn piano. "It was 1941, and I was in the Army at Fort Huachuca, Arizona. I used to go to the recreation room and listen to a pianist named John Lewis, not the famous John Lewis of the Modern Jazz Quartet. I'd look over his shoulder and ask him to teach me how to play. 'Can you read?,' he said. 'I don't want to have to take you from the ground up.' I showed him I could read and I used to meet him every day. We'd put the books up on the piano and he'd show me."

Another Army pianist, Lee Barnes, gave Garland further instruction, and by the time he left the service Red rarely found it necessary to play saxophone or clarinet. One of the artists whose influence guided Garland's stylistic development is barely remembered today as a pianist except by other pianists. That was Nat Cole, whose touch, phrasing, and conception impressed Red. Other players he studied were the stride giants James P. Johnson and Luckey

Roberts, the elegant Teddy Wilson, the mercurial Bud Powell, and Art Tatum.

"Tatum, of course, was the master. He was Mr. Piano. The first time I heard a Tatum record—I think it was 'Tiger Rag'—I thought it was at least three pianists."

Less than five years after that first piano lesson, Garland joined Hot Lips Page, perhaps the least celebrated of the truly great trumpet players, but one of the heroes of jazz in the Southwest.

"I was working in Dallas at a place called the Log Cabin with Bill Blocker, a tenor player. He's dead now. Lips came to Dallas to play a dance, and his pianist quit. Word spread around that Hot Lips Page was looking for a pianist. I was going to the dance anyway, and I went on up to the stand. Four of us tried out that night. I sat up there and read his book, and then I went on home. About five in the morning here comes a knock at the door—boom, boom, boom, boom—and my mother says, 'What have you done, Little William, must be the police, you must have done something wrong.' We opened the door and there were Hot Lips Page and Buster Smith. Lips said, 'You're the guy who sat in with me tonight? Well, I need you, man. Come on, throw somethin' in a bag and let's go.' That was it. That was the beginning of life on the road. Lips was beautiful. He was a good strong Dixie- and swing-style player, he had knowledge of music, and was a wonderful blues singer. I really enjoyed the man."

Garland was with Page until March, 1946, when a tour ended in New York and Red decided to take what jobs he could get there. Drummer Art Blakey happened to hear him in a small club and the next night returned with his boss, Billy Eckstine, known in the trade as "B," proprietor of a startlingly iconoclastic big band that had left the swing era behind. At one time or another, the Eckstine band included nearly every pioneer of the new music called bebop— Dizzy Gillespie, Charlie Parker, Fats Navarro, Dexter Gordon, Gene Ammons, Sonny Stitt, Miles Davis, Blakey—and Garland was asked to join.

"Blakey said to B, 'Let's get him. Let's get him. Let's take him.' B asked me to go, and I piled into the bus. I was only with them

about six weeks, but did I hear some music on that band! Then after
I left B, I started fooling around with Lockjaw Davis, the tenor
player, just going from club to club, this group, that group, this gig,
that gig."

From 1947 to 1949, Garland was part of the house rhythm section at the Blue Note, a bastion of modern jazz in Philadelphia. He
worked there with Charlie Parker, Miles Davis, Fats Navarro, Bill
Harris, Flip Phillips, Charlie Ventura, and Benny Green, among
others. Then he joined the seminal tenor saxophonist Coleman
Hawkins and trumpeter Roy Eldridge in their combo. "The name
jobs started coming. Hawk would say, 'Hey, get Red Garland. I
used him last week, he's something.' So I went from Hawkins to
Lester Young to Ben Webster, passed around among those great
tenor men. The word got around, and I got more work with good
players than I could handle."

By the early fifties, Garland was a big enough name to get steady
employment as the leader of his own trio. His reputation among
other musicians was firmly established. And the man who would
make Garland a part of the most celebrated and influential band
since Louis Armstrong's Hot Five was showing interest. "In 1953 I
was in Boston. Miles Davis came over to the club where I was working. He said he was going to form a group. He wanted me, Sonny
Rollins on tenor, Max Roach on drums. Oscar Pettiford would be
the bass player." But the group didn't materialize. Garland continued to work with his trio and with the eloquent tenor saxophonist Lester Young. He recorded with Davis and drummer Philly
Joe Jones in mid-1955, then returned to Young.

"In October of '55, Miles called and said he was ready. He said
he couldn't use Max Roach because Max had just formed his own
group with Clifford Brown. Could I recommend a drummer? I said,
'Yeah, Philly Joe.' Miles said to bring him. Rollins and Pettiford
were leaders now too, and he asked if I knew a tenor player, and I
said, 'Yeah, man, I got a kid here in Philly. He's bad. His name's
John Coltrane.' He said to bring Coltrane. Miles sent to Detroit for
a little bass player he knew of, Paul Chambers. I didn't know him.
The day of the opening, we all met at Anchor's Inn in Baltimore

about four o'clock. Miles ran us through four or five tunes, then we went back to the hotel and ate and fooled around, and we opened at nine, and that's how the group started."

Garland's account differs slightly from Philly Joe's. (The reticent Davis offers no account of anything.) Jones recalls that he and Miles had been barnstorming around the East in 1955, playing clubs with pickup groups of local musicians, virtually none of them satisfactory, and Davis was eager to find the right combination. Red may have gathered Jones and Coltrane together for the trip to Baltimore, but Davis was certainly familiar with Jones's work; they had played together sporadically since 1952. And he had at least heard of Coltrane, because 'Trane had worked with Dizzy Gillespie, Johnny Hodges, and other established musicians. At any rate, they agree that the first afternoon's perfunctory rehearsal was the final one of the new Miles Davis Quintet. Henceforth, everything was worked out on the stand, and the empathy of the group was uncanny. It is unlikely that any rhythm section has ever been so perfectly matched and so able to meet the needs and demands of soloists with styles as diverse as those of Davis and Coltrane.

Garland was Mr. Inside, the connecting tissue of the rhythm section, making it possible for the loud, eccentric but always swinging Philly Joe and the powerful, chance-taking Chambers to go outside with the horn players. His piano was always reliably there, providing the sturdy foundation for Davis's rhythmic and melodic departures and the rococo inventions of Coltrane, probably the most tirelessly searching improviser jazz has known. The few critics who looked for something to deprecate in Garland's playing chose to call him old-fashioned. What they failed to understand was that with a more "modern" pianist the group might well have flown off in all directions. Davis understood that perfectly, just as he knew or sensed that this combination of five disparate musicians would coalesce into a superior band.

In the first weeks of his return to regular playing in Dallas in 1977, all of Garland's skills were intact. If anything, he was performing with even more vigor. The lightning single-note lines were impeccable, sore fingertips or no, and the rhapsodic out-of-tempo introductions to ballads were as rich as ever. As for the legendary rhythmic qualities in Garland's work, terpsichorean testimony was given one Saturday night by a huge man in a slick red leisure suit who had been sitting near the piano for some time, bobbing and weaving. Finally, he sprang to his feet and broke into a kind of shaggy bear dance in front of the tiny bandstand. Garland applauded.

The band with Garland on a recent weekend was excellent. Marchel Ivery, the saxophonist, was once described in *Texas Monthly* as "competent." He is much more than that: a full-blooded, modern mainstream tenor man with abundant ideas and that peculiarly spacious Texas sound. Drummer Walter Winn slashes and crashes engagingly in the Philly Joe Jones manner, matching and inspiring Garland's swing. Winn is the painter of the Charlie Parker pictures in the club and the sculptor of the eighteen-foot bronze statue of Martin Luther King in the Dallas MLK Center. Charles Scott is an incisive and dependable bassist. Chuck Willis, who sat in on trumpet, showed genuine harmonic individuality on medium tempos and ballads and a fine liquid fluency on fast pieces. Willis is a graduate of the North Texas State lab band program and a musician to watch.

Outside the Recovery Room during an intermission, two women from Fort Worth chatted with Garland. "Did you know," one of them asked, "that a Juilliard professor once said you were one of the top five jazz pianists?"

"Yeah, I never could understand that. Art Tatum, Oscar Peterson, Errol Garner for originality, Earl Hines, OK. But me . . . that's always been a puzzle."

The lady wanted to know what he thought of his records.

"I don't listen to me. That's too egotistical. I listen to other artists. I think I have one of my albums, and my wife bought that. I can hear myself at work, but to sit and listen to me like I'm my own number one fan, I cannot do that."

Legions of listeners around the world can, however, and would like to, but most of his dozen or so albums as leader are out of circulation. At this writing, Don Schlitten of Xanadu Records is attempting to work out a Garland record date, the first in several years, and Garland is enthusiastic because he feels Schlitten is interested in capturing the *real* Red Garland. Others have tried to persuade him to follow the jazz-rock fusion path that has brought popular success to pianists like Herbie Hancock and Chick Corea, alumni of later editions of the Miles Davis group.

"Johnnie Taylor, the blues singer, called me up one day and said I ought to play some rock and roll. No. No way. The blues, yes, that's my heart. And let me play some Cole Porter, Rodgers and Hart, good standards, improvise on those. But play rock and roll? No sir, that just isn't music to me. I'd wash dishes first."

The record session with Don Schlitten did not materialize. But veteran producer Orrin Keepnews took Garland into the studio of Galaxy Records in December, 1977 for a reunion with Philly Joe Jones in a trio that also included bassist Ron Carter, another Miles Davis graduate. Over the next two years, Garland made several albums on Galaxy, whose parent company, Fantasy, also reissued virtually all of the pianist's recordings of the 1950s and 1960s for the Prestige label. Garland toured for a time, often with the band he used at the Recovery Room, playing festivals in the United States, Europe, and Japan. Then he dropped out again, and after a period of reclusion in Dallas, died there on April 23, 1984. The Recovery Room is out of business.

Woodrow Charles Herman was virtually born into the music business in Milwaukee, Wisconsin, in 1913. The son of a shoemaker father who sang in a group known as The White City Four, Herman was dancing in hometown theatres at the age of six, playing the saxophone in vaudeville at nine, and working in dance bands as a saxophonist and clarinetist during his early teens.

Before he graduated from high school, Herman was on the road with Joey Lichter's band. He returned to Milwaukee to earn his diploma and enter Marquette University. But in 1930 he left college to accept an invitation to join the enormously popular band of Tommy Gerun, with which he remained for three years. After a failed attempt to form his own group in 1933, he spent a little time with the studio band of Harry Sosnick and then with Gus Arnheim's slick outfit. For the next two years, Herman worked with Isham Jones and made his first recordings as instrumentalist and singer in the band of that successful leader and songwriter, whose compositions included "On the Alamo," "I'll See You in My Dreams," "It Had to Be You," and "There Is No Greater Love."

In 1936, at the age of forty, Jones quit the band business and opened a music store in Southern California. Herman and five other members of the Jones band formed a cooperative unit and hired musicians to fill out what came to be known as "The Band That Plays the Blues," with Woody elected leader. At twenty-two, Herman was launched on a remarkable fifty-one-year career in which his musicianship, leadership, development of young talent, relaxed personality, and openness to advances in musical thinking kept him and his bands at the very top of the profession.

The band struggled for a few years, burdened to some degree by a book packed with blues numbers, which did not thrill all of the ballroom managers upon whom Herman depended for work. Nonetheless, it was Herman's love of and loyalty to the blues that paid off in 1939 with the million-seller recording of "Woodchopper's Ball," his first and biggest hit. With World War II underway, the other partners in the band were successively drafted, and Herman bought all their stock, becoming sole owner.

As early as 1943, Herman's advanced ear tuned in the developments of bebop and he hired the young Dizzy Gillespie to write three arrangements, including "Woody'n You," which became a jazz standard but which, oddly, Herman never recorded. The original band did not dissolve; through personnel changes, it metamorphosed into the First Herd. The metamorphosis took place under cover of the infamous recording ban imposed during 1943 and 1944 by the president of the American Federation of Musicians, James Petrillo.

To many listeners who had lost track of the Herman band during the blackout, when the ban ended the First Herd came as a jolt, a stunning surprise. Packed with superb musicians, some of them dedicated young boppers, the band had drive, exuberance, and a joy in making music that were not quite like anything heard in jazz before. Veteran drummer Dave Tough and the almost unbelievably enthusiastic bassist Chubby Jackson drove and whipped the Herd in relentlessly swinging, even ecstatic, performances of pieces like "Apple Honey," "Northwest Passage," and "Caldonia." The arrangements by Ralph Burns and Neal Hefti were brilliant and, as it turned out, imperishable; forty years later they sounded less dated than some charts that had been in the Herman book only a few months.

The First Herd became an enormous success. It had its own network radio program. Its records sold well; "Happiness Is Just a Thing Called Joe," with the vocal by Frances Wayne, became a big hit. The band packed ballrooms and theatres. It won the most important polls and many of its players, including Tough, trombonist Bill Harris, and tenor saxophonist Flip Phillips, became stars.

At the end of 1946, at the peak of the First Herd's success, Her-

*man disbanded and returned to his new home in the Hollywood
hills to help his wife, Charlotte, through a medical crisis. When she
regained her health, he organized the Second Herd, often called the
Four Brothers band after the Jimmy Giuffre piece that featured
tenor saxophonists Zoot Sims, Stan Getz, Herbie Steward, and baritone saxophonist Serge Chaloff. If the First Herd had bebop leanings, this one was overtly a bop band and although it did not become as popular as its predecessor, its influence was felt for decades
as an incubator of talent and a symbol of the spirit of post-World
War II jazz.*

*After the brief, exciting life of the Second Herd, Herman occa-
sionally organized small groups to see him through hard times
when the vagaries of the economy and the music business would
not allow him to support seventeen pieces. Out of one of those periods in the early 1950s evolved yet another in the succession of
herds, this one known as the Third Herd. It, like those that came
before and after, was made up of youngsters with great talent who
were molded by Herman into an exciting unit whose sound, no
matter what the source of the arrangements, was unmistakably that
of a Herman band. Long after the numbering system had been
dropped and the generic name Thundering Herd was adopted, the
distinctive qualities imparted and inspired by the leader identified
his bands.*

Woody Herman: 1963

1974

Some jazz soloists travel around the country appearing with pickup
local rhythm sections. If Woody Herman decided to strike out as a
single, in many cities he could put together seventeen-piece bands

composed entirely of his alumni. Legions of musicians have passed through the Herman herds since "The Band That Plays the Blues" was formed in 1936. In New York and Los Angeles Woody could depopulate the studios by recalling the herdsmen.

There are so many Herman graduates in the lounges, pits, clubs, and sound stages of Los Angeles and Las Vegas that in his madder moments Woody dreams a scene DeMilleian in scope. Along the desert highway between the movie capital and the gambling mecca runs a line of horn players interruped every few miles by a rhythm section, a straight lineup band like the one Herman used to perch on the back bar at the Metropole in New York, but infinite. Woody patrols in a jeep, keeping the time straight and shouting out the number of the next tune.

The Who's Who quality of that imaginary lineup is staggering. Among the trumpeters are Conte and Pete Candoli, Sonny Berman, Bill Chase, Don Ellis, Nat Adderley, Shorty Rogers, Red Rodney, Ernie Royal, Cappy Lewis, Al Porcino; trombonists Bill Harris, Carl Fontana, Bill Watrous, Urbie Green; bassists Oscar Pettiford, Chubby Jackson, Red Mitchell, Red Kelly; pianists Jimmy Rowles, Vince Guaraldi, Lou Levy, Nat Pierce, Dave McKenna; vibraharpists Milt Jackson, Terry Gibbs, Red Norvo, Margie Hyams; drummers Dave Tough, Cliff Leeman, Don Lamond, Shelly Manne, Jake Hanna, Chuck Flores; guitarists Chuck Wayne and Billy Bauer; and of course the pantheon of saxophonists, Stan Getz, Zoot Sims, Herbie Steward, Gene Ammons, Flip Phillips, Al Cohn, Serge Chaloff, Al Belletto, Bill Perkins, Richie Kamuca, Don Lanphere, Sal Nistico, Joe Romano, Frank Tiberi, Leonard Garment. Leonard Garment?

The Old Man could undoubtedly make that serpentine L.A.-to-Las Vegas band swing. In the Metropole chorus line, it was impossible for a player to adequately hear himself, let alone anything definitive from the rest of the band. But the music was most often together, and supremely exciting. Woody Herman is a magician, a superb head coach who knows how to inspire team effort and individual brilliance under the most discouraging conditions. A miserable playing field like the back bar of a crummy New York tavern really presented no major obstacles. Herman once said admiringly of one of the herds that its men could adjust and attune to one another so well that they'd sound great in the men's room at Penn Station. That they would is a tribute to the musicianship and leadership of Woodrow Charles Herman.

Woody's wisdom as a leader is matched by his generosity as a friend. He has given material assistance to many struggling musicians and once incorporated Al Belletto's entire sextet into his band to save the career of a financially foundering fellow leader.

Except for a few brief periods, Herman has kept a big band together for nearly forty years. It has changed with the times, but to anyone with moderate listening experience and an adequate ear, there is simply no mistaking a Woody Herman band. Like Ellington and Basie, Herman puts the stamp of his personality on his organization, and that personality is so strong, so definite, that it transcends (as it shapes) material, instrumentation, and soloists. As Ralph Gleason pointed out in the notes for this album's original issue . . . "you know, even before the leader's clarinet is audible, that it cannot be anyone but Herman."

And his playing is timeless. He has made no discernible effort to "modernize" his improvising, but it never sounds dated. I recall meeting bassist Red Kelly, a Herman mainstay during the mid-fifties, after a particularly exciting concert by the edition of the Herd known as the Road Band. Herman has generated several boilersful of steam during a two-chorus blues solo on clarinet.

"Yeah," Red marveled. "The Old Man can still play."

The Old Man was then forty-one, and his musicians had been calling him the Old Man for years. As this is written in the summer of 1974, it seems to me that Woody is unquestionably the most consistently satisfying soloist in the current Herd.

Herman says he lost track of the number of Third Herds somewhere along the way. I can't recall whether the band still carried that subtitle when the music in this collection was recorded in late 1962. This was a newly formed band, one of the most exciting Woody fronted in the sixties. It had in abundance the qualities Woody is able to impart to seventeen men; vitality, joy, humor, a time feeling that seems to spring from a single pulse and that mysterious artful something that sets Herman apart as a leader.

It had marvelous soloists in Sal Nistico, one of the most exciting of those Italian-American tenor men who keep popping onto the jazz scene from upstate New York; trumpeter Bill Chase and trombonist Phil Wilson, high note specialists who were not only magnificent lead players but trenchant improvisers; and Nat Pierce, a pianist who also has provided some of Herman's most serviceable arrangements over the past two decades. The ensemble sound of this band was unfailingly bright and full. The superb rhythm section was sparked by drummer Jake Hanna, as perfect for this band as was Dave Tough for the First Herd.

When I last talked with Herman, he had just celebrated his fiftieth year as a bandleader. That and other recent conversations with him made it clear that he was as vital, charming, and opinionated as he had been ten years earlier when the following piece was published. His chronicle of frustrations in dealing with record companies is not unique to Herman. All but a very few jazzmen can relate stories about the record business that are at least as depressing.

Woody Herman on Musicians, "Civilians," Recording Companies, Etc.

1976

When Woody Herman speaks, even about the things that upset him most, there's a gleam in his eye and a smile in his voice that make it clear he enjoys what he's doing. Sometimes he enjoys it more than others.

The night I heard the band recently, Herman was playing a one-nighter at a cavernous road house called The Roaring Twenties.

Out among the mesquite and live oaks on the northern edge of San Antonio, this dine and dance emporium is operated by Larry Herman (no relation), whose own band usually supplies the music. The Roaring Twenties is made up to match its name, complete with a ball of mirrors throwing cheap glitter all over the place and waitresses in somebody's idea of flapper costumes. Saturday night at The Roaring Twenties is like five Elks Clubs in combined operation.

Woody packs the place with middle-aged San Antonians who remember Herman from the big band era and want him to sound like he did thirty years ago. There is a sprinkling of hip high school and college students, most of them aspiring jazz musicians, who want to hear "Giant Steps," "Corazon," "Spain," and "La Fiesta." On the night in question, Woody did his best to satisfy all comers. In sheer bulk of material, the oldies predominated. But Herman did a nice thing for the kids. He announced there would be no dancing for a while and played a concert set from the top of the book, including a sizzling "La Fiesta," a Chick Corea piece that is becoming a minor anthem among high school and college stage bands. Some of the Elks Club contingent looked a bit puzzled, although they applauded warmly.

"They're not sure," Woody said the next day, "but they figure if everybody else is cheering, there must be something to it. Long ago, I stopped trying to analyze what they like or don't like. You can really get yourself in a mess that way."

Herman said he gets a good deal of heat from fellow musicians about the rock-jazz orientation of some of his pieces.

"There are still hundreds of marvelous musicians who will come to me and say, 'Man, you still doin' that electronic shit?' Well, don't you think a Fender bass is here to stay, for certain kinds of things? I'm interested in almost everything that comes along until it proves we can't use it. Certain aspects of synthesizers can enhance what we're doing, and there will be some synthesizers on albums still to come out. I've always been interested only in the end result. We can all make mistakes, but I know when I make a mistake. The only thing I don't understand is how guys become so opinionated when they haven't delved into it. In many cases they've gone by the wayside because of their attitudes. They're scuffling, and when you hear them play, you know why. It's not that what they're playing isn't good. It's very good, but it was very good twenty years ago. I'm not saying that a style can't live, but I think an individual should grow, as long as he has a breath within his body and his mind is working. If you're not interested in moving with your music, then you can say, 'Well, this is jazz, and this is what I think, and the rest of that shit ain't nothin.' Then you'll have left the scene, 'cause the scene is what you come up with *now*."

That's Herman on the inelastic thinking of some of his colleagues. He also has strong opinions of the musical IQs of most of the customers who dine and dance at places like The Roaring Twenties.

"Most of them stop listening as soon as they leave high school. That's their last really firm connection with music. In that period of their lives, it's all-important, and from the time of their first responsibility on, it becomes background to everything else, which is very natural and correct, I guess. But then they still want to tell me how the band isn't making it now and it was so great then. And that really aggravates me. It's about the only thing that does."

But The Roaring Twenties audience seemed to enjoy the evening. They danced. They applauded. Nonetheless, they bugged Woody.

"Well, yeah. Because you can't hear the comments and requests. They're asking for ludicrous, ridiculous kinds of tunes. It could be 'Johnson Rag,' or 'Don't you have any Russ Morgan pieces?' or they're always getting your tunes mixed up with someone else's, so you get requests for 'Green Eyes' or 'Frenesi' or 'In the Mood.' And they get some very terse replies like 'No,' or 'He quit the business,' or 'I'll play that when I get to the big band in the sky.' It becomes a kind of standup routine. Certainly anyone had a right to ask for anything, but I can't for the life of me think why I have to do *those* tunes."

Herman is legendary in jazz for his ability to find and develop young players. Being surrounded by them continuously for decades has helped keep open the ears Woody uses as guides in assuring that his bands are flexible and new. It was Herman's early herds, after all, that provided catalytic big band settings for the transition from swing to bop. And he's been receptive to new directions ever since. His uncanny knack for scouting out new talent leads him frequently these days to the colleges and universities. His new rhythm section was pulled directly out of the North Texas State College class of 1975. Pianist Lyle Mays, drummer Steve Houghton, and bassist Kirby Stewart have Woody so enthused that he has recorded them and is shopping around for a record company to package and distribute their album. Trumpeter Jeff Davis and tenor saxophonist Sal Spicola came to the band right out of Berklee College of Music in Boston. Trombonist Dale Kirkland joined the Herd even before he was graduated from the prestigious Eastman School of Music in Rochester, New York. He was given special permission by the school to return later and pick up his degree.

"The Eastman School, that's no pushover boys' club, you know," Herman says. "There's a fantastic number of young players who are good and can be made available. You have to know your sources."

Woody is not certain of the average age of the herd, but says it compares with that of any band he's ever had. The herds have always been young, enthusiastic, and powerful.

"The youngest guy in the band is Mays. He's twenty-two. But we've got some guys with miles on them. Frank Tiberi, the lead tenor player, has a twenty-three-year-old son, so he can't be all that young. But these days you can jive it with the hair and the beards and mustaches, and as long as you keep in shape, who knows? And of course Bill Byrne has been in the band eleven years. He's the road manager, best one I've had in my entire career. I've had very few who've doubled; Bill's a very good legitimate trumpet player. He never solos. He's not interested in that. But he's got a hell of a background. He came out of the Cincinnati Conservatory and the Naval Academy band, and he's worked with a lot of good guys. He knows trumpet players. He can tell immediately whether they're right or wrong for the band.

"Lawrence Welk came to hear us when we were in Tucson the other night. He seemed to enjoy it, and he sure got his sinuses cleared, because he was at a front table. He had a comment when he got up with his friends to leave. He said 'Poy, ·Voody, haff you got some musicians.' So I guess he admired the musicianship. You have to."

Hundreds of musicians have passed through the Herman ranks

since "The Band That Plays the Blues" in the late thirties and early forties. Many of them have gone on to become famous and influential. Woody has warm appreciation of their contributions.

"I think the greatest aid to me in accomplishing what I was trying to do was the most prolific writer I've ever had, the greatest guy, Ralph Burns. His music is still being played in my book every night of the week. It doesn't sound dated, either, and that's the sign of true artistry. And of course there were guys who fit into any scene I ever got involved in. Take Bill Harris, the great trombonist. If I had a small group, he'd fit in with the small group. If I had a terrible band, he'd make his part of the band sound good. If I had a hell of a band, he'd move right with it. He was such an important facet of the First Herd, but I threw him a curve when I put him into the Second Herd, the bop band, the dirty beboppers. And, hell, he fell in like it was old home week. That takes some kind of versatility.

"It makes me sad, what they did to Bill in Las Vegas before he passed away. They had to chop off musicians, which they're always having to do in one hotel or another, and Bill Harris was the first to go. That doesn't make any sense to you or me, but to some pit boss and to some house leader who's afraid to breathe it doesn't matter. Vegas. It's like being in jail. Once musicians become too deeply involved there, they can't get out. James Moody was supposed to go on a jazz cruise with us last year. But he bowed out because he was afraid he'd lose his gig in Vegas if he went away for a week. And he probably would have. That's James Moody, a great tenor player."

In the early forties, Herman's band included for short periods such musicians as Ben Webster, Johnny Hodges, Juan Tizol, Budd Johnson, and Ernie Caceres.

"A lot of these people who were never with me very long were big influences in one way or another. Some of that had to rub off. People may come into the band for three months, and if they supply something we can really get our teeth into, we benefit. Shelly Manne was with me on drums for about six months in 1949. He replaced Shadow Wilson. Shadow was great, but we were doing some things in which he couldn't find us. Shelly jumped in and saved us, and I've always been grateful."

Herman's own musicianship has sometimes been overlooked. But there have been a number of occasions in recent years when he played far and away the most interesting solos of a given set. His sounds and styles on all three of his instruments—alto saxophone, clarinet, and soprano saxophone—are distinctive. He maintains them without practicing.

"I used to practice alto a little before arthritis hit my right hand, the one that holds the horn. It really hurts most of the time, but you learn to live with something like that. I tried a strap, but it's been so many years since I've played with one, it just threw the horn in the wrong direction. Anyway, I tend to play more soprano these days than alto or clarinet."

Herman played soprano sax for a short time when he was a child, then dropped it to concentrate on clarinet. Although he knew and often heard Sidney Bechet, the soprano master, he says Bechet intimidated rather than inspired him.

"We did some high schools and colleges in the Chicago area in the fifties, so I had a lot of exposure to him. The only thing is, he used to get so *el passionato* that he scared me. He was so warm and full of vibrato. The man could really express himself."

Later he heard a soprano saxophonist who turned him on to the point where he felt he had to take up the instrument again.

"I had been on the road with John Coltrane and we had done a lot of tours of Europe together. But one night when I went down to the Village Vanguard to listen to him it just struck me, wow, you can get a lot done with this axe if you pay attention and if you can control it. A lot of people who own 'em shouldn't mess with 'em at all because they can be just torturous. I knew I couldn't go in any direction that could by the most remote chance lead me to come out sounding like John. So it was just a question of doing whatever I could. I've enjoyed the axe. It's a saxophone if you treat it as one."

Woody has no encouraging words about the status or future of the clarinet in jazz. He says there are no new players who have impressed him.

"I had the good fortune last summer of doing a Canadian tour with Buddy DeFranco and his quartet. He's still the only guy who's coming up with anything new as far as that instrument is concerned. It's a very difficult instrument to play well. It's not the sort of thing you can just pick up and start making your own thoughts on, and I think that's one reason there aren't too many kinds interested. And then, too, it lost its place as a voice in jazz because it's connected in most younger people's minds with Dixieland."

Herman's recording plans are only partly settled. He is no longer under contract to Fantasy and has committed himself to a pair of one-shot albums for Groove Merchant. He is, shall we say, less than enchanted with the recording industry.

"There was no trouble with Fantasy, really, except that they ran out of gas as far as I was concerned with 'The Children of Lima.' They went for a bundle on that. The Houston Symphony didn't come cheap. I didn't stand there with a hatchet and say, 'Do this.' I never figured it would be a million seller, but I imagine over a period of years they'll get all their money back, and more. Our Fantasy albums won Grammies two years in a row. We must have been doing something right."

Some of Herman's Phillips albums from the sixties are being reissued on the Trip label under an agreement with Mercury, a fact about which Woody is artistically pleased and financially apprehensive. He hasn't heard from Trip, and he's afraid there is no one at Mercury looking after his rights.

"They'll make a lot of money. They've been out of print a long time. Those things have long since paid for themselves, so I think I should really put some heat on."

Herman has a number of tapes, "beautiful broadcast and concert stuff," he calls them, that he would like to have issued. But he says the musicians' union is making it economically impossible to release them as albums.

"The AFM put such a monstrous figure on what the guys would have to get that you'd have to do a hell of a lot of business to even hope to break even. It was triple or quadruple what recording scale used to be. They were really going to write the contract of the year on this one. Both Fantasy and RCA were interested, but they had to turn the deal down because of the bread. I don't want to see stuff like this go to the bootleggers. Jeez, six albums of my music showed up last year on bootleg labels. But my problem is small compared with Benny Goodman's. He's flipping out. I had a meeting with him to talk about whether we should get lawyers and try to track it all down. But when you figure it out, it comes to about a dollar-three-eighty anyway. There should be an agency connected with the union to collect what little there is to collect.

Woody says he is not interested in signing again with a major label.

"It would have to be something very special. First of all, they're very skeptical of people like me, because we've lost money consistently for everybody. But they also have a certain amount of respect and feel they should do something with us. So they get really uptight. I went back to Columbia after many years when my friend Ken Glancy (now president of RCA) was number two man. But before I got even the first album released, Glancy was switched to Europe to run CBS records, which he made into a giant. In the interim, I couldn't get to anybody. Teo Macero, my A&R man (artists and repertoire director), became my contact. Teo's a nice man, a lovely guy, with taste. The artistic understanding was fine. But nobody could talk to anybody about business. I had questions like 'Were any records shipped . . . ever?' No answers. So the minute that contract was up I had to get the hell out of there."

Herman's frustrations with record companies go back a long way. Once, in the mid-fifties, he and a friend decided to beat the system by forming their own label, Mars. They didn't beat the system. Mars lasted a year and a half.

"It was a big headache. We weren't making any money with it. My partner, a music publisher, had a gigantic business of his own going, yet he was wasting all his time with this turkey. We did some good music, though, so when Norman Granz came along and said he'd be interested, we said, 'Go, Norman, you got it.' My partner was spending all his waking hours trying to collect money from independent distributors, those [expletive deleted]. It's a nice business, the record business. It's lovely."

But he said it with a smile.

Herman's recording adventures became less peripatetic in the 1980s. He entered an agreement with Carl Jefferson's Concord jazz label that resulted in a number of excellent albums. His financial picture was bleak. An unscrupulous business manager had left income taxes unpaid for several years without Herman's knowledge, using the money for unprofitable investments. At seventy-two, Herman found himself in hock to the Internal Revenue Service for a million and a half dollars. Virtually all of his personal income was garnisheed by the IRS and he was forced to give up the Hollywood hills house he and Charlotte had bought from Humphrey Bogart and Lauren Bacall forty years earlier. With no possibility of paying his government debt in his lifetime, Herman kept up a schedule of one-nighters that would be punishing for a man thirty years younger. Friends and admirers started a fund to help defray the back taxes.

Early in 1987, his fragile health collapsed and he was hospitalized in Detroit for several months while his band, under the direction of saxophonist Frank Tiberi, continued to tour. When he had rallied enough to be moved back to Los Angeles, Herman was allowed to rent his former house from the man who bought it after the IRS seized it. He remained there under 'round-the-clock nursing care. But he had no money and when news reports of his destitution and his back-taxes dilemma reached the public, entertainment industry figures including Frank Sinatra, Tony Bennett, and Peggy Lee offered to help with his medical expenses. The Los Angeles jazz radio station KKGO-FM paid his back rent. Benefit concerts, many of them organized by former band members, were held across the country. Representative John Conyers of Michigan introduced a bill in Congress that would direct the IRS to erase Herman's tax debt and fines. In late September, 1987, Herman's condition worsened and, suffering from emphysema, pneumonia, and congestive heart failure, he was again hospitalized and placed on life support machinery. He died on October 29.

Bass Hit / Gene Ramey

1981

The new jazz bassists have achieved the agility and speed of guitarists. Their solos are full of slides, double stops, triple stops, and dazzling rubato tricks of all kinds. But in their preoccupation with virtuosity, many of these young acrobats of the fingerboard have not acquired the ability that was long considered the first requirement of jazz bass: to swing.

The original master of the bass—and of the tuba and the baritone saxophone—was Walter Page. Gene Ramey was Page's student and disciple and now, forty-nine years after they met, Ramey still thinks of a Page as his musical father. Page's Blue Devils, the most influential small band in the Southwest during the twenties, was absorbed into the Bennie Moten band, which in turn became Count Basie's, the heartbeat of Kansas City jazz in the thirties. Page was the core of the Basie rhythm section, the motor drive of a perfect swing machine.

Ramey was Page's heir, the second great master of the pulse that made the best Kansas City bands artistic standard bearers of the swing era. For half a century Ramey's playing—powerful, precise, silken—has put him in the company of an astonishing variety of musicians who have all demanded steadiness, dependability, and swing. They have ranged from blues singers to the most adventurous beboppers and they include Charlie Parker, Thelonious Monk, Jay McShann, George Shearing, Luis Russell, Horace Silver,

Lester Young, Lennie Tristano, Jimmy Witherspoon, Fats Navarro, Count Basie, Billie Holiday, Ben Webster, Stan Getz, Art Tatum, and Miles Davis.

Today Ramey lives quietly in Austin, a few blocks from where he was born. His brother and sister live nearby. He rarely sees his six children (from the first and last of his three marriages). His household companions are three generations of dogs, which amuse him, and his bass, which he plays every day, sometimes for hours. Ramey is trim and just under medium height, with a high forehead, gray hair, and a substantial mustache. He no longer wears the rimless glasses that made him look so studious in early photographs, and his customary expression is one of gentle bemusement. He has the sardonic humor typical of jazz musicians. He moves with the grace of an athlete, although he discounts his ability in sports. "I set a record of nine minutes flat for the hundred-yard dash," he told me.

Ramey spends a part of each day with a group of neighbors who have converted a garage into a domino parlor. He has a small pension from the Chase Manhattan Bank, where he worked as a safe-deposit officer during his final decade as a musician in New York before he returned to Austin in 1976. He lives in a big white house notable for its neatness, and he owns a half-acre just outside Austin that serves him as a small truck farm.

He occasionally travels to Chicago, New York, and Europe to perform, but he does not play much music in Austin outside his practice room. Nor does he think that situation is likely to change . . . "You've seen a map of the world? You can pick out the landlocked countries. Well, Austin is jazzlocked.

"I was born in 1913 on the site of Brackenridge Hospital," Ramey said over a grape Nehi. "My father, Curry, has been described in my biographies as a chauffeur. But he was an animal trainer, and he was working on a farm in Round Rock when he died. I think he was forty. My mother refused to remarry. She said she wasn't going to take a chance on having a mean stepfather for us children. She went on and fought it out to raise us.

"My grandmother Glasco remembered being brought over on the ship from Madagascar when she was five. She taught Mother and all the kids to play the piano and the organ. My grandfather played

the violin. My family sang. We used to set the whole community on
fire for miles around with that singing. People still remember us as
the family that sang so well. My brother Joe sang in the Capitol City
Quartet. They sang at the Governor's mansion, the Driskill Hotel,
the Stephen F. Austin Hotel. They had Austin sewed up, they were
making so much money singing for senators and doctors. I sang in a
quartet in school.

"I also hustled. I knew how to make money. We used to go over
to Tom Miller's turkey house and pluck turkeys, ten cents for toms
and eight cents for hens. In the spring and summer we'd chop
cotton and pick corn. We had a little wagon, and every morning
we'd put the lawn mower on top of it with a hoe and a rake, and
we'd go all over Austin mowing. Later I shined shoes."

Ramey's first instrument, acquired when he was eight years old,
was a ukulele, which he continued to play through high school.
There was a succession of others.

"I had some temple blocks, and I tried to play trumpet for a
while. My cousin was commander of the Boy Scouts, and when I
got in he made me a field drummer. I got hold of a baritone horn,
then I got a bass horn. I took a few lessons on that from a barber
named Mr. Timmons. It was a helicon, a big E-flat horn with a bell
you couldn't detach. We got a little band together at Anderson High
School with the same name as our social club, the Moonlight Serenaders, and learned to play "Should I" and "When the Moon
Comes over the Mountain" and "Dinah." We had stock arrangements, but we always had to put in little optional notes. Oh, boy, let
me tell you, we tore up the town."

The Moonlight Serenaders also began tearing up Taylor, Bastrop,
Elgin, and a smattering of other small towns and earning as much
as a dollar and a half apiece each night. At the same time, Ramey
was playing tennis, football, and baseball, plucking turkeys, and
shining shoes. In 1930, he was one of the first students to amass
enough credits to graduate from Anderson High at midyear.

After high school he went to work at the Maverick Cafe as a porter and played at the Austin Club two nights a week. Then, in 1931,
he joined George Corley's eleven-piece band, remaining until 1932,
when he entered Western University in Kansas City. There he joined

the school band, and his musicianship and professional experience soon had him involved in the yeasty Kansas City jazz scene. He acquired a string bass and was learning to play it when he encountered the best possible teacher.

"All I was doing at first was slapping it—bang, pow!—the way guys used to do. I didn't know what notes I was playing, but folks said, 'This boy's sure got a good beat.' Then I met Walter Page, and every evening I'd go watch him play with Basie. Pretty soon I knew what notes to play, and I had a good enough ear. Page would tell me, 'Play something that's going to make a line. You're supposed to tell a story just like that soloist out front is doing.' And he spoke about the diatonic scale, which involves a lot more than simple chords.

"Page had the ability to charm that rhythm section, to make it think about restraint. He kept Jo Jones in tow. Jo was full of pep and ready to tell off the world on those drums, and Page held him in. He pulled the section together so that you could hear the guitar, the drums, the bass, the piano. It was so smooth, consistent and even, that there has never, ever been anything like it. After two years of staying around him, I got the chances; he would try to get me up there to jam. But after I saw what happened to Bird, I wouldn't dare go up there."

Bird was Charlie Parker, the quicksilver genius of modern jazz alto saxophone. But when Ramey met him he was short of his midteens and struggling with music. "What happened to Bird" is part of the folklore of American music, and no one knew better than Gene Ramey the aspirations and shortcomings of the boy already nicknamed "Yardbird." Ramey met Parker in 1934.

"I was at the university," Ramey remembers, "but the guys in a high school band would come get me to play with them because they needed a bass player. I was still playing bass horn then. We had a battle of the bands with a high school band from across the river in Missouri and Bird was in that band with Lawrence Keyes, who later became famous as Lawrence '88' Keyes. From then on I began to see Bird at jam sessions and things. We got to know each other pretty well."

What was the fourteen-year-old Parker's playing like? "It wasn't too good. I've been quoted so many times it seems my word has been gospel. He had a Lucy sound." Sweet Lucy was the poor man's wine, cheap muscatel and port sold by the gallon. "You ever see a guy when he's really drunk and he's trying to talk? *Uhyeealyuh*—that's how he sounded on his horn. So we said Bird had a Lucy sound, which is natural anyway for a beginner finding himself."

Parker worked on his sound, Ramey switched from tuba to string bass, and the spring of 1936 found both of them playing on Twelfth Street, Parker for little or no pay at the Greenleaf Garden with a group of other youngsters and Ramey with the grownups at the Bar Le Duc. Kansas City had dozens of nightclubs with live music, all flourishing as if the Great Depression were fictional. Basie had the band at the Reno. It was the standard by which all other Kansas City bands were judged.

"He had two trumpets, a trombone, three saxes, and three rhythm, with Lips Page on trumpet and Jimmy Rushing singing as extra attractions. Every intermission at the other clubs, every night, all the musicians would go over to the Reno to hear Count Basie. They were attracted by Lester Young. Some nights the management just cleaned up on musicians drinking and listening to the band. They'd bring their horns and sit in and jam. But the majority of them came to look and listen, and to learn. You'd see arrangers sitting there writing on their sleeves what the guys were playing. It was like a research laboratory."

One night when they were through at their own clubs Ramey and Parker met at the Reno for the nightly jam session. The club was packed with musicians. On dozens of similar occasions the two had been content to listen, to study, but tonight, though Ramey tried to dissuade his friend, Parker thought he was ready for the big leagues. The formidable Basie drummer Jo Jones was on the stand.

I asked Ramey about the version of the jam session story in *Bird Lives*, Ross Russell's quasi-factual biography of Parker. Russell writes that Parker's downfall came during a performance of "I Got Rhythm."

"Now they've got it as 'I Got Rhythm?'" Ramey said, laughing. "Nobody remembers what the tune was. It would be amazing for anybody to remember. There were dozens of tunes they used to jam.

What that particular song was, we'd never be able to remember. That shows you how things can be stretched. Russell got most of his information from me. I've seen some of the stories I'm supposed to have given. I look at 'em and say, 'Oh, boy.'

"Whatever the tune was, Bird was doing pretty well until he attempted something that took him out of the correct chord sequence, and he couldn't get back in. He kept getting lost, and Jo Jones kept hitting the ball of the cymbal like a gong, Major Bowes style—remember on his amateur hour on the radio Bowes hit the gong if somebody wasn't making it. Joe kept hitting that cymbal, but he couldn't get Bird off the stand. So finally he just took the cymbal off and dropped it on the floor. When it hit, it skidded a little. I read one story where Jo was supposed to have thrown the cymbal all the way across the floor. But he just dropped it at Bird's feet, and that stopped him.

"I guess the story in itself is so dramatic that people kept taking it and enlarging it and spreading it out. But enough of it was true, and it was comical but still pitiful to see the reaction on Bird's face. He was dumbfounded. He came over and I said, 'Well, Bird, you almost straightened it out. I remember you made that turn back, but somewhere down in there you got off on the wrong thing.' We kidded about it, and he kept telling me, 'Oh, man, I'll be back. Don't worry, I'm comin' back.'"

Ramey felt that his young friend was hesitant for a long time after. That summer Parker took a job with the George Lee band at a resort in the Ozarks. He spent his time learning harmony from the older musicians and studying the recorded solos of Lester Young on Basie's Jones-Smith Incorporated records until he had them memorized. When he returned to Kansas City in the fall he was able to jam competently in fast company. A few years later he emerged from Jay McShann's band to become a dominant influence in jazz and a founder of the new music eventually labeled bebop.

Ramey, eight years Parker's senior, was a close friend and more. He kept tabs on him and bailed him out of trouble for twenty years. He was tuned into Parker's habits, including the drinking and drug addiction that ultimately brought him to a premature death.

"Bird was, I should say, my project. I couldn't stand to see a guy that good be wasted away. So every time he was in trouble I couldn't help but try to get him out. He was a good guy. He did have a heart, but he had a tendency to be spiteful, like a little baby would be, to get your attention. He might pawn his uniform jacket just because you didn't let him have some money. We played together a lot in New York in the forties. The last time was at Birdland in 1954. He had very few jobs at Birdland, although the place was named after him. They said they wanted no part of him, not because he was so much trouble but because he was continually wanting money, even though he might have a pocketful.

"I had the band at Birdland on Monday nights, and I persuaded Oscar Goodstein, the boss, to let me hire Bird for two nights. His problems didn't affect his music at all. He could still cook. Even that short a time before his death, he was playing well. The last time I saw him was the middle of February 1955. He came into the Embers when I was working there with Teddy Wilson and Jo Jones. Then, in March, Dizzy Gillespie called and told me that Bird was dead."

After Count Basie's band left Kansas City in 1936 for the New York big time, Ramey and Bus Moten moved into the Reno club briefly, and then Ramey joined the Countess Johnson band at the Stateline Tavern. "The Stateline straddled the line between Kansas City, Kansas, and Kansas City, Missouri. When the Kansas closing law was in effect, everybody would go over to the Missouri side of the club and get drunk again. After the Countess Johnson band broke up I was instrumental in getting every member into the Jay McShann band."

McShann, an accomplished pianist, organized in 1939 what was to become Kansas City's last great big band. It never achieved the long-term success of the Basie organization, but it had a million-seller in "Confessin' the Blues." And it provided the first national exposure for its nineteen-year-old star soloist, Charlie Parker, who by then was essentially formed as an improvisational genius. Ramey thinks the roots of bebop were growing in Kansas City long before Parker's solos with McShann began to electrify musicians. He says the Kansas City players, notably Lester Young of the Count Basie band, were verging on bop in what they called "running out of key."

"It's the same variations as bebop," Ramey said, "but the bass player had to keep the basic line. If you were playing 'Sweet Sue,' for example, the bass player used the chords to 'Sweet Sue,' not altered chords, and that gave the horns a chance to go out, to play alternates. So sometimes the horn player would sound like he was in another key, using flatted fifths and so forth. That sort of thing was already going on. About that time Bird and I had met this guitarist named Effergee Ware who was showing us the relationship of chords. So Bird and I would go off and the two of us would jam. My duty was to tell him if he got too far out. If it sounded too strange I said 'Whoa.' When we got with McShann we would jam on trains, in the back of the bus, when we got to the dance hall early. When Dizzy Gillespie and Benny Harris and those guys came to Kansas City they knew about Bird. They would look us up, and about eight of us would go out and jam. Buddy Anderson from McShann's band was really the first bop trumpet player. Dizzy began to see what we were doing then. So bop began much earlier than the critics believed. That's *another* mistake they made. The critics are always late."

Ramey was with McShann until early 1944, when McShann's Army induction led to the band's dissolution. The two had agreed that the bassist would keep the band alive. They wanted to call it "the Jay McShann Band under the Direction of Gene Ramey, Featuring Walter Brown." Brown was the band's blues singer. But the Rockwell-O'Keefe agency, which handled the band, informed Ramey that it was to be known as "Walter Brown and His Band under the Direction of Gene Ramey," eliminating the founding father's name entirely. Ramey refused to go along with that. He quit and joined the Luis Russell band at the Reno Club, then went on tour with Russell as a featured soloist, an experience he considers the height of his accomplishments.

"We played Chicago, Washington, Detroit, Baltimore, and the Apollo in New York. Each time I soloed, there was a standing ovation. We did five shows a day, and each time I had to come back and take another bow and sometimes play an encore. I was with Russell until October 1944, long enough to become established in New York."

In January 1945, when Ramey was working out his six-month probation period as a member of the notoriously restrictive New York Local 802 of the American Federation of Musicians (AFM), word came that McShann was out of the Army and interested in re-forming his band. Ramey claims that powerful manipulators in the jazz world ordered him to abandon his 802 membership, reinstate himself in the Kansas City AFM local, and rejoin McShann. Ramey refused and, coincidentally or not, from that time on he was never able to secure a solo position. He worked on 52nd Street, the nerve center of New York jazz life in the forties, but leaders would not allow him to solo, and he claims record producers would let him play only in the rhythm section, never as a soloist. He thinks that when the McShann band died for lack of a leader, considerable money was lost and he was identified as the cause. When he refused to help McShann regroup, a jazz business establishment conspiracy kept his work opportunities scarce.

Certainly there are no Ramey solos on records, even though he worked with many of the leading artists in jazz for another thirty years. His sturdy, resourceful bass lines were heard behind Art Tatum and Billie Holiday at the Famous Door, Teddy Wilson at the Embers, Eddie "Lockjaw" Davis at Minton's Playhouse, Ben Webster at the Onyx Club, Miles Davis at Birdland, and his old Kansas City buddies Charlie Parker and Lester Young at a number of New York clubs. Because of his dependability, Ramey was even called upon to back players thought of as avant-garde, out of the jazz mainstream, including the enigmatic pianist Thelonious Monk.

"For a long time I was the only bass player who could work with Monk," Ramey claimed. "If we were playing 'Humph,' I would play those chords only; no experimenting. And that gave him a base to work from. If I had tried to do what he was doing—go out—the musical balance would have been ruined.

"One time I was called to make a record with that other strange piano player Herbie Nichols. It was me and Herbie and Art Blakey on drums. When we rehearsed, he started playing the first tune in C and wanted me to accompany him in D-flat. Now, those keys are at war. If he had wanted me to go in E-Flat or even in E, it might have been interesting. But that's a bad marriage, C and D-flat. So I made everybody mad, refused to do it. I called Al McKibbon and he made the record.

"I was supposed to record with Ornette Coleman, the alto player. But I went to hear him in a rehearsal, and I backed out. I couldn't figure it out. I knew I couldn't give him what he needed."

Ramey listens to what younger musicians are doing these days. He keeps up, he says, but for the most part he is puzzled. "In our day, music was a message. Now you can get the beat from rock 'n roll, for example, or the avant-garde groups, but it's hard to follow the message. In the olden days, the guy picked up his horn and started blowing, and you could feel what he was trying to say on his instrument. You must remember that there has got to be some kind of message sent. John Coltrane, for example, a great tenor player. He could blow when he first went with Miles Davis. But he started playing this avant-garde or whatever. To me, it gave the impression of a fierce battle in the jungle, like all the animals are stampeding. It's frantic, and it can be moving, but what is it saying, unless it's saying that there's torment in the world? Somebody has said that jazz describes the system, and science is moving faster than the human brain can adjust, so maybe that's what the music is trying to tell us, that we haven't been able to keep up with what the world is doing."

Even in semiretirement, Ramey is eager to play. He is exploring the possibility of getting a group together to perform for the residents of nursing homes in the Austin area, a project that will require either some form of government support or help from the musicians' union trust fund. Last summer he traveled to San Antonio to work with the Jim Cullum band, which he praises, and he occasionally joins clarinetist Herb Hall, who lives in Boerne. But in jazz-locked Austin, there's nothin' shakin' for Gene Ramey.

Shortly after this piece appeared in Texas Monthly, *Austin began opening itself up to jazz and to Ramey in particular. He found him-*

self in demand not only as a player but as a mentor to developing musicians. Through his quartet passed several impressive young players. When I last saw him in Austin in September of 1984, he was preparing for a reunion concert with Jay McShann in Chicago the following January. But in December he died suddenly, at home, of heart failure. He was seventy-one.

Freddie Hubbard

Freddie Hubbard came out of Indianapolis in the late 1950s. He was one of a group of dazzling young trumpeters of the period that included Lee Morgan, Booker Little, Carmel Jones, and the slightly older Donald Byrd. Like the others, in his developing years Hubbard's playing was modeled on that of Clifford Brown, who was inspired by Fats Navarro, who learned from Dizzy Gillespie. So in the compressed evolution of jazz, Hubbard was a member of the fourth generation of bop trumpeters, and all four generations had existed in a span of less than a quarter of a century. Follow the progression backward through the forties, thirties, and twenties from Gillespie to Roy Eldridge to Louis Armstrong, and you have virtually the entire history of jazz trumpet playing in a forty year period.

Through the 1960s, Hubbard was a mainstay of hard core post-bop music in the bands of Art Blakey and Max Roach, in his own groups, and in the recording studios of New York. He was particularly identified with the Blue Note label, whose stable of artists included many young players who developed a recognizable and widely influential approach to modern jazz that came to be known as "the Blue Note sound."

In the seventies, Hubbard's popularity made him attractive to Columbia Records, which recorded him in semi-jazz settings designed to appeal to the new audience for crossover or fusion music. Understandably eager to make capital with his ability, Hubbard stayed with the Columbia format for several years. But in the late seventies, it became increasingly apparent that, in Hubbard's internal war, jazz was winning over commerce. By 1981, he had returned to the full-time production of serious music.

Freddie Hubbard Live at Rosy's

1979

Having moderated if not forsworn the disco approach of his *High Energy* and *Liquid Love* albums, Freddie Hubbard wheeled his tight little band into New Orleans this past December very much in the spirit of *Super Blue,* his latest Columbia album. Those who watched the rhythm section setting up its electronic arsenal at Rosy's club may have felt some apprehension that they were in for a crossover audio onslaught. But it became apparent with his cadenza leading into "Super Blue" that Hubbard had come to play, and only rarely after he switched to flugelhorn for the main body of the piece did the decibel level of the accompaniment become distracting.

If there is a general belief that Hubbard has been influenced by Rex Stewart, it is not often discussed. But during "Super Blue" the half-valve phrases, buzzes, and flutters he used so effectively in the middle register called to mind no one as much as the great Duke Ellington cornetist. It is an aspect of Hubbard's technique that greatly adds to the humor and warmth of his playing.

His front line partner, tenor saxophonist Hadley Caliman, soloed on "Super Blue" in the tradition of John Coltrane's middle period and worked beautifully with Hubbard in the ensembles. As the evening progressed, Caliman's playing took on much of the intensity and coloration of Coltrane's later work, but he is a more directly rhythmic player than Coltrane was toward the end of his life and from that standpoint is reminiscent of Dexter Gordon. Whatever his influences, Caliman is an inventive and cheerful soloist. When he is not playing, his good nature finds an outlet in dancing. His disco moves on the stand were impeccably and exuberantly executed, giving him the air of the young Gilbert Roland in one of his macho roles, celebrating newly found riches in the oil fields or on the shrimp boats.

Hubbard, too, occasionally dances on the stand, always briefly and somewhat bearishly. For the most part, in the craft of occupying space while not playing, his forte is striking poses. Being a handsome and self-assured man who dresses well, he does so quite effectively. His poses are created during short promenades across the stand, often preceded or followed by quick jumps into the air at crucial moments in the music. The leaps are employed to give cues to the rhythm section, triggering changes in intensity or direction. Watching this band is not boring.

"Her Ladyship," like "Super Blue," had disco-crossover tinges, but that aspect was underplayed. Again there were several choruses of Hubbard at his most fleet and inventive. Perhaps he has worked through the exhibitionism that has diluted his work in the past few years.

Gino Vanelli's "The Surest Things Can Change" is hardly one of the great melodies. But Hubbard, on flugelhorn, invested it with a wistful sadness that had the audience thoughtfully attentive during his first chorus, which was taken out of tempo. As the rhythm section joined him, they applied themselves a bit too rigorously and the leader called for "space, space, space." Pianist Rodney Franklin thinned out the electronic accompaniment, to the unquestionable benefit of the performance.

Hubbard and Franklin did a vocal duet on the latter's "I Like the Music, Make It Hot," the set's only outright concession to commercialism. The object was promotion of Franklin's recently issued album, and the piece was replete with string synthesizer effects from the electronic circuitry of the composer's Arp.

Franklin has an almost Rachmaninoffian technique on acoustic piano and performed impressive rhapsodic passages. He was stimulating during his solo on Hubbard's "Black Magic," which has a line much like some of the numbers Art Blakey's Jazz Messengers played during the sixties when Hubbard was a member. But Franklin's most satisfying playing came on the fast blues that closed the set, the only straight ahead 4/4 piece of the evening. Hubbard played with a controlled, fierce intensity that had the crowd applauding during his solo. It may have occured to him that the more trendy pieces did not get that kind of response. After all, New Orleans audiences, by and large, go to Rosy's to listen to *jazz*, and when they get it, they show their appreciation.

Unfortunately, drummer Kirk Farquar, who had been impressive during the rhythmic convolutions of the crossover pieces, got hung up trying to negotiate straight-time blues. Nevertheless, Franklin forged ahead with his flying single-note lines. Caliman wailed with a series of keening high notes, and alternating forays into the lower register of the saxophone.

It would have been interesting to hear Larry Klein, a good electric bassist, play the acoustic instrument. With that alternative, Hubbard would have the option of occasionally going all the way into the hard bop he flirted with on "Black Magic" and entered in that marvelous fast blues. There is something manifestly unconvincing about the electric bass in uncompromising bop.

One cannot avoid the suspicion that deep down inside, Hubbard is longing to pull out all the stops. It would be a welcome development, but he has young audiences to please and a living to make. Perhaps it is enough to be grateful that one of the most gifted jazz soloists has returned so far toward the center of the music.

George Benson and
Jack McDuff

The guitarist and singer George Benson became a best-selling popular music performer in the mid-1970s with an album called Breezin'. *He has built on that success and is one of the world's best known pop music figures, rarely absent from the upper reaches of the commercial charts. To his pop fans, Benson's guitar playing is secondary. To jazz listeners, the dominance of his voice and formulized instrumental work in the pop field mean they are seldom allowed to hear him demonstrate his improvisational powers. On those rare occasions, however, it is clear that he is one of the master jazz guitarists.*

Benson was born in Pittsburgh, Pennsylvania, in 1943. Taught the ukelele when he was a very young child, by the age of eight Benson was earning money playing. At age eleven, when he was learning the guitar, he recorded as a singer. In his early teens, he played in a cousin's rock and roll band. Then he heard records by Charlie Parker and guitarist Wes Montgomery and became interested in jazz. He first received the serious attention of the jazz world at eighteen, when he was in the band of organist Jack McDuff. Later, he led his own group and, through a series of successful albums for the CTI label, began crossing over from mainstream jazz into mainstream pop.

McDuff, one of the most tasteful and powerful of the jazz organists, was born in Champaign, Illinois, in 1926. He worked in the early 1950s with such leaders as Porter Kilbert, Eddie Chamblee, and Willis Jackson but has led his own groups since 1959.

1977

Toward the end of 1976, when George Benson had beaten the odds
and gods of public taste and the music business and became a genuine pop star, he was part of a jazz all-stars program put together by
down beat magazine for public television. Most of the musicians
involved were, like Benson, men who had paid their dues in jazz
and were making it big in fusion, or crossover or jazz-rock.

The natural concern of a dedicated jazz lover was that the music
on the program would find the lowest common denominator of the
best-selling albums Benson, Chick Corea, Stanley Clarke, Billy
Cobham, and Jean-Luc Ponty had ridden to commerical success.
The fear was that, despite the proven creative musicianship of all
concerned, eagerness to please the mass audience that had made
them famous would draw the level of performance downward into
boredom. Indeed, there was a brief opening period of obligatory
jazz-rock get-the-money-and-run shuckin'. Then the all-stars settled
down to serious business, and there were fine moments from all of
the above, plus Thad Jones, Sonny Fortune, Bill Watrous, and Gary
Burton. Benson's solo feature had all the elements, including those
borrowed from Wes Montgomery, for which the top-40 devotees
admire him. It was pleasant.

But when Benson and Ron Carter combined for a guitar-bass
duet on "Lover Man," the real George Benson stood out. Reducing
his amplification nearly to that of an acoustic instrument, George
constructed a filagree accompaniment to Carter's solo, ultimately
melding with the bassist in a stretch of mutual improvisation that
was uncanny in the way the two men anticipated one another. His
comping behind Carter's rubato flight at the end of the piece was
a model of what guitar accompaniment should be. The performance was worth warehouses full of Benson's hit album, and it was
a reminder that when a superior musician achieves success with
watered-down material he doesn't necessarily dilute his art, however rarely he may choose or be allowed to work at it.

Besides, before we get too exercised about this business of popular acceptance versus artistic integrity, it may be well to keep in mind that Benson set out years ago to become a popular performer, not a jazz musician. His public career began when he was an eight-year-old singer. His first recordings in 1954, the year he began learning to play the guitar, were vocals. He has often said that he considers himself an entertainer who became a musician out of necessity.

That makes Benson something of a hangover from an earlier era, when jazzmen like Earl Hines and Louis Armstrong, for all their artistic genius, never discussed their music in terms of art. They saw their task as entertaining, making people happy. It would take a mighty effort of critical dissembling to convince anyone with ears that Hines and Armstrong were not among the most important creative musicians of their time. And it would be foolish to seize upon Benson's commercial appeal as proof that his worth as a serious musician has diminished. The Armstrong of "West End Blues" and the Armstrong of "Blueberry Hill" dwelled not in separate planes of existence, but together. The Benson of "Lover Man" and the Benson of "Breezin'" don't seem to be at war with each other, certainly not in the mind of Benson.

Be that as it may, given a choice, most serious listeners would take Louis's "West End Blues" and George's "Lover Man" every time, whatever the entertainment merits of "Blueberry Hill" or "Breezin'." Armstrong went through periods when he succumbed, or was conditioned, to his popular repertoire, but he still loved to blow, and there were times almost to the very end when he stunned his colleagues with his imagination. Benson, even if he achieves Armstrong's commercial success, is incapable of jettisoning his artistic sensibility which, however much he proclaims his artistic innocence, is ingrained through years of development as a creative musician.

Until he was seventeen, Benson was his own teacher, guided by basics picked up from his stepfather, Thomas Collier, an amateur guitarist and avid fan of Charlie Christian, the seminal jazz guitar stylist. Benson had a rock and roll band in which he played guitar. But his vocals were the main attraction. Benson loved Christian, but he says it was the late Hank Garland's only jazz album that made him "realize all the possibilities of the guitar." Garland, one of the most recorded country guitarists in the Nashville milieu of the fifties and early sixties, was a phenomenally gifted musician who could have had a stellar jazz career if he had been willing to take the pay cut. In 1960 he recorded a quartet album (*Jazz Winds from a New Direction*, Columbia CSP ACS 8372) with young Gary Burton on vibes, bassist Joe Benjamin, and drummer Joe Morello. Among other things Benson learned from the Garland record was the effectiveness of single-note lines, an aspect that he quickly began to absorb into his own style. Inspired by Garland, Benson now began earnestly to pursue guitar knowledge.

When guitar players came through his hometown of Pittsburgh, George studied their techniques and quizzed them endlessly about fingerings, chords, improvisational methods, amplifiers, strings . . . the full range of guitar lore. His persistence paid off in instruction from Grant Green, Eddie McFadden, Eddie Diehl, Thornel Schwartz, and John Pisano. Then, in 1961, when Benson was eighteen, Jack McDuff asked Benson to join his quartet, which was riding the wave of soul-jazz popularity.

A number of organists rose to fame after Jimmy Smith showed the way for them in modern jazz. McDuff has been one of the most admired, popular, and durable. He began his jazz life as a bassist and was working with tenor saxophonist Johnny Griffin in Chicago when Art Blakey asked him to join the Jazz Messengers. McDuff recalls that it was during a period when Blakey was enamored of fast tempos on tunes that would often last an hour and a half. He didn't think he had the stamina a bass player would need for that kind of marathoning. Shortly after, he switched to piano and worked steadily with trios that included bassists Leroy Vinnegar and Richard Evans long before they became well known.

The change to the instrument that would be his vehicle to fame came about not because of inspiration from Jimmy Smith but as a matter of economics. He kept getting gigs at clubs that turned out to have organs, not pianos. If he wanted to keep the contracts he had no choice but to play the organ. As he spent more and more time at the electronic keyboard, McDuff began to discover what he has since demonstrated thousands of times, that the organ is "a hell of an instrument, a complete instrument, a dominant instrument."

Most organ groups did not include horns at the time McDuff left tenor saxophonist Willis Jackson to form his own quartet. But McDuff had developed a taste for the tenor-organ sound and has almost always included at least one saxophonist. One of his bands had two tenors.

McDuff told Dan Morgenstern in a *down beat* interview a few years ago that among all the bands he's led he had a special feeling for the quartet that included Red Holloway on tenor and the neophyte George Benson on guitar. Benson was definitely not a finished product when McDuff took him on.

"When I first met George," McDuff told Morgenstern, "he didn't know any complete tune, not even the bridge to 'Moonlight in Vermont,' which all the guitarists were playing because of Johnny Smith's record. But he could play blues, and he was so fluent that it was clear you could show him things. I had my electric piano, so I'd tape five or six tunes, and the next day he'd be playing them like he'd been reading them. . . . In fact, Red Holloway was a good reader, and I'd write out parts for him, but George would be playing them before him! People started to recognize that he was a bitch, and he hasn't looked back since."

Benson developed awesomely during the three and a half years he was with McDuff. The simple opportunity to do steady work in a highly professional band was probably all that a musician of his natural gifts needed to become a rounded soloist. But McDuff is much more than a journeyman organist. He is one of the most vital blues players on any instrument and has few equals in his knowledge of the harmonic makeup of the standard song. His example was unquestionably important in Benson's growth.

Without getting into an enervating discussion of the merits of the performances on the records at hand, it is instructive to contemplate McDuff's solo on "Will You Still Be Mine," in which he swings his young colleague out of the room. At this stage, Benson was still bedeviled by an inability to make his notes last as long as he wanted them to, and had a way to go in interpreting standards at fast tempos.

The McDuff experience, naturally, made a solid impression on Benson. When he left the organist to form his own group, the instrumentation was the same, except that Benson used a baritone saxophonist, Ronnie Cuber, instead of a tenor. Benson had wanted to work out some of his own ideas as a leader, and he did, beautifully. But the sound of the new Benson quartet was virtually that of "Rock-A-Bye" on this album, the sound of the McDuff quartet.

With the formation of his first band, George Benson was off and running. Despite McDuff's assertion that his protégé "hasn't looked back since," Benson has frequently been quoted as warmly remembering the days with Brother Jack, happy times in the careers of two fine musicians.

The Dave Brubeck Quartet

Dave Brubeck's musical activities over the past two decades have encompassed the composition and performance of cantatas, oratorios, and tone poems, and appearances with symphony orchestras. Simultaneously, he has kept his quartet in business with sidemen like baritone saxophonist Gerry Mulligan, drummer Alan Dawson, clarinetist Bill Smith and, for a time, three of his sons. Nonetheless, for many—perhaps most—people, "The Dave Brubeck Quartet" means the long-running group with Paul Desmond, Eugene Wright, and Joe Morello which disbanded in 1967. Although much of the history of that band is covered in the second of the following pieces, it may be helpful to know something of the early careers of its members.

Brubeck was born in 1920 in Concord, California, a town that, coincidentally, is now the site of a jazz festival and headquarters of Concord Records, for which Brubeck records. Taught by his mother, he began piano lessons at four. During his teen years he played with local bands, mostly for dancing in situations that required him to master a range of styles including dixieland, swing, and hillbilly. Majoring in music at the College of the Pacific in the early 1940s, he formed his own band, created jam sessions, and began to develop a style. He was influenced by Fats Waller and Earl Hines and by the boogie-woogie pianist Cleo Brown. With the U.S. Army in Europe in World War II, Brubeck managed to organize his own band and to continue his composition studies, with no less eminent a teacher than Arnold Schoenberg.

When he returned to the States following active duty, he went to Mills College to resume his study of composition with another leading figure of twentieth century music, Darius Milhaud. In 1946, he put together an octet which was a workshop for ideas stimulated in

Brubeck, Dave Van Kriedt, Jack Weeks, Bill Smith, and other young composers by their studies with Milhaud. Although lack of employment caused the octet to disband in 1949, the daring, complexity, and joyousness of its music brought notice from Bay Area visitors like Duke Ellington and George Shearing and the enthusiastic championship of KNBC disc jockey Jimmy Lyons. The octet's rhythm section, with drummer Cal Tjader and bassist Ron Crotty, began appearing, as The Dave Brubeck Trio, on Lyons' radio program. That resulted in an offer of two weeks in an Oakland nightclub. The two weeks became a six-month engagement, and further steady employment followed. In 1951, alto saxophonist Paul Desmond, another alumnus of the octet, was added and The Dave Brubeck Quartet was created.

Desmond was born in San Francisco in 1924 and grew up there except for his grade school years, which were spent in New Rochelle, New York. He took up clarinet in high school and continued to study it when he attended San Francisco State College as a creative writing major. He began to play alto saxophone in 1943, the year he entered the Army. He was assigned to the 253rd AGF Band in his hometown and remained with it for three years. During that time, he developed his jazz skills and at a jam session met Brubeck, who was on his way overseas as a rifleman. The two did not see one another again until after the war, when Brubeck was working in San Francisco with a tenor player named Darryl Cutler and Desmond sat in. In an interview for a 1960 down beat article, Desmond told Marian McPartland that the two had instant rapport, on the spot developing the counterpoint approach that was to become central to their collaborations.

Shortly, Desmond hired away Cutler's sidemen, including Brubeck, for some dates in Palo Alto. Over a period of months in Desmond's group, the pair's musical compatibility and senses of adventure coalesced into a remarkable partnership which continued through Desmond's membership in the Brubeck octet and seventeen years of the quartet. Desmond was not to be a leader again until the 1970s, and then rarely. He worked with the Jack Fina and Alvino Rey bands in 1950 and 1951 before joining Brubeck's quartet in 1951.

Eugene Wright grew up in Chicago, where he was born in 1923. He taught himself to play bass and at the age of twenty had his own big band, the Dukes of Swing. He gave up his band in 1946 to join the group of fellow Chicagoan Gene Ammons, the tenor saxophonist son of the boogie pianist Albert Ammons. Wright also worked in the 1940s with Count Basie and by the beginning of the fifties had a considerable reputation as a bassist whose time, sound, and harmonic conception were rock-solid. He played with tenor saxophonist Arnett Cobb, then in 1955 joined the highly regarded quartet of clarinetist Buddy DeFranco. After working with the Red Norvo Trio, Wright joined Brubeck's quartet in 1958. Following the group's breakup in late 1967, he led his own bands, played with pianist Monty Alexander, and did television and motion picture work in Los Angeles. He also taught music, privately and as chairman of the jazz department of the University of Cincinnati.

Joe Morello, regarded by fellow percussionists as one of the fastest and most powerful of drummers, was born in Springfield, Massachusetts, in 1928. After working in the Boston area, he played for a time with Glen Gray's big band. His first New York City engagement was in 1952 with guitarist Johnny Smith. He worked with Stan Kenton, then spent three years in the trio of pianist Marian McPartland. He joined Brubeck in 1956. Plagued by worsening lifelong eyesight problems, since 1967 Morello has spent much of his time conducting drum clinics and teaching. He has also published instruction books for drummers and recorded under his own name.

THROUGH THE YEARS
WITH DESMOND AND BRUBECK

The first item I wrote about The Dave Brubeck Quartet was for the University of Washington Daily *in 1955, four years after the group was formed in San Francisco. Although some of these thoughts*

*about musical quotes have been incorporated into the "Common
Language" section of the introduction to this book, the article itself
is an embarassing example of youthful excess and will not be inflicted upon the reader. The following three pieces deal with the
quartet's members and music over a period of fifteen years. In the
first, the word "hippy" is used in its original sense, describing a fan
immersed in the subcultural trappings of the jazz life, the sort of
person immortalized in Dave Frishberg's song, "I'm Hip" ("I even
call my girlfriend 'man,' 'cause I'm hip"). The flowerchild application of the word came a few years later.*

Take Five with Paul Desmond
Or an Intermission Spent at Wit's End

1962

During much of the summer, Dave Brubeck keeps his cheerful band
of music makers on the cross-country trail from outdoor concert to
tent show to county fair, helping satisfy suburban America's newly
found, fashionable need for jazz.

The crowd at the summer jazz concert, which is not to be mis-
taken for the larger and more confusing jazz festival, is composed of
college students who would much rather hear Johnny Mathis but
are too cool to admit it, local distributors for Columbia Records,
drummers who come to watch Joe Morello's feet, and actors who
will do a "Broadway" musical in the tent that night and have nowhere to go following afternoon rehearsal.

Not long ago at a performance in the Musicarnival tent in Cleveland, Brubeck broke into what for him was a frenzy of good natured
chatter.

"We were at the Hollywood Bowl last night, San Francisco the
night before, at the Aqua Theater in Seattle the previous three eve-

nings . . . that's a vacation, three nights in the same town . . . New Jersey on Monday and a week ago on 'The Ed Sullivan Show.'

"Sullivan brought us on for three minutes at the end of the show. That gave us a chance to watch the acrobats. You have to be there to appreciate it. Sullivan likes to run them through their act five or six times to decide if he'll use them or cut the bit out altogether. It's kind of exhausting. There was a fella there who did back flips with a set of drums. I didn't think he'd make it when the show went live.

"Well, enough of this. On with the music."

At intermission, alto saxophonist Paul Desmond expressed mild amazement at his friend's oratory.

"Really quite garrulous. Came on like Mort Sahl. Dave's punchy— no sleep."

An attractive blonde approached. The interest in Desmond's eyes turned to curiosity when she asked what kind of horn and mouthpiece he uses.

"The horn is a Selmer and the mouthpiece is a Gregory," he answered. "It was invented by Pope Gregory. Do you play alto?"

The girl said no, giggled and edged away into the crowd. A pair of young brothers arrived, programs in hand, and asked Desmond the whereabouts of Gene Wright. They wore identical striped blazers and were around five and seven years old. Desmond didn't know but said he thought the bassist might be in the dressing room. The young fans ran, yelling, at top speed toward the low building housing the dressing room, ten feet away.

Desmond and an old friend were about to reminisce, but one of the Musicarnival actresses had a question.

"I don't want to show my ignorance," she chirped, "but do you know what you're going to play before you sit down, or do you just sort of make it up as you go along?"

Desmond gave her a long look to be sure he wasn't the victim of a put-on, decided he wasn't, and explained.

"First of all, I never sit down. But I do try to follow a general plan, which we've all discussed on the plane. Chords and things."

"Oh, you mean sort of like harmony."

"Yeah, something like that."

As Desmond turned to resume his conversation, up shuffled a

man easily identifiable as a hippy even before he opened his mouth. He slouched, his eyes were downcast, his dress was conservatively ostentatious.

"Hey, man," he whined, "what about Art? Like is Art in for good after his last bust? I mean, Art's too much and they shouldn't keep him in there."

Desmond explained that he wasn't too familiar with Art Pepper's legal problems but had always admired his playing.

The hippy apparently felt he hadn't made his point, removed his extremely dark glasses and moved closer to whisper in Desmond's ear. Desmond nodded gravely and thoughtfully and watched the hippy slip away toward a hot dog stand.

A Marine Corps private reached out to shake hands. Desmond saluted and introduced him as a youngster who had been attending Brubeck concerts in Cleveland since 1956, "always came back after the show," decided to become a jazz player, and purchased an alto. Desmond told him the uniform was becoming, but:

"Why did you do it?"

"My folks didn't understand jazz, so I joined the Corps to get away. Three more years. There's a pretty good band at Camp LeJeune."

The blonde was back. She asked Desmond what his mouthpiece was made of. He asked if she were collecting the information for Cannonball. The name didn't register. She pointed to a man a few yards away. He stood grinning and waving. Desmond told her the mouthpiece was made of hard rubber. She trotted off dutifully with the answer.

The young autograph hounds returned, reported proudly that they had Wright's autograph and asked Paul for his. They got it, and Desmond used his own name. A few years ago it was his custom to sign all autographs, "Good luck, Chet Baker."

A couple of twenty or so appeared and were introduced by the Marine, who explained he had been trying to get them to a Brubeck concert for months.

The newcomers said the music was "just great, no kidding." Desmond thanked them very much. Who was the bass player, the man wanted to know, on the *Jazz at Storyville* album.

"Which one, Fantasy or Columbia?"

"Fantasy."

"There wasn't any."

"Oh."

Embarrassed silence, interrupted after a few seconds by Desmond.

"Bull Reuther was supposed to be there, but he was upstairs asleep in the shower. Later they made it a 12-inch LP and added a track or two from an air check. I guess Ron Crotty was on them, but I really don't remember."

More silence. The young man decided to try again.

"Well, 'Sunday Afternoon in Boston' was about the best thing you've done, wasn't it?"

"No, not really."

Intense silence. Equally intense thought by the young man.

"Well, on the back it said you were just warming up for the evening when they recorded that."

"That was just Ralph Gleason warming up for the liner notes."

With that, the fellow said it was nice meeting Desmond, took his girl's arm and retreated, his show of jazz knowledge a failure.

The blonde messenger returned.

"My boyfriend would like to know is that hard rubber mouthpiece specially made and what is its number."

Desmond told her the number and said it was not a special model but was no longer available. She looked disappointed, walked away and doubled back. She had forgotten the number. Desmond repeated it. She returned to her companion, who waved to Desmond. Desmond waved back. The messenger said something to her boyfriend and pointed at Desmond. Desmond pointed back. They walked away.

Others walked up to the altoist and asked about the size of his mouthpiece and the inevitable "Where do you go from here?" After answering the questions about his instrument and accessories and repeatedly explaining where the group was to play next, Desmond excused himself.

"See you next time," he announced.

He backed into the dressing room, smiling, and disappeared.

Twenty-Fifth Anniversary Reunion

1976

The Dave Brubeck Quartet was on the road again; twenty-five cities
in twenty-five days, one for every year since Brubeck organized the
band. For the last eight of those years, the quartet existed only on
records and in memory, although each of its members was thriving;
Brubeck composing, touring, recording; Paul Desmond writing a
book, accepting a few club dates, doing an occasional album; Gene
Wright leading his own ensemble and playing with Tony Bennett,
Monty Alexander, and others; Joe Morello teaching and recording.
"I hadn't seen Joe since the night we broke up, December 26,
1967," Brubeck recalls. "Joe and Gene hadn't seen each other at all.
I ran into Gene once in an airport. We had time to shake hands be-
fore we dashed off to catch our flights. I think Paul and Joe met in
New York once. Of course, Paul and I got together fairly often."
Brubeck and Desmond were charter members. They had known
each other since 1944, had played together in assorted combina-
tions around San Francisco and formed the quartet in 1951. Cal
Tjader and Ron Crotty were the original drummer and bassist. Joe
Dodge, Herb Barman, and Lloyd Davis were among the men who
carried out the percussion duties until Morello took over in 1956.
Wyatt Reuther, Joe Benjamin, and the Bates brothers, Norman and
Bob, were some of the bassists who worked with Brubeck until
Wright arrived in 1958. From then until the group disbanded, the
personnel was fixed. On the occasion of a previous anniversary, in
1961, a New Yorker profile said: "The Brubeck Quartet, which is
ten years old, is the world's best-paid, most widely-traveled, most
highly publicized, and most popular small group now playing improvised syncopated music."
And they dominated the field until the end—or what everyone
assumed would be the end.
The reunion tour began at Alfred College in Alfred, New York,

where they had played eight years ago, shortly before the Quartet disbanded, supposedly for all time. But a tireless promoter finally got Brubeck to propose the tour to the other three and, to his surprise, they eagerly agreed.

Much of the travel was by bus. But what a bus. It was equipped with eight beds, two television sets, a kitchen, two bathrooms, a shower, two audio systems and a citizens' band radio.

"The CB kept us in constant hysterics," Dave says. "I'm still saying 'ten-four' a lot. The police with CB units aren't supposed to talk to civilians, but they would always get curious about the bus, and they'd talk to the driver, and he'd get directions from them, or they'd lead us into town, which they are also not supposed to do. We ate mostly at truck stops because we had to refuel with diesel, so we got into that whole truckers' scene. Those are great people."

The tour included the Two Generations of Brubeck unit made up of Dave and his sons Chris, Danny, and Darius, as well as the reconstituted quartet. Standard practice in the concerts was for the Brubeck family group to play a few tunes, followed by Brubeck-Desmond duets. Then the youngsters would rejoin Dave and Paul for a couple of numbers, often "Brandenburg Gate" and "It's a Raggy Waltz." The second half of the program was an hour or more by the quartet.

"St. Louis Blues" opened the concerts in most cases, as it did in the last several years of the quartet's previous incarnation. The old empathy is obviously still intact in this version, but it becomes immediately apparent to a practiced Brubeck listener that there is something different in the bass section. Wright's swing has been nonpareil since he began recording with Sonny Stitt and Gene Ammons in the late forties. But his sound has taken on crispness and clarity that make him a good deal easier to hear, and his technique is more sophisticated than it was in 1967. Listen, for example, to his double stops on this piece. But then, Wright has always concerned himself with artistic growth. Backstage between halves of a Brubeck concert at the Seattle Civic Auditorium in 1960, Gene and the late, brilliant young bassist Freddie Schreiber were discussing the trend toward gospelizing and funkifying that was nearing its crest in jazz. Lectur-

ing Schreiber gently, Wright said: "Come on, man, get past that
funk thing. Once you get that out of your system, you'll find music
opening up to you. There's a lot more beauty in store. That's what's
exciting about working with this band. We're into 5/4 time, for instance. This band is where it's all happening." Then Gene gave a
little lesson to Freddie and all of us who were gathered around.
"1,2,3—1,2 . . . that's how to count it." So we went back to our
seats for the second half and counted along as the quartet performed "Take Five," which was to become Desmond's most famous
composition and most dependable annuity.

"Take Five," like "St. Louis Blues," is a part of every Brubeck
concert. The quartet's approach to it is considerably looser that it
was fifteen years ago, when we all had to count along.

"The first recording in 1959 was a little stiff," Dave recalls. "I
didn't take a solo. I had to keep that vamp locked in because we
weren't used to playing 5/4, although Paul could solo well in it from
the start. To this day, Joe likes me to keep the vamp going behind his
solo. Some nights on the tour I changed it, and he'd say, 'Hey, Bru,
just keep that vamp simple. It gives me more freedom to move
around and get cross-rhythms going.' And I feel the same way;
somebody has to mind the store, to give the improviser more freedom to get out on his own. I have four or five tapes of it from the
tour, and they're all completely different. It's the kind of tune you
can play differently on, because it's on a pedal. Jazz is moving more
and more toward getting away from chord changes, and this is not
only one of the earliest tunes in 5/4 but one of the earliest to set a
precedent for improvising on one chord change."

Since then, of course, jazz musicians have improvised on no
chord changes at all, occasionally with success. And there are legions
of young players who can negotitate all manner of strange time signatures. The Brubeck group graduated to 9/8, 7/4, 10/4, and some
divisions of 13 and 15. Don Ellis has done serious work in 19/4,
32/8, 7/8, and so help me, 3-and-a-half/4. Max Roach and a few
others were early experimenters with unusual rhythms, but it was
Brubeck's success with "Take Five" that led to popular acceptance.
Even some of the rock groups have adopted unconventional time

signatures, and it is not too startling these days to see a hall full of kids dancing in 7/8 under the psychedelic lights.

Desmond's solo on this version of "Take Five" is structurally fascinating and typically lyrical ("Paul's the greatest lyrical player there's ever been," Brubeck says). During his final chorus the swing takes on a passion unusual even for this group. It's actually something of a relief when the ball is passed to Dave and the intensity comes down a peg. Brubeck builds up to another kind of intensity, the kind critics used to identify as bombast. He is . . . always was . . . often unabashedly heavy handed. Perhaps this can be best explained by something he told me years ago during a drive to or from an airport in one of the cities in which we kept running into one another. We were discussing jazz criticism, which he tolerates, barely.

"The word bombastic keeps coming up," Brubeck said, "as if it were some trap I keep falling into. Damn it, when I'm bombastic, I have my reasons. I want to be bombastic. Take it or leave it."

Just in case you need help counting, Morello keeps that 1,2,3— 1,2 going on his hi-hat during the solo, while his hands and the free foot work astounding variations. Dave, following instructions, keeps the vamp going.

"Three to Get Ready (and Four to Go)" combines time signatures, 3/4 for two measures, then 4/4 for two, throughout the piece. It's one of Dave's most charming compositions. For years it was an outlet for Desmond's ingenuity with quotes, and the night of the recording at hand, Paul seemed delighted to be up to his old tricks. Before his solo ends he has quoted from or alluded to "Auld Lang Syne," "Drum Boogie," "The Gypsy," "52nd Street Theme," "Taps Miller," and "Organ Grinder Swing." It would seem logical that any solo with all these disconnected phrases packed into it would be entertaining, possibly, but confused, certainly. Desmond, however, carries logic a step further than almost anybody, connects the disconnected and makes his solos entertaining and lucid. This one excels in both departments. Morello and Wright, known in the band as "The Section" because of their teamwork, demonstrate why. Brubeck's solo begins with the light, single-note lines he has shown a greater fondness for in recent years, then moves into locked-hands technique and some mild bombast. I'll take it.

"Salute to Stephen Foster" is not Brubeck's first recorded encounter with the great nineteenth century American composer, whose work is enjoying something of a renaissance. His 1960 *Southern Scene* album contained two Foster songs, and his concert repertoire has included Foster for twenty years.

"Foster's tunes are well suited to jazz much more than, say a Broadway show tune," Brubeck says. "They're great for improvisation. I think of this as a kind of Bicentiennial tribute to an important composer, even though the one-hundredth anniversary of his death was twelve years ago. The tune is very polytonal, with G in the left hand and B-flat and D-flat alternating in the right."

One of the most gratifying things about the Brubeck group has always been that the high esteem in which the members hold one another is evident to the audience. Never cool or disdainful on stage, these guys love to listen to one another. There is delightful evidence of this mutual admiration in Gene Wright's free-association performance called "African Times Suite." Gene, while demonstrating his awesome abilities, quotes from "You Stepped out of a Dream." For whatever inside reasons, this breaks up the other three, and you can hear Brubeck urge Gene on with "Yeah," a word which among jazz musicians speaks volumes of approval. You can detect the audience enjoying not only the performance but the rapport among the players. I'm not sure this phenomenon has been adequately considered in evaluations of the success of the Brubeck quartet.

With one exception, these pieces were recorded in a single concert at Interlochen, the music academy in Michigan that was attended by two of Brubeck's sons and his daughter Catherine. Brubeck has a number of friends on the Interlochen faculty, and the audiences there have always been extraordinarily knowledgeable about and receptive to his music. The tapes are from a campus radio broadcast. Dave had hired one of the finest mobile recording units for this album, with Fort Wayne, Indiana, targeted as the primary night of taping.

On the way to Fort Wayne, Joe Morello began going blind.
Morello has had deficient eyesight since he was a child, and it has
worsened over the years. Shortly before the reunion tour, he lost the
sight of one eye. A detached retina could not be repaired. But his
eye specialist in Boston advised Joe to make the tour for its psychological benefits. The doctor had a warning, though; if Morello de-
tected any change in the partially sighted eye, he was to leave the
tour immediately and return to Boston for treatment. Twenty-two
days into the tour, on the car trip to Fort Wayne, Morello thought
something almost imperceptible was happening to his eye. By the
time the concert was underway, he was sure.

While they were playing, Morello asked Wright if one of the spot
lights was green. Wright said it wasn't. "Was the auditorium lit in
green?"

"No, Section, it's white like it always was."

"We finished the set," Brubeck says, "and I knew something was
wrong. You can have a night when things aren't cookin' as well as
usual, but this was different. As soon as it was over, Joe said he had
to talk to me. We stood in the corner of the stage, and he said he
hadn't been sure all day, but tonight it had really happened. He said
it was like being under water. Everything took on a green, bubbly
look and faded to a deeper and deeper green, then went out. He
said 'Bru, I can't even see you right now.' So I said, 'Okay, you gotta
go to Boston.'"

Brubeck, Desmond, Wright, and Morello sat up most of the night
talking.

"In the morning, when we had to leave, Joe shook hands with me
and said, 'One thing you've got to promise me. If I come out of this
and can travel, we'll play together again.' I had planned this as a
one-time reunion, one concert, not even a tour. But Joe, who continued to shake my hand, has a drummer's strong grip and I wanted
to continue to play piano, so I hastily replied, 'Okay, Joe, as soon as
you get out of the hospital, we'll plan on another tour.' So now we
have a tour of Europe coming up, if everyone can make it. Joe's last
words to me were, 'Don't worry about me.'

"When we got in the bus to go to the next town, I told the driver to honk as we passed Joe's motel room. He did. Nothing happened. So I took over and beat out the rhythm of 'Blue Rondo a la Turk' on the horn, and immediately the curtain opened and this huge man in his jockey shorts stood there and waved. We knew he couldn't see us. That was the last time we saw Joe. One of his drum students who travels with him, Steve Forster, saw that he got back to Boston. Maybe we should call that tune 'Salute to Steve Forster.'"

Morello had another operation in Boston. Slight vision—mostly color perception—has been restored.

Brubeck had prepared a number of new compositions for the tour and had planned to revive some selections the group hadn't performed even in the latter days of the quartet's formal existence. Most of them were to be played the nights following the Fort Wayne concert. However, the mobile recording unit was sent back to New York and Dave's son Danny slipped into Joe's seat next to Eugene Wright. No substitute could have better credentials than Danny Brubeck. Not only has he heard Morello and the Quartet almost from the day he was born, he has become one of Desmond's favorite drummers. So, no concerts had to be cancelled. The tour was completed, but the opportunity to record the special material had been lost. "Don't Worry 'bout Me" was the only track done at Fort Wayne.

"That last track on the album has great significance to me," Dave says, "because of the circumstances under which it was recorded, because of Joe's parting words, and because of the concern we had for him and we all had for each other that night.

"As the leader of a group, you throw people into situations every day, different countries, different cultures, different environments, different playing conditions. And you're the reason everybody's there. Sometimes they wish they were someplace else. I remember the year Gene joined the group, 1958, we were in India. One of the first quotes he played was 'What Am I Here For' and I thought, 'Jeez, I've gone and uprooted everybody.' But I think we all felt those years were worth it, and we were all glad to be back together. What I sensed out of the reunion was a great love among four terribly independent individuals. No matter what we put each other through over the years—and believe me, the emotions ran the full gamut—there was deep love and regard."

As might have been predicted, the offers rolled in, even before the twenty-fifth anniversary tour ended, offers from Europe, Japan, Australia, the Middle East. The members of the Quartet are not inclined to revert to the steamroller schedule of yore. Ninety cities in ninety nights; they remember the life and are not eager to live it again. But there is that promise to Morello. He's a persuasive man with a strong personality and a strong grip.

Remembering Desmond

1977

We were in an elevator in the Portland Hilton, waiting for the doors to close, when the car jerked and dropped slightly and a bell sounded.

"What was that?" a startled woman asked.

"E-flat," Paul Desmond and I said simultaneously.

I think that's when he decided we could be friends.

We had been acquaintances since a decade earlier when The Brubeck Quartet was playing a concert at the University of Washington in 1955 and I was writing about music for the UW Daily. During intermission, Desmond and I discussed cameras and books. We picked up the conversation later that night at a party given for the band and it continued until toward the end of May, 1977. He told me then that the doctors had decided to discontinue radiology and chemotherapy, that the treatment had become worse than the disease, and the disease was pretty bad. His liver, however, was still perfect.

The liver thing had becoming a running gag. Desmond and good scotch were, shall we say, not strangers. It amused him that after a physical examination in early 1976 turned up a spot on a lung, his liver was given a clean bill of health. He enjoyed the irony.

"Pristine," he said, "perfect. One of the great livers of our time. Awash in Dewars and full of health."

I think he was even amused by the circumstances of the discovery of his nemesis. He had gone to the doctors about foot trouble, and they found the cancer. The swelling of the feet turned out to be temporary and unimportant.

His mother was Irish and literate, his father German and possibly Jewish, and musical, so it was probably inevitable that Paul Breitenfeld's verbal and musical selves would be witty, warm, and ironic. The name Desmond came from a phone book.

"Breitenfeld sounded too Irish," he told me.

Among those who knew him, his word play was as celebrated as his soloing. He was quiet, quick and subtle, and some of his remarks have become widely published, like the one about his wanting to sound like a dry martini. One night at closing time at Bradley's, the quintessential Greenwich Village piano bar, Jimmy Rowles was packing his fake books and Bradley Cunningham remarked that if Peter Duchin could have access to all those chords, his prayers would be answered.

"Unfortunately for Peter Duchin," Desmond said, "all of his prayers have already been answered."

Hanging on our dining room wall was Barbara Jones's large oil painting of four cats stalking a mouse. Seeing it for the first time, Paul said, "Ah, the perfect album cover for when I record with the Modern Jazz Quartet."

"You'll notice that the mouse is mechanical," I pointed out.

"In that case," he said, "Cannonball will have to make the record."

Like all true lovers of language and humor, Desmond knew that the only good pun is a bad pun. He and the guitarist Jim Hall conspired to conceive a sort of "Jazz Goes to Ireland" album with outrageous song titles like "Fitzhugh or No One," "The Tralee Song," "Mahoney a Bird in a Gilded Cage" and "Lovely Hoolihan."

Paul loved to visit our house in Bronxville, a half hour north of Manhattan. The place was on a hill with huge rocks, a pond, pine trees, and a stone veranda that looked down on the street. "The real estate deal of the century," he called it, never failing to marvel that such rural-seeming territory existed so close to "ground zero," his neighborhood at 55th Street and 6th Avenue in Manhattan. After dinner, we sat on the veranda and talked, often for hours but never non-stop. There were long, comfortable silences.

And there was always talk about books. He rarely left on a trip of more than thirty minutes without at least one paperback. He was a rapid and consuming reader. Long before, in 1955, he had alerted me to J. D. Salinger's *The Catcher in the Rye,* and I was gratified in the sixties to turn him on to Walker Percy. Paul said he found a lot of himself in *The Moviegoer,* that beautiful Percy book about loneliness and grace. He chuckled for five minutes one night as he recalled his favorite episodes from John Updike's *Bech: a Book.*

Paul loved to discuss things, objects, consumer goods. We had long conversations about cars, cameras, tape decks, blue boxes (he dropped that idea after Robert Cummings was busted in Seattle for using a blue box to defray his long distance phone bill). He was fascinated by sound equipment and had Charley Graham rig him a superb system on which only Charley was allowed to work. No sooner had Desmond bought a top-of-the-line TEAC tape deck than someone offered him a deal on the finest Revox, and he couldn't pass it up.

In the years following the dissolution of the Brubeck Quartet, Desmond was semi-retired, playing only when he was presented the opportunity to work with musicians he admired or, in at least one case, to help someone. He was one of the first to play the Half Note when it moved from among the warehouses and garages of lower Manhattan to the expensive midtown real estate that was to prove the club's undoing. Desmond maintained that he was accepting the gig only because it was around the corner from his apartment and he could pop out of bed and into the club. He never admitted that he wanted to help the Canterino family launch the new joint successfully; to do so would have been to admit that he had the drawing power of a star.

Never has there been a star less eager for the role. He received the
interruptions and compliments of strangers graciously, but there
was often a wince of recognition as he saw some real estate sales-
man from East Orange approaching his table at the French Shack,
his favorite restaurant, even more accessible from his apartment
than was the Half Note. Once when he and I were dining, a cor-
pulent, polyestered middle aged couple planted themselves next to
us and announced to Paul that they recognized him from an album
cover and just wanted him to know that his music sure was good to
make love by. Desmond took a long look at the flabby woman in
her beehive hairdo and caked makeup and the man with his hefty
paunch and cigar stub, and said, "Glad to be of help."

He appeared fairly often with the Two Generations of Brubeck
troupe, hit the road with the old quartet in the twenty-fifth anniversary reunion tour in the winter of 1976, and traveled now and then
to Toronto to work at Bourbon Street with guitarist Ed Bickert,
bassist Don Thompson, drummer Jerry Fuller, and sometimes Terry
Clarke on drums. In 1969, Paul was in the all-star band assembled
by Willis Conover for Duke Ellington's seventieth birthday party at
the White House, the only domestic affairs high point of the Nixon
administration. That night, as I have recounted elsewhere, Paul did
an impression of Johnny Hodges that was so accurate that it caused
Ellington to sit bolt upright in astonishment, an effect that gave
Desmond great pleasure when I described it to him. At the New Orleans jazz festival the same year, there was a memorable re-creation
of the Gerry Mulligan Quartet with Desmond as the other horn.

In New Orleans, Paul and I hung out virtually without pause for
four days, closing the French Quarter every morning shortly before
sunrise. We avoided the strip joints and pseudo-jazz clubs and concentrated on little bars known to tourists only if they stumbled in.
And we listened to all the music we could absorb at that remarkable
festival, still remembered by musicians and audiences alike as the
finest jazz festival ever and described by Desmond one night on a
television program I was conducting as "the most civilized I have
attended." That was the year before New Orleans became just another stop for the Newport road show.

Taking in one incredible jam session in the ballroom of the Royal Orleans Hotel, we witnessed Roland Kirk surpassing himself in one of the most inspired soprano sax solos either of us had ever heard. Kirk used Alphonse Picou's traditional chorus from "High Society" as the basis of a fantastic series of variations that went on chorus after chorus. We were spellbound by the intensity and humor of it and Paul announced that henceforth he would be an unreserved Roland Kirk fan even unto gongs and whistles. In the same session, Jaki Byard rose from the piano bench, picked up someone's alto saxophone and began playing, beautifully.

"I wish he'd mind his own business," Desmond said.

About his own playing he was modest, even deprecatory. "The world's slowest alto player," he called himself, "the John P. Marquand of the alto sax," and he claimed to have won a special award for quietness. He was reluctant to listen to his recordings, although once after dinner when we'd had enough Dewars he agreed to hear a Brubeck concert I had on a tape never issued commercially. I intrigued him into listening by insisting that his solo on "Pennies from Heaven" was some of his best work. In my opinion, Paul's solos tended to be too short, but on this piece he stretched out for ten choruses of some of his most architectonic playing, full of inventive figures, sly rhythmic twists, and ingenious quotes.

He nodded along with himself, laughed a couple of times (in the right places, obviously) and when it was over said, "I agree." And that's the closest I ever heard Desmond come to approval of his own playing.

During those final nine years, after the breakup of the original Brubeck group, he was allegedly working on a book about his life and times in music. It was to be called *How Many of You Are There in the Quartet?*, after a question asked by airline stewardesses around the world. There were periodic negotiations with agents and publishers, but little of the book actually made it onto paper. The only chapter to get into print was in *Punch,* the British humor magazine. In an account of the Brubeck group's engagement at a county fair in New Jersey, Desmond, in a montage worthy of S. J. Perelman, melded a horse show, volunteer firemen's demonstrations, Brubeck's only known appearance on electric organ, and a marathon Joe Morello drum solo that frightened the livestock. The book, he now and then claimed, was mainly a cover story that allowed him to hang out with the writers at Elaine's. That two-page cadenza, his liner notes, and a very few letters remind us of Paul's literary ability. He was a creative writing major at San Francisco State College in the forties, but he got sidetracked.

We talked by phone fairly often in the last year of his life. When calls came to San Antonio, they invariably began with his cheerful greeting, "Hi, it's me, Desmond." The last time, we found the conversation tapering off into an uncomfortable succession of commonplaces, a sort of shadow boxing that grew out of what he knew and I guessed. We should both get mildly bombed the following Friday night, he suggested, and he would call me from Elaine's. The call didn't come. His housekeeper found him dead on Monday.

Thelonious Monk

Like Art Tatum, to whom he bore virtually no pianistic resemblance, Thelonious Monk stands aside from the stylistic categories of jazz. He is his own category. His technique as a pianist was long denigrated by most of his colleagues. His work as a composer was for years truly understood by a mere handful of musicians. In the jazz establishment, only a few critics and executives of small record companies sensed the importance of his music, even as they were often baffled by it.

It wasn't until the late 1950s, years after his contemporaries Charlie Parker, Dizzy Gillespie, and Bud Powell became public symbols of jazz, that Monk had generated enough recognition to encourage a major record company to offer him a contract. In the 1960s, after Time *put him on its cover, there was a flurry of interest in Monk. Much of the attention resulted from emphasis on his personal eccentricities, but the publicity widened his audience. At the same time, it was beginning to dawn on musicians who had dismissed him that Monk ran considerably deeper than the surface peculiarities of style that had occasioned in them so much derisive merriment.*

Gillespie has praised Monk for his pioneering harmonic discoveries in the developing days of bebop in the early 1940s and for being a superb, though remarkably unverbal, teacher. Powell was equally effusive about the importance of Monk's influence. There is a difficulty, however, in conceiving of Monk as a bop musician. Certainly, he didn't think of himself as one. In 1947, in an interview in Metronome, *he said, "They think differently harmonically. They play mostly stuff that's based on the chords of other things, like the blues and 'I Got Rhythm.' I like the whole song—melody and chord structure—to be different. I make up my own chords and melodies."*

A *few other musicians of his generation understood Monk's importance and how to play his music almost from the time he became a mature pianist, certainly by the time of his first Blue Note recording sessions in 1948. That understanding required absorption of the concept of improvising not merely on the harmonic structure of a piece but on the melody as well. Those insightful players included vibraharpist Milt Jackson, drummers Max Roach and Art Blakey, bassists Gene Ramey and Al McKibbon, saxophonist Sahib Shihab and the grossly underappreciated trumpeter Idrees Sulieman. Among critics, George Simon of* Metronome *and Orrin Keepnews of* Record Changer *wrote seriously in the forties about Monk's music. Indeed, Keepnews became an important factor in Monk's success when he signed him to the Riverside label in 1955, by which time the jazz world was beginning to awaken to Monk's genius.*

Monk *was born in Rocky Mount, North Carolina, on October 10, 1917. When he was four, his family moved to New York. Within a couple of years, he began teaching himself to play the piano. Formal lessons started when he was eleven or twelve. By fourteen, he was playing rent parties and hearing many of the legendary Harlem stride pianists, such as James P. Johnson, who was to become a profound and permanent influence on his music.*

On *the road in his teens playing for an evangelist, Monk spent some time in Kansas City and became involved in its incredibly active jam session scene. Years later, pianist Mary Lou Williams was to recall that Monk in the mid-1930s in Kansas City had essentially developed the style he worked in all his life. After a short period of formal study at Juilliard, Monk played through the latter half of the thirties in whatever contexts he could find, from dance jobs to beer halls, always experimenting, always developing his harmonic ideas and unique approaches to rhythm.*

When *Minton's Playhouse in Harlem became headquarters in 1940 for Gillespie, guitarist Charlie Christian, trumpeter Joe Guy, drummer Kenny Clarke, and other young musicians with new*

*ideas, Monk was advanced enough that Gillespie remembers him as
a source of instruction. It was around that time that he composed
his most famous piece, "'Round Midnight," as well as "Ruby, My
Dear," "Rhythm-a-ning," and other works that would become jazz
standards more than a decade later. Although Monk worked fairly
steadily with the bop innovators through the 1940s, his own music
was not received with anything approaching the welcome given
bop. It wasn't until his Blue Note recordings of 1948 became known
that Monk's reputation began slowly building, and not until his af-
filiation with Riverside in 1955 that he achieved much measurable
public appreciation. In 1949, for example, he received no votes in
the* down beat *readers poll.*

*For many young players of the 1960s, it wasn't until their univer-
sal hero, John Coltrane, put the stamp of approval on Monk that
the pianist became a factor in the way they thought about music.
Reflecting on his intensive development during his engagements in
Monk's quartet at the Five Spot in New York in 1957, Coltrane was
widely quoted as saying, "Working with Monk brought me close to
a musical architect of the highest order. I felt I learned from him in
every way—through the senses, theoretically, and technically."*

*After his considerable successes of the 1960s, Monk's career went
into decline. Columbia Records, which had enticed him to move
from Riverside, at first allowed him to record in his preferred small
band format, which resulted in a series of very good, if not great,
albums. By 1968, Columbia was forcing him into square holes, and
his last project for the label was an affair the quality of which was
symbolized by the hucksterish nature of the title,* Who's Afraid of
the Big Band Monk? *He emphatically rejected Columbia's sugges-
tion that he do an album of Beatles tunes.*

*After a couple of years of regular work marked by recurrent side-
man problems in his quartet, Monk agreed in the fall of 1971 to
join an all-star group called the Giants of Jazz, with Gillespie,
McKibbon, Blakey, tenor saxophonist Sonny Stitt, and trombonist
Kai Winding. The band's world tour was a business success, but for
all the potential of such a collaboration little happened musically.
During the tour Monk made a superb series of solo, and with*

McKibbon and Blakey, trio recordings for the British label Black
Lion; the initial Giants of Jazz experience was not a total artistic
loss. The group was reassembled in 1972 for further concerts and a
studio recording in Switzerland in which Monk is heard soloing by
rote and not so much accompanying the horns as dispiritedly and
monotonously dabbling.

Monk seldom worked during the next decade. A long club engagement in New York in 1973 was followed by just four more
public appearances, one of them a stunning and unexpected performance at a 1974 New York concert designed to honor him. After
mid-1976, Monk went into total seclusion, rarely seeing old friends
and even more rarely speaking. Those who knew him best suggest
that the emotional problems of his final years stemmed from a conviction that his music was insufficiently appreciated, and that he no
longer cared to maintain his lifelong struggle to remain true to his
values and artistic standards. Monk died on February 17, 1982,
after suffering a stroke.

In the 1980s, the depth, power, wisdom, humor, and universality
of Thelonious Monk's music became steadily more apparent to,
greater numbers of people, a classic case of an artist's being ahead
of his time or . . . more accurately . . . of the times catching up
to him.

The following reviews deal with some of Monk's Riverside recordings and with his appearance at the tribute concert of 1974.

Thelonious Monk
In Person
Milestone M-47033

1977

Monk, piano; Donald Byrd, trumpet; Phil Woods, alto sax; Pepper Adams,
baritone sax; Charlie Rouse, tenor sax; Eddie Bert, trombone; Robert

Northern, french horn; Jay McAllister, tuba; Sam Jones, bass; Arthur Taylor, drums (record one). Monk, piano; Joe Gordon, trumpet; Charlie Rouse, Harold Land, tenor sax; John Ore, bass; Billy Higgins, drums (record one).

"Thelonious"; "Monk's Mood"; "Off Minor"; "Crepuscule with Nellie"; "Little Rootie Tootie"; "Friday the 13th" (record one). "Let's Call This"; "Four in One"; "I'm Getting Sentimental over You"; "San Francisco Holiday (Worry Later)"; "'Round Midnight"; "Epistrophy" (record two).

This review was sent to RFJ somewhat later than it was expected because I have been tied up in a project that required a good deal of listening to free jazz from 1968 to the present. Although free or New Thing playing seems to many to be anarchic and disconnected, serious listening discloses that the music has roots, antecedents, a vocabulary, and common influences among its various branches.

One of the most universal of these connecting elements is the music of Thelonious Monk. I have discovered in all this listening to Ornette Coleman and Cecil Taylor and Archie Shepp and Roswell Rudd and John Coltrane and Sun Ra and their stylistic children that Monk's compositions are sometimes played and often quoted but, more importantly, that his concepts have permeated and inspired the new music. As Robert Palmer points out in his excellent notes for this reissue of two Riverside albums, Monk was unafraid either to open up a chord to the point of what in his early days seemed to many listeners idiotic simplicity, or to indulge in the most outrageous dissonances. Outrage, of course, is what he often generated. But, to Monk, dissonance could be beauty, and he knew its uses. His mastery of rhythm was such that he could break its rules to enhance swing. I have a feeling that a good, solid musicological case could be made that free jazz could not have developed as it has without Monk's trailblazing.

Well, all of that comes to mind as I listen for perhaps the five-hundredth time to *Monk at Town Hall*, one of the most delightful recordings in his career and a tribute not only to Monk, as the 1959 concert was intended to be, but to the late Hall Overton, who orchestrated some of Monk's most intriguing compositions for the occasion. Overton was far and away the most successful of the men who attempted to transfer to paper the subtleties and idiosyncracies of Monk, giving these performances by a medium-sized band much of the urgency achieved by the best of the pianist's quartets. He was abetted in the realization of his charts by ten musicians who were just right for them, including one who was moved to play far above his usual level.

He was Donald Byrd, inspired by something in Monk's music to abandon his routined finger-flicking and find the meaning of these pieces. That is especially true of his solo on "Off Minor," in which Byrd gets into harmonic adventuring worthy of Thad Jones or Art Farmer. His work here is less clean, in the sense of "good" trumpet playing, than on those dozens of jam session recordings he was making in the late fifties. But he plays more interesting ideas in "Off Minor" than in any other solo I've heard from him. Monk has had that salutary effect on a number of musicians. It is no coincidence that one of John Coltrane's most dramatic periods of artistic development came during and immediately after his membership in Monk's band.

Charlie Rouse, of course, is one of Monk's favorite tenor companions, and he solos well throughout the concert. Pepper Adams and Phil Woods were having a brilliant night and displayed an affinity for the music that makes one wish they could play with Monk more often. Adams is formidable on both takes of "Little Rootie Tootie." Woods's work in the fifties was never wittier nor more energetic than it is here on "Friday the 13th." Woods repeated in a Monk-Overton collaboration in 1964 (reissued on Columbia KG 32892), as did Eddie Bert, who was also featured in the Monk big band presentation by the New York Jazz Repertory Company at Carnegie Hall in 1974. Bert, obviously a favorite of Monk, has a gloriously trombonish trombone sound perfectly suited for the lead in "Monk's Mood." Sam Jones and Art Taylor, once Monk regulars, offered the most suitable accompaniment the leader has had since he recorded more or less regularly with bassists like Percy Heath and Al McKibbon and drummers Art Blakey and Max Roach.

The ensembles, a tad sloppy here and there, are nonetheless executed with a spirit few pickup groups have ever achieved. "Little

Rootie Tootie" is a joyous, romping tour de force. Full of good solos by all the horns and Monk, the piece has an orchestrated out-chorus transcribed from Monk's solo on the original trio recording. It is one of the highlights of recorded music of the fifties, a favorite of knowledgeable musicians and listeners. And now, with this re-issue, a second take is included, as good as the original release and with equally incendiary solos. This LP should be considered a basic item in everyone's jazz collection.

The second record, also unavailable for years, was made slightly more than a year after Town Hall at the lamented Blackhawk club in San Francisco by Monk's working quartet plus trumpeter Joe Gordon and tenor saxophonist Harold Land. It is one of the regret-tably few recorded appearances by Gordon and a reminder that we lost a brilliant trumpeter when he was taken by an apartment fire in 1963. Gordon and Land both had a feeling for Monk's music. That is obvious not only in their excellent, relaxed solos, but in the en-sembles; the three horns blend harmonically and spiritually. Land was in one of his most attractive periods here and had not yet allowed his earthy, personal style to be engulfed in the ideas of others, notably those of John Coltrane. Land and Monk are the most consistently interesting soloists on the date, but the overall level is very high.

The recording quality is superior for a location session, and if you close your eyes you might imagine that you're back in the good old Blackhawk. You should be so lucky.

New York Jazz Repertory Company

Carnegie Hall
1974

Monk, piano; Hal Dodson, bass; Thelonious Monk, Jr., drums; Charlie Rouse, tenor sax; Budd Johnson, soprano sax; Charles McPherson, alto sax; Julius Watkins, french horn; Cecil Payne, baritone sax; Jack Jeffers, tuba; Charles Stephens, Eddie Bert, trombone; Charles Miller, Charles Sullivan, Richard Williams, trumpet; Paul Jeffrey, conductor, tenor sax; thirteen strings, including bassist David Holland.

The few listeners who went to Carnegie Hall for an evening of the music of Thelonious Monk played by members of the New York Jazz Repertory Company heard an unexpected guest soloist, Monk himself, in a superb concert. In his first New York appearance in more than a year, the seminally influential pianist and composer joined a thirteen-piece band augmented by strings on some numbers, and sparked one of the most satisfying offerings of the repertory company's season.

The band was extremely well rehearsed by conductor Paul Jeffrey, a tenor saxophonist who has played in Monk's quartet in recent years. The collective rhythmic thrust applied by the ensemble to the late Hall Overton's arrangements of Monk compositions sent them forward with the kind of chugging, churning swing achieved by Monk's best quartets. Although beset by illnesses of late, the pianist appeared hearty and healthy. His solos were full of skipping high-energy passages and eccentric good humor that had his fellow musicians beaming at Monk and exchanging knowing smiles.

The string section negotiated Jeffrey's sketches with accuracy, aplomb, and feeling for the music. The only exception came when two of the violinists entered late after having been mesmerized by Monk's lovely solo on "Pannonica."

Of the other soloists, sixty-four-year-old Budd Johnson was the most consistently interesting, playing soprano saxophone with fire, imagination, inventiveness, and a composer-arranger's understanding of the core of Monk's music. Johnson's choruses on "Evidence" showed total mastery of the maverick soprano sax with breathtaking doubletime passages and flawless swing. A young trumpeter named Charles Sullivan also demonstrated affinity for Monk in excellent solos on "Oska T" and "Evidence." Alto saxophonist Charles McPherson seemed victimized by an inability to achieve momentum in the early numbers, although he tried to gather steam in several overlong solos. By the end of the evening he was less dependent on his bag of Charlie Parker phrases, hit his rhythmic stride, and produced superior solos on "Evidence" and "Epistrophy."

Cecil Payne cajoled Jeffrey into letting him solo on "Epistrophy" and gave a magnificent, rolling baritone saxophone performance that was one of the highlights of the evening. Eddie Bert imparted his glorious trombone sound to the ballad "Monk's Mood," embellishing the melody only slightly but putting his unmistakable personal stamp on it. The veteran Monk tenor saxophonist Charlie Rouse soloed consistently well, teaming up with Jeffrey and the rhythm section in a quintet version of "Straight No Chaser," the classic Monk blues line. Rouse's dry, cool, somewhat detached style contrasted with Jeffrey's juicier, R&B-tinged improvising. Richard Williams brought his spacious classical tone and his boppish linear conception into play in an impressive trumpet solo on "I Mean You."

Had Monk not shown up at literally the last minute to play the concert, the pianist was to have been Barry Harris, who helped Jeffrey organize the musicians and rehearse the arrangements and who took a deserved bow before intermission.

As usual at concerts of the New York Jazz Repertory Company, there was no written or spoken announcement of the names of the compositions and only the mostly fleeting (and nearly inaudible) introduction of the musicians. If the listener could not identify the tunes by ear and the players by sight, he was kept in ignorance. Producer George Wein might contemplate the effect on attendance of this information blackout before his next speech on stage deploring the public's lack of support for the repertory concerts.

Charles Mingus

As bassist, composer, and leader, Charles Mingus was one of the most powerful forces in jazz in the 1950s, 1960s, and 1970s. A virtuoso on his instrument, he continued the work of liberating the bass begun by Jimmy Blanton of the Duke Ellington band in the early 1940s. Blanton moved the bass beyond its 1930s role as a stolid timekeeper. In his hands it took on a bright, clear tone and, because of Blanton's harmonic genius and unprecedented facility, became an improvising solo instrument. Blanton died in 1942 at the age of twenty-one, but in his two years with Ellington he had become the hero and model of virtually all jazz bassists. Oscar Pettiford and Ray Brown, his most prominent and talented disciples, continued the Blanton tradition, as did hundreds of other bassists, Mingus among them.

But Mingus did more than carry on or extend the time-keeping and harmonic functions of the bass that Blanton pioneered. Without abandoning either of those duties, Mingus brought the bass into the center of the music as a catalyst of continuous action, reaction, and interaction. In his swirling, surging, stormy performances of his works, the bass is the central nervous system as well as the heart of his music, all but inseparable from his composition and orchestration. Mingus inspired Scott LaFaro, who in the early 1960s perfected a polyphonic style of bass playing that influenced a whole new generation of bassists and became a central element in the development of the free jazz movement of the 1960s and 1970s.

Indeed, Mingus's entire approach to music, rooted in the jazz tradition and particularly in Duke Ellington, involved the melding of traditional and new elements. In his early arrangements he often followed Ellington's example in letter as well as spirit. Later, his

always powerful individuality blossomed and he became more ad-
venturous with voicings, tempo changes, and an eclectic mixture of
elements from field hollers and early gospel music to Jelly Roll
Morton, Ellington, Lester Young, Charlie Parker, the quasi-classical
approach of Third Stream music, and free jazz. All of this was put
together with Mingus's fine musical sensibility and powered in per-
formance by his compulsive energy, which more than one observer
has likened to that of a volcano.

In the late 1960s, disgusted with the commercialization and com-
plications of the jazz scene and in poor health, Mingus dropped out
for a couple of years in Lower Manhattan and concentrated on
completing his autobiography, Beneath the Underdog *(Alfred A.*
Knopf). The book created a good deal of interest in him, and he
again became active in 1972 with a concert at Philharmonic Hall in
New York City. He recorded several albums of new music dur-
ing the 1970s, toward the end conducting and supervising from a
wheelchair when he had become too debilitated to play.

Requiem for a Heavyweight

1979

Charles Mingus was attempting to exhaust the San Antonio Palacio
Del Rio's store of Ramos gin fizzes. The bartender told me with a
note of awe that the night before, Mingus had thrown down twenty
and never shown an indication of disequilibrium. Tonight, he was
apparently gearing up to establish a new record. I braced myself for
the competition.

It was February 1977, two years before his death. Although
Mingus was hardly well, the bassist and composer was still work-

ing. Not enough, however, and that was why he was in San Antonio at a convention of student bookers who buy talent for college and university concerts. Getting on the circuit to entertain tomorrow's leaders is lucrative, so Mingus and his quintet had been up there on the stage of the Theatre for the Performing Arts with all the rock bands, comedians, jugglers, magicians, and tumblers who hoped to cash in on the campus show-biz bonanza.

The showcase experience past, Mingus was explosively propounding the proposition that his agent had erred. His band had performed over a misaligned sound system to an audience attuned to top-forty drivel, had played a set trimmed to twenty minutes by a producer whose only professional guideline was quantity, and had been received with reserve. Nothing was going to come of it, he said (if anything did, I never heard about it); it was a waste of time because no one listened, and if they had they wouldn't have known what they were hearing, he should have known better, he'd been misguided, he should have rid himself of his agent long ago, can't trust anyone, should have stayed out of music when he holed up on the Lower East Side, shouldn't have had a woman for an agent in the first place. All of this was delivered in a mumble at approximately the speed of light, none of the thoughts uttered without a lathering of creative obscenity. At no point was there the slightest allusion to the fact that the person he was slandering, the person solely responsible for this embarassment, this current agent he should be getting rid of, was also his wife.

Along about the seventh Ramos gin fizz, Sue Graham Mingus joined us in the hotel's purple-upholstered bar. She is a striking strawberry blonde, a classy woman. Mingus acknowledged her arrival with a noise deep in his throat, a long pull from his glass and a refill signal. The reason for our meeting had been to do an interview for an article. It required no feat of perception to conclude that tonight drinking with Mingus would be more productive, and possibly safer, than asking him a lot of damn fool questions. He had been known to hit people. That was something Sue discussed after Mingus suddenly retired, not having broken the fizz consumption record. The bartender looked disappointed. Mrs. Mingus looked relieved. This was the woman who had inspired the composition "The I of Hurricane Sue."

Charles had never gone around looking for fights, she said. In the notorious attack on Jimmy Knepper, Mingus had been upset over the trombonist's failure to make Mingus's musical point. The lesson cost Knepper considerable expense in dentists' fees. I recalled other such incidents; Mingus had a reputation for threats, intimidation, and occasional violence in rehearsal and on the bandstand. All true, she said, but people didn't understand that it was because he so passionately wanted the music to succeed that he drove, pushed, screamed, and sometimes struck. He refused to let his musicians accept less than the best from themselves, refused to let them play clichés and get away with it. He had so much love for his music that he would do anything to make it work the way he conceived it.

If Mingus rose to towering rages, he also reached the sustained joy achievable only by musicians of the highest rank. It is a fact that all the musicians he abused, all those he screamed at and humiliated in public—even those he assaulted—forgave him, worked with him again, and in most cases gave him credit for their development.

He was already a perfectionist when he came out of Los Angeles's Watts district in the early 1940s to work with drummer Lee Young. He was an awesome bassist by 1947, when he recorded with Lionel Hampton. By 1955 he had become a major composer, indeed, a creative force influencing the development of jazz. His recordings from the mid-fifties disclose luminous musical intelligence and energy that was sometimes barely controlled.

Atlantic's Mingus retrospective, *Passions of a Man* (SD 3-6000) includes his 1956 "Pithecanthropus Erectus," a work with passages of elemental force and an orchestral concept successfully carried out by only five musicians, demonstrating Mingus's skill with tonal organization, an ability honed by his study of Duke Ellington. His quintet and sextet recordings almost always had the sound of a bigger combo. For the first several hearings, I assumed that the celebrated 1959 Columbia eight- and ten-piece recordings were the work of a full-sized big band and was astounded when I eventually looked at the personnel listings.

Some of the best of the 1959 Columbias have been reissued in a two-record album, *Nostalgia in Times Square* (Columbia JG 35717), that includes not only solos left out of the original issue but also four complete performances never before released. With the exception of an atypically so-so John Handy alto saxophone solo on "Pedal Point Blues," all the new material is historically and musically important. Handy and fellow Texan Booker Ervin, a heaven-storming tenor saxophonist, are present on all fourteen performances on the album. On most of them Willie Dennis or Jimmy Knepper or both are heard on trombone. Dennis, a fine soloist, was little known when he died in 1965, except to musicians, who universally loved him. Knepper, still flourishing, has all the super-charged facility of the J. J. Johnson school of bop trombone, plus a more traditional kind of slippery, off-the-wall humor that Mingus admired. He used Knepper frequently, before and after punching him in the mouth. Drummer Dannie Richmond, who was to Mingus what Sonny Greer was to Ellington during Duke's heyday, is omnipresent on both the Atlantic and Columbia reissues, except for the earliest Atlantics, which were made before Mingus discovered this uncanniliy attuned musician.

The three-record Atlantic album runs from 1956 to 1978. Consistent through Mingus's two-decade off-and-on relationship with Atlantic was the passion of his music-making, whether in the tightly controlled format of a quintet or at the helm of a tempestuous twenty-six-piece band. Gospel fervor, flamenco tinges, fog-bound moodiness, bebop complexity, the joy and despair of the blues, Schoenbergian atonality, were all bound together by Mingus. A driven skipper, sometimes more crazed than Ahab, he conducted from the bridge, shouting praise, condemnation, and love.

"Haitian Fight Song," a 1957 masterpiece for quintet, is twelve minutes of fierceness worthy of its name. Rooted in the same religious inspiration as "Better Git It in Your Soul" and its genre companions, it is more directly expressive of the hatred the composer nurtured because of a lifetime of racial mistreatment. He once told critic Nat Hentoff that he couldn't play the piece properly unless he made himself angry by thinking about the injustices he and other blacks had suffered. This version is introduced by a virtuoso out-of-tempo bass passage of superbly ordered construction. Mingus's anger was never unfocused or unstructured.

Nor were his humor and good feeling. "Eat That Chicken," for example, is a high-spirited tribute to Fats Waller. "Jelly Roll," on the Columbia album, is a fond, intelligently informed reflection of his love for Jelly Roll Morton. Although reviewers sometimes concluded that both pieces were satire, neither is. Mingus revered Waller and Morton, as he did Duke Ellington, Lester Young, and Charlie Parker. He memorialized those giants in "Duke Ellington's Sound of Love," "Goodbye, Porkpie Hat" and "Reincarnation of a Lovebird," all in the Atlantic release.

The Atlantic "Goodbye, Porkpie Hat" is a remake from 1977. It features two guitarists, Larry Coryell and Phillip Catherine, and has electronic overtones Mingus never would have dreamed he'd use when he made the original version in 1959. In that recording, Booker Ervin and John Handy carried the sadly evocative melody, which has become a jazz standard. Handy's solo is the most plaintive he has recorded. This earlier "Porkpie" is included in a 1975 Columbia reissue of the 1959 recordings, *Better Git It in Your Soul* (Columbia CG 30628). It has the original, edited versions of the pieces restored in JG 35717, plus the titles from 1959 not reissued in the newer album. In other words, for the complete 1959 Columbia sessions, you must get both CG 30628 and JG 35717.*

All of Mingus's recent Atlantic albums are available, but the three-record anthology gives a rounded picture of his activities with the label. Of course, the serious collector will want everything from the Atlantic sessions.

The strange evening in the bar of the Palacio Del Rio was the last time I saw Mingus. He did not get rid of Sue Graham. She remained his wife, agent, and pillar until his death of a heart attack January 5, 1979, in Mexico. He had gone to Cuernavaca in search of treatment

---

* The vagaries of record company catalogues being what they are, it might be helpful to know that in 1987 Columbia issued a digitally remastered version of the original 1959 collection, *Mingus Ah Um* (Columbia 40648).

for amyotrophic lateral sclerosis, known as Lou Gehrig's disease. The last photographs I saw of Mingus were made in June 1978 as he sat in the wheelchair to which his ailment restricted him. He was on the south lawn of the White House, surrounded by many of the world's best jazz musicians, who had gathered there for a festival. A tribute to Mingus had just been spoken. The arm of the President of the United States was around his shoulder. And he was in tears.

Charles Mingus
New Tijuana Moods
RCA Bluebird 5635-1-RB

1987

Mingus, bass; Jimmy Knepper, trombone; Curtis Porter (Shafi Hadi), alto sax; Clarence Shaw, trumpet; Bill Triglia, piano; Dannie Richmond, drums; Frankie Dunlop, percussion; Ysabel Morel, castanets; Lonnie Elder, voices.

"Dizzy Moods"; "Ysabel's Table Dance"; "Tijuana Gift Shop"; "Los Mariachis"; "Flamingo"; plus alternate takes of all titles.

It has never been explained, at least publicly, why the *Tijuana Moods* tapes languished in RCA's vaults from 1957, when they were recorded, to 1962. It was Mingus's contention that if the album had been given a timely release, Clarence Shaw would have become a star. We can wish the trumpeter had achieved fame; then there would be more of Shaw to hear than his incomparable solos with Mingus. His own album on the Argo label long ago disappeared.

Thanks to RCA's revitalized Bluebird reissue program, not only is the *Tijuana Moods* album available again, it is accompanied by a second LP of alternate takes. More accurately, producer Ed Michel has used base takes to carry previously unissued solos. When the solos are of the quality of those recorded in two eventful summer days by Shaw, Shafi Hadi, Jimmy Knepper, Bill Triglia, and Mingus, there is reason to celebrate. The recording sessions were supercharged with levels of energy and emotion unusually high even for a Mingus unit. The combination of raw rhythmic passion and lyrical improvisation is all but unequaled in the work of Mingus or anyone else. He called it "the best record I ever made."

In each of the five alternate performances, the restoration of unused material from the session results in a longer track than that in the original release. In nearly every case, the "new" solos match the "old" in quality, and dramatically differ from them in content. Knepper, Triglia, and Porter/Hadi are consistently inspired. This is unquestionably some of Knepper's best early work. Hadi is listed as playing only alto, but he is on tenor in "Dizzy Moods" and, particularly on the alternate take, an earthy brand of tenor it is.

The fluidity of Shaw's expression, which occasionally stops just short of sloppiness in execution, is stunning on the alternate take of "Los Mariachis." He dallies with a phrase from "For All We Know" in the opening bars of his solo on the alternate take of "Dizzy Moods," taking an approach to the piece that is totally different from his work on the original issue. The astonishing beauty of Shaw's famous solo on "Flamingo" is not matched in the alternate. But a lovely one by Knepper is added.

We now get all of Dannie Richmond's solo in "Dizzy Moods," rather than just the snippet left in for the original album. The quality of Richmond's playing throughout is amazing in light of the fact that Mingus had converted him to drummer from tenor saxophonist only a few weeks earlier. But, then, this is amazing music in every respect. By the way, it is not monaural, as the record labels announce. It is in excellent two-channel stereo.

John Handy

In the 1980s, saxophonist John Handy has remained headquartered at his home of nearly a quarter of a century, a rambling old house in San Francisco's Western Addition. From there, he occasionally ranges the world with all-star bands like Mingus Dynasty and the Bay Area group known as Bebop and Beyond. Mostly, however, he stays close to home, working with local players, teaching, and composing.

A formidable soloist known for the grit and passion of his work with Charles Mingus and for the fiery little avant-garde band he maintained in the latter half of the 1960s, Handy was for a time extremely popular. Simultaneously, he was admired by his peers for his innovative musicianship. Those two facts rarely coincide.

1983

John Handy was shaped by Dallas and the blues. Their influence runs through his music from the R&B of his days as a fledgling professional to his symphonic works and collaborations with Indian classical artists. His Texas blues roots are obvious in "Hard Work," his 1976 hit record that sold nearly half a million copies and put him on the pop charts. In his tenor and alto saxophone solos with Charles Mingus and in the daring and sophisticated work of his celebrated small groups of the sixties, the blues furnish the flavor and foundation of his music.

John Richard Handy III was born in Dallas in 1933. Some of his earliest memories are of music played by family members, and for the most part the music was the blues. His mother and all of her brothers and sisters played the piano. Handy says one of his uncles was a remarkable amateur blues guitarist. His maternal grandmother had been a dance-band pianist in her youth.

He got his early education in the Dallas public schools until 1944, when he and his sister Shirley entered St. Peter's Academy, a small North Dallas school operated by Dominican nuns. There, at twelve, he began to play the clarinet. A teacher told him to get a self-instruction book, and Handy taught himself to read music. Three days later, he joined the school band. After his second rehearsal he was playing first-chair clarinet and became involved in a small student swing band.

"My best friend and I started to learn about improvisation," Handy recalls. "And I began paying close attention to the people I heard on the radio—Count Basie, Duke Ellington, Lester Young, Billy Eckstine, the Dorsey brothers, and Benny Goodman, of course. Actually, my hero as a clarinet player was Artie Shaw. But the person I started to imitate first was Louis Jordan. I tried to play clarinet like he played alto saxophone." Handy memorialized Jordan's influence in "Blues for Louis Jordan" on his *Hard Work* album.

Handy's student swing band rehearsed, worked on improvisation, and played for assemblies. It gave no performances outside of school. Handy did, however, encounter a boy his age who was working professionally.

"This guy was big, and he had a moustache. He was in a band at Playfair, the big dance hall. I thought he was twenty-one or so. I remember telling him I played the clarinet, and we talked, and I learned that he was also fourteen. That was David Fathead Newman."

Tenor saxophonist Newman was soon working with blues artists like Lowell Fulson and T-Bone Walker and by the late 1950s had achieved stardom as a sideman for Ray Charles. In recent years Newman has led his own bands and recorded extensively in a blues-drenched modern style.

When John was fifteen the Handys moved to Oakland, California, where he was enrolled in McClymonds High School, an incubator of musical and athletic talent. Among his schoolmates were baseball star Frank Robinson, basketball great Bill Russell, and Michael White, the violinist from Houston who was to become an important part of Handy's most famous band. Shortly after his arrival in the West, Handy began to play professionally.

"I borrowed a saxophone from the school on a Wednesday and I had my first job, a dance, on Friday. I could play almost anything I could hear. I got into three different bands in school, and from then on it was all music. There went the academics."

In his mid-teens, Handy found himself jamming on the bandstand of San Francisco's Bop City with Dizzy Gillespie, Art Tatum, and other international jazz stars like Kenny Dorham and Benny Bailey, from Lionel Hampton's trumpet section, and Duke Ellington tenor saxophonist Paul Gonsalves.

"It was Gonsalves who showed me what the saxophone could be. When I was jamming with him, I realized the saxophone could be practically devoured. I actually thought he was going to eat the instrument. And there were so many other incredible saxophone players I learned from. However, the person who influenced me the most, and whom I admire most, I got to hear only once. I sneaked in the Say When club to hear Charlie Parker. He was working with a local rhythm section and only one of the guys could really play, so the tempos had to be kept slow. So, unfortunately, I heard Bird under the most uncomplimentary circumstances."

At nineteen, Handy entered San Francisco State College. Shortly before he was drafted in 1953, he recorded with Lowell Fulson and was working with a big band led by Gerald Wilson, the former arranger for Jimmie Lunceford, Dizzy Gillespie, Count Basie, and Duke Ellington. Wilson's own considerable success was some years in the future. Just when Handy had been offered an engagement with the combo of bassist Oscar Pettiford, the Army called him for a two-year stint. After discharge he married, spent three more years at San Francisco State, compiled a book of original compositions that he tried out on the job with local groups, then moved to New York in July 1958.

"I immediately started to make the rounds of the jam sessions and clubs. I starved for a couple of months, but I knew a lot of people, so through my contacts I began to get work. Christmas week of 1958 I joined Charles Mingus. I was with him only three and a half months, but during that time we made at least five albums, so people tend to think we were together much longer."

Since his discharge from the Army, Handy had been playing tenor sax exclusively. But with bassist Mingus he began doubling on alto. He and Booker Ervin, the wild and wooly tenor saxophonist, formed the front line of a quintet that could run the range of expression from tenderness to ferocity in one performance. During this period the twenty-five-year-old Handy was being honored not only with employment in the band of a respected jazz leader but with rave notices by New York jazz critics.

"There were good days with Charles," Handy recalls, "but there were some stormy days. His temper is well known. I used to make him cry simply by telling him how nasty he was. It's amazing how he could change, storming one minute like he was going to kill someone and blubbering with remorse the next. But he had beauty, a little child's beauty, about him."

Handy is present on some of Mingus's best-known and most influential recordings. The *Wonderland* album for United Artists includes masterful Handy alto solos on "Nostalgia in Times Square" and "I Can't Get Started." He and Ervin share tenor sax duties on the 1959 Mingus sessions for Columbia, calling up their Texas blues and gospel antecedents to provide the gritty preaching on two irresistible church-based pieces in 6/8 time, "Better Git It in Your Soul" and "Slop." Handy is the moving tenor soloist on "Goodbye, Pork Pie Hat," Mingus's tribute to Lester Young, one of the most influential tenor men in the history of jazz.

During his more than three years in New York, Handy led bands made up of an assortment of outstanding players. His quintet and quartet recordings on the Roulette label, made from 1959 to 1962, find him playing with the same bittersweet inventiveness that characterized his work with Mingus, but his forays into modal compositions and improvisation foreshadow his achievements with what came to be known as the "Spanish Lady" band.

"I came back to San Francisco for a three-week visit in 1962," Handy says. "I've been here ever since. I returned to San Francisco State, got my degree, and eventually ended up teaching there. I was on the faculty for twelve years." Handy also taught at Stanford; the University of California, Berkeley; California State University, Hayward; and Merritt College in Oakland. His academic pursuits paralleled his music-making and his involvement in the civil rights activism of the sixties. He was in a Bay Area contingent that traveled to Washington, D.C. for the 1963 civil rights march. The same year, he was arrested in a civil disobedience protest against a discriminatory San Francisco real estate firm. He formed a ten-piece group called the Freedom Band that played at rallies, demonstrations, and civil rights fundraisers.

Handy was disturbed then, however, and is disturbed now at what he sees as blacks' rejection of jazz. "For the most part, they've totally abandoned us. Whites may be to blame. On the other hand, if whites hadn't been our audience, we wouldn't have had anybody to play for, and the music wouldn't exist as it does today. As an educator I've seen two thousand student musicians at college jazz festivals and maybe thirty of them were black. I spent twelve years trying to get this music and the knowledge of it into the universities. Now I see a few young blacks coming to hear the music, but just a few."

Handy was so impressed with the playing of two young Canadian musicians he had worked with in Vancouver that in 1965 he arranged to have bassist Don Thompson and drummer Terry Clarke move to San Francisco to join his band. They spent that summer rehearsing and playing at the Both/And, a club whose proprietors and audiences encouraged adventurous music. By the time the quintet appeared at the 1965 Monterey Jazz Festival, it was tightly rehearsed and as exciting as any small band in jazz history. Handy, Clarke, Thompson, guitarist Jerry Hahn, and violinist Michael White, Handy's old school chum, were the sensation of the festival, stealing honors from Mingus, who had hoped to repeat his triumph of the 1964 festival. Handy's "Spanish Lady" was an expansive treatment of an eight-bar theme, with a stunning alto saxophone cadenza, astonishing collective improvisation, and a sustained release of joyful energy. Handy was a known quantity, but the other players were established virtually overnight as important musicians. After two and a half years with Handy, the Canadians faced a Viet Nam-era choice: return home or be drafted. They went back to Canada. Through the rest of the sixties Handy worked with various combinations, including a quintet featuring White, Mike Nock on piano, drummer Larry Hancock, and bassist Bruce Cale. Then, when Handy was in the hospital for treatment of a tennis injury, the other musicians re-formed and began calling themselves The Fourth Way, which became one of the first jazz fusion bands. Handy did not play for almost two years after that. Then in 1968 he began teaching and by 1970 was touring as a single, mostly on college tours. That year Handy wrote his Concerto for Jazz Soloist and Orchestra and performed it with the San Francisco Symphony. He has also performed the concerto with the New Orleans Philharmonic, the Santa Barbara Symphony, and the Stockton Symphony. Until 1975, Handy concentrated on his academic pursuits, private teaching, studies with the Indian sarod master Ali Akbar Khan, and his tours as a solo artist. Then came "Hard Work."

"I decided that since black people weren't coming to jazz, I was going to take jazz to black people," he explains. "I wanted a wider audience. I was a little tired of playing for those who sit all night saying 'yeah, yeah, yeah,' all thirty-five of them. I wanted to know what it was like to play for a stadium full of people. I wanted to see black women in the audience. And it happened. The record hit."

"Hard Work" is Louis Jordan for modern audiences: simple, catchy, funky, old-fashioned urban blues with a backbeat, sung and played by Handy with wry humor and an affectionate regard for the tradition. It made him rich, for a while.

"After 'Hard Work' I had a contract with ABC/Impulse. I made a lot of fast money, and I lost it just as fast."

Handy was recording and on the road, following his *Hard Work* ethic, until 1979, when he joined Mingus Dynasty for a year of worldwide touring. Mingus had died in January 1979, and the Dynasty was a group of all-star musicians who had worked with him at one time or another and felt a bond.

"It was a band Charles could never have afforded," Handy says. "I felt I could contribute by playing with the Dynasty and making more people aware of Charlie Mingus. Secondarily, it was a chance to work with great players."

Handy took time out from Dynasty to join a State Department tour. He was one of the Western soloists to perform in Bombay with Ravi Shankar, India's leading classical musician, and a thirty-piece orchestra. Following the Dynasty tour, Handy resumed barnstorming in Europe and the United States as a single, using local rhythm sections.

In the summer of 1982 he began rehearsing with three young women violinists and a rhythm section. The group is known as John Handy with Class. The musicianship is high, the ensemble sound of the four instruments is not unlike that of a perfectly melded sax section, and the visual impact is considerable.

For all of his accomplishments and activities since he left Texas, John Handy's thoughts keep returning to Dallas. He has never worked there professionally, but he remembers a jam session he took part in twenty-five years ago during his only visit since moving to California.

"I stopped there for two days on the way to New York. I was invited to a session at the American Woodmen Center. It was summertime, hotter than blazes. We stepped into that beautifully air-conditioned hall and there were all kinds of people playing their tails off. On an integrated bandstand. In the South. In 1958. It was amazing and I've never forgotten it. I'd never seen James Clay before, but I recognized his playing from records. I got my horn out, and he and I had a wonderful tenor battle. It was a great afternoon."

Four Tenor Saxophonists

Since the early 1920s, when Coleman Hawkins virtually reinvented the tenor saxophone and made it a jazz instrument, it has been an essential voice in the music. Hawkins was a grand romantic who played with passion, brashness, and sweeping inevitability. His aggressive style and huge tone constituted the major model for saxophonists and were primary influences for at least thirty years.

In the early 1930s, Lester Young was removed from the Fletcher Henderson band for not playing like Coleman Hawkins. But from his first recordings with Count Basie in 1936, Young's lightness, buoyancy, rhythmic daring, and harmonic subtlety established him as a hero of forward-looking musicians. He provided an evolutionary step between Louis Armstrong and Charlie Parker in the freeing of the jazz soloist from the arbitrary restrictions of time divisions. In his solos, Young flew weightlessly over bar lines. He saw deeply into chord changes. He helped lay the rhythmic and harmonic keystones of bebop.

Budd Johnson was a superb tenor saxophonist, if not an innovator like Lester Young. He had great influence as a catalyst through his composing, arranging, and organizational ability.

John Hardee was active for only a short time on the national jazz scene, but his impressive playing made him a memorable figure in the jazz of the 1940s. During the 1980s, reissues of his recordings attracted a good deal of attention.

Ike Quebec's tenor saxophone style was under the influence of Hawkins and Ben Webster, but in the mid-forties he was exploring the possibilities of bebop. Quebec was consistently creative despite a life of self abuse.

1981/1985

There is no music more therapeutic for these agitated times than that of Lester Young, the gentle, bedeviled genius whose vision of beauty found expression even though he was hounded throughout his life by nearly every demon the twentieth century has managed to spawn. The tenor saxophonist whom Billie Holiday nicknamed "The President" is often erroneously remembered as a talent who flared brilliantly during brief spans in the thirties and forties, then deteriorated into an echo of himself. He died in New York City in 1959 at the age of forty-nine.

Young was drafted in 1944, even though he was in bad health and admitted he had used dope for the past decade. The Army confiscated his horn, refused to let him play in the camp band, and later arrested him on drug charges. He was dishonorably discharged, but first he was imprisoned for ten months at an Army base in Georgia, an experience with devastating emotional consequences. In spite of his experience in the military, his attempts to recover from its dehumanizing effects, and his efforts to build his own withdrawn world of sweetness and love, Young was capable of playing tenor sax with inventiveness, relaxation, and swing never achieved by any other jazz soloist. He had some periods of embarassing playing, but he had very good years as well, some near the end of his life, when the conventional wisdom was that Pres was a burned-out case.

One such year was 1956. In *The Jazz Giants '56* (Verve VE-1-2527) Young was reunited with other heroes of the swing era for a session in which he did some of the best playing of his later career. The album has been reissued and is now available from, among other sources, the Book-of-the-Month Club, possibly a favorable sign for the improvement of culture in America. At the time of the album's original release there was much talk of Young's work on it being a fluke, a kind of remission in his supposed artistic illness. Now, however, Pablo records has issued four volumes of Young that were recorded for private use during a 1956 nightclub engagement in Washington, D.C. They disclose him at a high level of creativity, entirely comfortable with his pickup rhythm section. The supporting trio is led by Bill Potts, a celebrated arranger and somewhat enigmatic figure who, it turns out, was a more than respectable piano soloist and accompanist.

The albums—*Pres* (Pablo 2308-219), *Pres Vol. II* (Pablo 2308-225), *Pres Vol. III* (Pablo 2308-228), and *Pres Vol. IV* (Pablo 2308-230)—include twenty-one pieces of the repertoire that Young rarely departed from in his last few years, but there is nothing routine about his playing. Although Louis Armstrong may have been the first soloist to erase bar lines and smooth out jazz improvisation with long, logical, flowing passages, Pres is the man who brought total relaxation to the process and yet managed at the same time to extend the boundaries of rhythmic propulsion. No one has ever done more swinging while creating beautiful ideas, and it is clear from these remarkable recordings that in December 1956 his ability had not been lost.

Young's oblique approach to familiar melodies and his ultra-relaxed rhythm may at first create the impression that he was having trouble finding his way. Quite to the contrary, his habit of lagging behind the beat was the product of assurance and of comfort with his surroundings. The result is unhurried enjoyment for the listener who is willing to accept that Pres in 1956 was not the Pres of 1938. They had changed, but through distillation, not regression.

Happily, not only are Young's live D.C. recordings being made available for the first time but his classic Commodore albums have also been reissued in their most complete and intelligently produced form on LP. His 1938 recordings with the Kansas City Five and Kansas City Six, including alternate takes, are available on *Kansas City Six and Five* (Commodore XFL 14937) and the 1944 Kansas City Six sessions on *The Kansas City Six with Lester Young* (Commodore XFL 15352). They are among the crown jewels of the entire jazz discography and are essential to any serious collection. The reissues in the Commodore series were overseen by the original producer, Milt Gabler, who has done a superb job of organizing the material.

John Hardee couldn't handle the competitiveness and uncertainty of the New York jazz scene of the late forties, so he went home to Texas to teach school. Budd Johnson left Dallas at fourteen to go on the road as a drummer, switched to tenor sax two years later, and thrived on the jazz life, becoming one of the most important figures in swing and the transition to bebop. Both men were Texas tenors in the grand tradition of spacious tone, irresistible rhythm, and the vocabulary and emotion of the blues. Hardee died at sixty-five in 1985 in Dallas, Johnson at seventy-three the same year in Kansas City, Missouri.

Hardee went into exile after only five years of playing in New York, and his small recorded legacy, entirely on 78s, was buried by the LP revolution of the fifties. A few selections have popped up on Blue Note anthologies over the years, but it quickly became almost impossible to find any of the recordings he made for Savoy, Regent, and Castle or his work on Atlantic with Tiny Grimes. Hardee was such an indistinct figure in the recent history of jazz that books on the subject either fail to mention him or offer little of substance about his career.

The shortage of recordings and of information are both satisfyingly addressed in *The Complete Blue Note Forties Recordings of Ike Quebec and John Hardee* (Mosaic MR4-107), which includes all of the music Hardee recorded for the Blue Note label. He is heard in the company of such musicians as guitarist Grimes, bassist Gene Ramey, trombonist Trummy Young, pianist Marlowe Morris and the protean drummer Sid Catlett. Hardee's most obvious attributes are power and gruffness, which give way to a churning tenderness in ballads and slow blues. His presence is so riveting that it takes the listener a while to appreciate his mastery of time. Regardless of the tempo of a performance, Hardee is assuredness itself. In "Idaho," as his lines move forward with the inevitability of a rolling river and the intensity builds, Hardee becomes more, not less, relaxed. In seeming contradiction, the swing increases. Hardee and several other swing era tenormen, such as Lester Young, Ben Webster, Chu Berry, and Coleman Hawkins, had this ability to lay back yet swing hard, but few tenor players of succeeding musical generations inherited it, Zoot Sims being a glorious exception.

On many of these recordings Hardee's conspirator in the buildup of intensity is Sid Catlett, a drummer who used simple press rolls on soloists the way an experienced ranch hand uses a cattle prod. With wire brushes on a snare drum, Catlett could elevate a performance to heights out of the reach of ordinary drummers using sticks with the most elaborate drum kits. The relentless, ever-increasing swing that he and Hardee achieve in "Blue Skies" is as elemental as the movement of the tide. The excitement Hardee generates in his solo on both versions of the fast blues "River Edge Rock" can be credited in great part to the arsonist drumming of Big Sid.

Also present is Trummy Young. He was relegated for a short but highly visible phase of his career to a supporting role in Louis Armstrong's All Stars. Perhaps out of boredom, he took to showboating in his trombone solos, and he is often thought of as a clown. But in the mid-forties Young was a virile soloist whose role as a transitional figure between swing and bop was important in the evolution of the music. Teamed with Hardee in the front line of the Tiny Grimes Swingtet, Young gave some of his best jump band performances of the period. His energy was a match for Hardee's. Together in "C-Jam Blues" and "Flyin' Home," they construct one inventive riff figure after another. The effect is like that of a big band—say Count Basie's early one—in full cry.

Mention must be made of Hardee's slow playing in this collection. As a balladeer in "Tired" and "Sweet and Lovely," he is nearly in a league with Ben Webster, who was perhaps the ballad master among tenors. Unlike so many jazzmen who double the tempo in ballads, Hardee maintains the integrity of the solo. From the evidence here, he did not fall into the common double-time trap of merely playing convenient notes around the song's harmonic changes but had the ability to play fast without being glib. The surge and flow of his slow blues in two versions of "Hardee's Party" are hallmarked by the moan with which all Texas tenormen seem to be born.

Considering the short time he was active in jazz, John Hardee's degree of development was remarkable. His Blue Note recordings indicate that if he had stayed in New York and fought the jazz wars, he would have become one of the best-known tenormen of his generation. According to the excellent Michael Cuscuna biography that accompanies the Hardee-Quebec album, Hardee lived a full life as a Dallas middle-school band director, with no regrets except that he never became a member of the Duke Ellington Orchestra. He thought that he should have been Ben Webster's successor with Ellington. This record tells us he could have filled the chair.

The Ike Quebec recordings that make up the balance of the four LPs in the Mosaic set present another relatively little-known tenor saxophonist in sessions from 1944 to 1946. Quebec, also possessed of a big sound, had more pronounced bebop leanings than Hardee, and his bop ideas can be heard germinating here.

A pianist when he first played professionally in the very early 1940s, Quebec was a tenorman in 1942 and by 1944 had worked with trumpeters Frankie Newton, Roy Eldridge, and Hot Lips Page, and with Benny Carter, Coleman Hawkins, and Sammy Price. His tone was round and full, with a fast vibrato. A compelling tension was set up by the contrast between his essentially legato delivery and his rhythmic energy. Even at slow tempos, as in Quebec's hit blues "Blue Harlem" or a ballad like "She's Funny That Way," his playing transmits an energizing urgency. At fast ones, as in the two takes of "Indiana," his drive and swagger are almost overpowering.

In the Mosaic Blue Note recordings of Quebec there are also fine moments from trombonist Keg Johnson, Budd's brother; trumpeter Shad Collins, an unsung hero from the Count Basie band; trumpeter Buck Clayton, another Basie alumnus whose celebrity is as deserved as Collins's anonymity is unfair; guitarist Tiny Grimes; and bassist Oscar Pettiford, who, like Quebec, was beginning to feel the effects of bop.

Long ravaged by his use of heroin, Quebec disappeared from major jazz activity and led a more or less nomadic life during the 1950s. But in 1959 he surfaced to again become intimately involved with Blue Note as it entered one of its most important periods and recorded with some of the leading lights of the Blue Note stable of young post-boppers. Quebec died of cancer in 1962, at the age of forty-four.

At twenty-three, Budd Johnson was in Chicago co-leading a band with pianist Teddy Wilson, a fellow Texan. They got a call from Louis Armstrong and both joined the most famous jazzman of the day. A year later, in 1934, Johnson left Armstrong to become musical director for pianist Earl Hines. With Armstrong, Hines had made a handful of records that changed the course of jazz. He was leading a big band at Chicago's Grand Terrace, and its broadcasts were becoming nationally famous. The dissemination by radio of Johnson's arrangements gained him a reputation among musicians as one of the most innovative writers in the increasingly important big band field.

Johnson's eminence also won him the respect of the young revolutionaries who in the early forties were developing what came to be called bebop. His advanced and receptive ear told him that great changes were in the making, and in 1942 he brought alto saxophonist Charlie Parker and trumpeter Dizzy Gillespie into the Hines band. The orchestra became an incubator for the new music, with not only Parker and Gillespie in its ranks but also such important players as Wardell Gray, Benny Green, Shadow Wilson, and Benny Harris, and vocalists Billy Eckstine and Sarah Vaughan. Johnson is also credited with organizing the first bebop recording session—under Coleman Hawkins's name—for the Apollo label in 1944.

Thus, even if he had never played a note, Budd Johnson would have made an enormous impact on the development of jazz. But there was more to Johnson than his arranging, composing, and entrepreneurial skills; he was at the forefront of the second rank of jazz saxophonists. Though not a major stylistic innovator like Lester Young or Coleman Hawkins, Johnson was a supremely gifted tenor saxophonist who also played also, baritone, and clarinet and in his later years became one of the two or three top soprano saxophonists when that maverick instrument enjoyed a revival. Disappointingly, little of Johnson's work is available.

A happy exception is an Earl Hines album, *The Legendary Little Theatre Concert of 1964, Volumes 1 and 2* (Muse MR 2001-2). On the second LP of this previously unissued set, Johnson is at the top of his form. In "Lester Leaps In," he pays tribute to Lester Young with a series of building choruses that lead Hines to shout encouragement. "Out of Nowhere" finds Johnson employing his roomiest tone. The first and last choruses, played at a super-slow ballad tempo, leave the performer with only his imagination and taste for protection. His Southwest roots are fully exposed on a number he and Hines dreamed up on the spot, "Blues for Jazz Quartet." Johnson's playing on this piece is full of shouts, moans, low-register honks, and some of Young's patented false fingerings of repeated notes. The Little Theater concert marked Hines's return after several years of obscurity and launched what amounted to a new career. Johnson worked with his old boss frequently through the sixties and seventies, and the fireworks ignited that night were a preview of a felicitously renewed partnership.

Ten years later they recorded in France, and the result was issued in this country as *Linger Awhile* (Classic Jazz 129). It is one of the few latter-day Hines-Johnson collaborations still obtainable. In "Blues for Sale," Johnson has a blistering soprano solo and a tenor solo that smolders with blues feeling. "Gone with the Wind," taken at what the labels on 78s used to describe as a medium bounce, gives Johnson an opportunity to display his double-time capabilities while Hines literally bounces along in accompaniment. In "If You Were Mine," another of those ballads so slow they would be agonizing in lesser hands, Johnson barely embellishes the melody and thereby enriches it. His a cappella introduction to "The Dirty Old Men" is a classic exposition of the ability of the tenor sax to relate to the basic emotions in a way no other instrument can. Johnson growls, grunts, and all but speaks with the horn. *Linger Awhile* will no doubt be hard to find, but it is more than worth the search.

One of the finest examples of Johnson's small-band writing is on *Budd Johnson and the Four Brass Giants* (a 1960 Riverside album reissued as OJC-209 in Fantasy's Original Jazz Classics series). Johnson is on tenor with a trumpet quartet made up of Clark Terry,

Harry Edison, Nat Adderley, and Ray Nance, daunting soloists who team up magnificently behind Johnson.

Divided equally between standards and Johnson compositions, the collection includes a blues called "Trinity River Bottom," named after what Johnson remembered from his youth as a perennial Dallas troublemaker. With his characteristic melding of toughness and tenderness, Johnson delivers a memorable tenor solo over trumpet shout choruses. The riffs are definitive examples of his command of the written jazz idiom.

But the jewel of the album is "Driftwood," a mournful melody created for Nance's violin and buoyed by some of the most richly textured writing in the remarkable sixty-year career of Bud Johnson, one of the least-known major artists in the history of jazz.

Ben Webster

Tenor saxophonists Paul Gonsalves, Ike Quebec, Zoot Sims, Charlie Ventura, Georgie Auld, Eddie "Lockjaw" Davis, Lew Tabackin, Archie Shepp, Lucky Thompson, Harold Ashby, Jimmy Hamilton, Scott Hamilton, and Bennie Wallace have something in common: the inspiration of Ben Webster. Webster was one of the most powerful and influential soloists in jazz and one universally admired and respected by musicians, listeners, and critics of all generations.

Born in Kansas City in 1909, Webster was a silent movie pianist in 1929 when he heard Budd Johnson play tenor saxophone. He asked Lester Young's father to teach him to play the instrument. He learned quickly, at first on alto sax, and after a brief stint with the Young family band worked in a succession of bands led by Gene Coy, Jap Allen, Blanche Calloway, and Andy Kirk. He arrived in New York in 1932 as part of the Bennie Moten band and later played with Benny Carter, Fletcher Henderson, Willie Bryant, Cab Calloway, and Stuff Smith. Under the spell of Coleman Hawkins from the beginning of his saxophone career, Webster developed into one of the most accomplished and individual of the many disciples of Hawkins, the father of jazz saxophone.

In the beginning his playing was modeled closely on the dramatic, sweeping, even grandiose, style of Hawkins. But over time, Webster pared away embellishments and rococo elements, while maintaining warmth and a big tone, and created a style that appeals with force and clarity directly to the emotions. Or, as the critic Martin Williams put it, Webster became a great soloist when "he accepted the limitations of his fingers and embouchure and became a simple and eloquent melodist."

He became best known as a member of the Duke Ellington band.

*Some of his hallmark works with that organization are discussed in
the following piece.*

Unabridged Webster

1984

On the day my friend Swartz turned forty, he had a revelation. Entering my office at what for him was a gallop but for most of us would be a saunter, he announced that he had just heard on the radio a saxophonist named Ben Webster. He accurately described the fullness and the breadth of Webster's tenor saxophone sound, his unmatchable phrasing, his gruff softness. Swartz added, with the sheepishness of one who realizes that he has just discovered something obviously long in the public domain, that there must be a lot of Ben Webster to catch up on.

For many years Swartz had made his living playing music, mostly rock, in lounges and clubs. No collection of musicians is more isolated from the mainstream than are professional rockers. I have known folk guitarists barely out of the three-chord category who revered Stravinsky. Jazz players are likely to be deeply in love with classical music. Country musicians like Willie Nelson and Waylon Jennings have a broad knowledge of and a healthy respect for jazz and rock. Classical artists listen to Charlie Parker and Art Tatum. But the rocker's is a limited listening environment, for a variety of sociological, psychological, pharmacological, and business reasons.

Swartz long ago left the rock milieu and has since been discovering other kinds of music. When I mentioned Webster's imperishable solo on Duke Ellington's "Cotton Tail," though, Swartz looked blank. This was proof; he really had just heard Webster for the first time. This made him an object not of pity but of envy. A first en-

counter with Webster equals whatever else you experienced for the
first time that gave you the greatest pleasure.

Webster died in 1973, but the joy of coming upon his music is still
possible through records. Originally a pianist from Kansas City (he
once played movie-house piano in Amarillo), he had switched to the
saxophone by the early Depression years. During Webster's longest
stint with Ellington, from 1939 to 1943, "Cotton Tail" was recorded. Webster's solo, an architectonic creation on this variant of
"I Got Rhythm," had universal application to the process of jazz
improvisation. Forty years later, it is still quoted and alluded to; it
has been absorbed into the jazz language in the same way that some
idiomatic phrases are absorbed into the spoken language.

Both "Cotton Tail" and "All Too Soon," with another monumental Webster solo, can be heard on *Duke Ellington 1940* (Smithson-
ian Collection R103) and on *Duke Ellington: The Webster-Blanton
Band* (RCA Bluebird 5659-4-RB). Another fascinating performance
of "Cotton Tail" on *Duke Ellington at Fargo 1940* (Book-of-the-
Month Records 30-5622), this one live, disproves the canard that
Webster's solo was a memorized set piece. "Star Dust," from the
same album, displays Webster's celebrated ballad style, with its
counterpoised elements of tenderness and power. None of his imitators has ever got it exactly right.

Throughout the fifties and sixties, Webster recorded copiously
for the Verve label, and some of that work is available today on reissues. On *Jam Session #1* (Verve UMV-25300) he rounds out a
formidable quintet of saxophonists that includes Flip Phillips, Benny
Carter, Johnny Hodges, and Charlie Parker. In the ballad medley he
follows Parker's perfectly limned "Dearly Beloved" with a one-
chorus exposition of "The Nearness of You" that is pure, straight
melody. With only the slightest departures in phrasing and with
his enormous, breathy tone, Webster engraves his personality on
the song.

Webster and the alto saxophonist Benny Carter shared an affinity
that generated two superb albums. *Benny Carter, Jazz Giant* (Contemporary 7555) had Carter and Webster in the front line with
trombonist Frank Rosolino in a 1957 session. Webster's solo on
"Old Fashioned Love" is one of his best two or three on record and

is among the finest medium-tempo statements ever recorded. *Opening Blues* (Prestige MPP 2513), recorded in 1962, brought clarinetist Barney Bigard and the underestimated trumpeter Shorty Sherock together with Webster, Carter, and a sterling rhythm section headed by Jimmy Rowles, one of Webster's preferred pianists. Everything works so well that what is essentially a jam session sounds as though it were the product of careful orchestration. Webster's warmth and power and Carter's urbane lyricism serve as the cornerstones of this remarkable achievement.

In the early sixties, Webster and the young Austrian Joe Zawinul developed a deep, lasting friendship. Zawinul—then Cannonball Adderley's pianist, now musical director of Weather Report—had been influenced years earlier in Vienna by Webster's recordings. Although Zawinul was awestruck on meeting his idol, he was nonetheless spunky enough to take advantage of the opportunity to collaborate. The resulting recording has recently been reissued as *Ben Webster and Joe Zawinul* (Milestone M 47056). Initially released by Riverside just before the company went out of business, the album has been virtually unknown until now. This unlikely fusion of a fairly green European bebopper who had yet to develop a personal style with an out-of-fashion tenor player made music that twenty years later is not dated; indeed, it is fresher than much of today's music.

Zawinul knew how to provide the kind of space and timing that Webster wanted from an accompanist, and Webster responded with some of the most gorgeous playing of his final decade. The album includes two versions of Ellington's "Come Sunday" that may be mentioned in the same breath as those of another star Ellington saxophonist, Johnny Hodges. Two blues pieces and the standards "Love Walked In" and "Like Someone in Love" are extraordinarily vigorous, even for Webster. Drummer Philly Joe Jones supplies a good part of the drive, but even more is generated by Webster himself; he was one of those rare jazz players who could swing hard from the first note of a solo. The album also includes, in its entirety, Webster's 1957 date with trombonist Bill Harris, whose wry jollities and fund of melodic inventiveness made him a perfect, if unexpected, foil for the saxophonist.

In *Gerry Mulligan Meets Ben Webster* (Verve UMJ–3093) the seasoned young baritone saxophonist and arranger encountered the grizzled veteran. Mulligan was thirty-two at the time of his 1959 session and had been an active professional jazz artist since his teens. Steeped in the full range of the jazz tradition, he adapted his playing to Webster's without altering his own style, and the older man felt comfortable with Mulligan and the stalwart rhythm section of Jimmy Rowles, Leroy Vinnegar, and Mel Lewis. The result was the best of the *Mulligan Meets* series and is a highlight in the discographies of both men. Webster is evocative of his Ellington days on "Chelsea Bridge." But his masterpiece of the date, and one of the major solo constructions of his later career, is on "Sunday." The solo captures and holds one's attention with its spontaneous development of logic and through a symmetry of ideas borne on exquisite rhythm. It is Webster surpassing himself.

Mention must also be made of an album of 1960 Webster performances not released until 1985, Ben Webster at the Renaissance *(Contemporary C–7646). It presents Webster with a band he employed as frequently as possible during his few years in Los Angeles. Jimmy Rowles was the pianist, with guitarist Jim Hall, bassist Red Mitchell, and the elegant, effervescent drummer Frank Butler. All of it is wonderful, but Webster's "Star Dust" here is in the class of his very best work. In conversations through the years, Hall and Rowles have remarked at length about the remarkable empathy of the group and their respect for Webster. The evidence on this record bears out their contention that this combination of soloist and rhythm section was a rare perfect musical relationship. That Webster felt the same way is apparent in a wistful remark made to producer Lester Koenig when they were listening to tapes of the session some years later. With tears in his eyes, Webster asked Koenig, "Why can't I get to play with guys like that anymore?"*

Phil Woods

In 1973, the alto saxophonist Phil Woods formed a band with drummer Bill Goodwin, bassist Steve Gilmore, pianist Mike Melillo, and guitarist Harry Leahy. Eventually, the guitar was dropped. Later, Melillo left and was replaced by pianist Hal Galper. Woods maintained his quartet unchanged for nearly a decade, molding it into a stunningly cohesive and expressive group. When trumpeter Tom Harrell joined in 1983, the band took on added character, dimension, and excitement. It is in many respects a classic bebop quintet, although its repertoire and style go beyond bop and are very much attuned to, in fact help define, the mainstream jazz of the late eighties.

While the reputation and marketability of his own group were being established, Woods recorded in various situations. There were albums with other artists, including a memorable collaboration with Lena Horne, and several of his own in settings ranging from combo to full orchestra.

Phil Woods was born in Springfield, Massachusetts, in 1931. He moved to New York City when he was seventeen to pursue the clarinet and saxophone studies he had begun at home. Following lessons with the brilliant, eccentric pianist and theorist Lennie Tristano, Woods spent a semester at Manhattan School of Music before moving to Juilliard for four years as a clarinet major. During his Juilliard years, he made his presence known at jam sessions and through sitting in at clubs. The vigor and dash of his playing on recordings with guitarist Jimmy Raney in 1954 brought him the opportunity to record as a leader and, quickly, Woods had established himself as a journeyman soloist in the tough New York jazz community.

During the 1950s he worked with Ramey, Charlie Barnet's big band, Friedrich Gulda, and the George Wallington Quintet. He traveled overseas with Dizzy Gillespie. He co-led a combo with fellow alto saxophonist Gene Quill, appeared for a short stint with Buddy Rich, and became a part of the Quincy Jones band that toured Europe in the show built around Harold Arlen's blues opera, "Free and Easy."

During the next decade, Woods was in the Benny Goodman band that made a tour of the Soviet Union, composed and recorded a critically acclaimed suite called "Rights of Swing," and freelanced extensively before moving to Paris in 1968. There, he formed a small group, The European Rhythm Machine, with which he toured and recorded, occasionally appearing in the United States. In 1972, he moved to California for ten months, then returned to the East Coast.

From the days of his first sessions in New York, Woods has been admired for the no-holds-barred quality of his playing. He is a thoroughly schooled musician with subtle harmonic intelligence, but force, authority, and smoldering emotion are the hallmarks of his work.

Few musicians relish the process of studio recording. Even what is intended to be a simple blowing session of blues and other familiar harmonic patterns usually requires more than one version or "take" of each tune before a usable one is captured on tape. The musical, mechanical, and electronic vagaries of sound recording can make the most successful recording experience long, arduous, and frustrating. When a meticulous leader and a demanding producer are involved, the quest for a faithful musical document that will also be a viable commercial product can be a memorable adventure. This following is an account of Woods's January 1974 record session with pianist Jaki Byard, bassist Richard Davis, and drummer Alan Dawson.

1974

Long-haired and full-mustached, booted, mackinawed and gloved against the raw New York day, Phil Woods looks like a visitor from a nineteenth-century lumber camp as he steps into a chrome-lined elevator in the RCA building at 6th Avenue and 44th Street. On the seventh floor, the cavernous studio B and a supercharged rhythm section have been placed at his disposal for the afternoon. Woods has moved to New York after a few months of working the Los Angeles film, television, and record studio circuit. His reason for leaving L.A. is succinctly put: "I couldn't stand it." Born in Springfield, Massachusetts, in 1931, Woods is a veteran of the Dizzy Gillespie, Quincy Jones, and Benny Goodman big bands and a star of countless recording sessions over the past two decades. He is best known for his alto work, of course, but he majored in clarinet at Juilliard and in 1963 the *down beat* critics declared him "deserving of wider recognition" on that instrument. He still is. This will be his first record date as a leader since his return to the United States from a five-year stay on the Continent, where he invented and perfected the formidable European Rhythm Machine, an engine of swing so powerful that it helped silence once and for all the canard that Europeans were rhythmically deficient, perhaps genetically.

There is certainly little cause for a lack of propulsion on this occasion. Richard Davis is in studio B, chatting with Alan Dawson, who has flown in from Boston for the session. Dawson's drums are in place, and Davis begins tuning his lion-headed bass. Woods, Davis, and Dawson shake hands not with the cool slap that has been appropriated from musicians by pseudo hipsters of all stripes, but with hearty grips straight out of the Tuesday Rotary meeting. The phraseology is considerably more rarified.

"Gooseneck Jones," Woods says to Dawson, "howya feelin', baby?"

"Pretty good, baby."

"Hey," Davis salutes Woods.

"All right, Richard."

Jaki Byard wanders in, looking, as always, slightly bemused and mystical. He greets the others and sets about testing the piano. Asked how he likes it, Byard says, "It's a piano. I had a good one once, in France." The universal suffering of jazz pianists; an endless chain of inadequate instruments binds them together as surely as their love for Art Tatum.

After a round of exchanges concerning recent travels and mutual acquaintances, Woods repairs to a chair facing a microphone, unpacks his alto, assembles it, performs the ritual of the reed, and launches a few experimental notes. Producer Don Schlitten and RCA engineer Paul Goodman enter and leave several times, alternately adjusting microphones in the studio and levels in the control room. Pictures are being taken. The rhythm section is having a reunion. Schlitten has used its members frequently over the years, notably on a stunning series of Booker Ervin albums in the sixties, and they have a lot to talk about.

Dawson, one of the most admired and least showy of drummers, was born in Marietta, Pennsylvania, in 1929. There are very few of his major contemporaries who have not worked with him and none who would not like to. He has been Dave Brubeck's drummer for several years now, fitting tours and recording dates with Brubeck into an incredibly demanding schedule as teacher at the Berklee School of Music in Boston. Alan is available for few bar mitzvahs or weddings. Byard is also gracing the academic world these days, as head of the jazz department at Boston's New England Conservatory. Born in Worcester, Massachusetts, in 1922, Byard has worked with Charles Mingus, Maynard Ferguson, Eric Dolphy, Roland Kirk, Charlie Mariano, and Don Ellis and has led his own bands, large and small. He is best known as a pianist who encompasses literally the entire history of jazz, but he also plays drums, vibes, trumpet, trombone, bass, and saxophones. Brubeck recalls having first heard Byard at a jam session as an impressive alto saxophonist who laid down the horn to play an even more impressive piano solo. Davis was born in Chicago in 1930. He began attracting widespread attention in 1961 as a member of the Eric Dolphy-Booker Little group and in almost no time at all other musicians were call-

ing him the world's greatest bass player. He is astoundingly versatile
and constantly in demand for every kind of music, from Streisand
to Stravinsky (at the late maestro's request).

Woods has extracted from his saxophone case the music for two
original compositions and is prepared to distribute it.

"You guys didn't come here to have a good time, did you?" he
inquires.

"Uh, oh, work time," Dawson says, belying the anticipation in
the air.

The music is received and examined. Woods offers a few rudi-
mentary instructions, and the rundowns of "Samba du bois" begin.
Woods says he can't hear the others; headsets are suggested and all
but Byard accept them. Woods now looks like a lumberjack wear-
ing earphones. It is decided to depart from the samba rhythm on the
bridge of the tune; it will be played in straight 4/4 time. Woods says
he's ready to try one, the tape machines are started and Schlitten
intones, "'Samba du bois,' take one."

Take one is short-lived. The piano mike has gone dead.

"I did it," Goodman humorously confesses to Schlitten. "I did
that on purpose, you know."

"Yeah, I know. 'Samba,' take two."

Davis smiles widely at a particularly robust Woods run. Byard
solos primarily in block chords. During playback the pianist sits
palm to brow, wincing. The take ends on a magnificent bass slide
over cymbals. "Sounds a little nervous," Woods reflects, "not
settled yet."

The studio lights are lowered. The control room is beginning to
fill with friends of the musicians and members of the critical community who have looked forward to the date as one of the major
events of the winter season. Woods's inventive and forceful playing
during his engagement at the Half Note over the holidays has caused
a wave of excitement among the cognoscenti, one of those periodic
"rediscoveries" of a major talent.

"The idea of the bridge being in four was nice," Dawson inter-
jects during the planning for the next take, "but. . . ."

No one comes to the defense of 4/4 for the bridge, and it is

banished from the work in progress. Davis gets into an extraordinary mixture of sliding and walking under a ripping Woods solo
which includes an uproariously funny modulation around the first
four bars of "Flying Home." Byard hasn't abandoned his chord
clusters, but now the shade of Tatum is beginning to make itself
heard in the form of a few lightning single-note lines. Woods accompanies Davis during the bass solo, blowing little jets of rhythm.
The ending becomes a vamp, with Davis wildly free and rubato. Engineer Goodman holds up his hand for silence until Dawson's cymbal has rung its last.

Woods has heard something amiss in the rhythm section and
wants a fourth take.

"Did you all goof?" Byard asks the other three. Much laughter.

Woods decides to develop the bass-and-alto idea he played with
in take three.

"Richard, let's you and I do one after Jaki. I'll kind of play under
you—a duet. Jaki and Alan lay out."

Take four. Byard joins Dawson in the percussion section, punching out chords in metronomic 4/4 time as he accompanies another
superb Woods solo. This time the chromatically-manipulated quote
is from "All God's Children Got Rhythm." Byard's solo is almost
exclusively single-note lines, with some maniacal excursions up and
down the top octaves of the keyboard. Laughter and shaking of
heads in the control room. The planned duet becomes a trio; Dawson
has forgotten to lay out. But Woods doesn't stop, and the interplay
is fascinating. The vamp ending takes on the joyous spirit of car-
nival in Rio. Schlitten asks Woods if he wants to hear it.

"Dare we?"

After the playback, Schlitten approves. "Crazy."

"Why not?" Woods replies.

"I can dig it," puts in the ever-cautious Dawson, "but let's do another one, just out of spite."

"All right, let's be spiteful," Woods agrees.

Take five is aborted. Woods finds the bridge too static.

"Don't plan it," he suggests.

Take six opens with just Woods and Davis, vamping. Into his

solo, Woods toys with a phrase from "52nd Street Theme," evidently finds inspiration there, and tears off into a succession of majestic choruses. Byard churns and swirls, producing what sounds like a solo for four hands. Woods is free, soaring over the rhythm section on the vamp ending. Dawson concludes with a little waltz figure. The playback draws chuckles from the musicians. There has been a remarkable evolution during the six takes, a casebook in the development of a piece of jazz music.

"Keep that spite going," Woods says.

"The Last Page" is harmonically involved and rhythmically complex, with a mixture of 5/4 and 4/4 time. It requires eleven attempts, including section inserts which will be assembled during the mixing and editing later in the month. The introduction is balladic, the main body faster and extremely rhythmic. Davis is much taken with the composition, and his playing is inspired.

"Pretty song, man," he beams at Woods.

The pretty song fights back. Woods cuts several takes short to deal with its obstacles. He finds the tempo for the introduction a bit soggy. And the harmonic development is not to his liking. Byard wants Woods to explain a certain progression.

"Forget the B-7th. You know where to get to the E? . . . bah, dah, dah."

"Oh, yeah, I'm hip."

"You stayed on the A too long. Can we make a cut there? Let's check the front section. If it's cool, we'll just pick it up on the 5/4."

Dawson finds himself longing for some forgotten equipment.

"I wish I had my mallets."

"Yeah," Woods agrees, "mallets would be nice. How about a couple of stale rolls?"

A take with a marvelous Woods solo full of throaty tremolo passages and a quote from "Parker's Mood" is terminated. Dawson has misinterpreted a hand signal. Several more attempts are scrapped after premature entries. By the seventh take, the piece is beginning to jell and Woods, more relaxed, is producing low growls and overtones that shake the control room. He plays a ferocious solo incorporating the "Stranger in Paradise" lick from Borodin. After a series of eight-, four- and two-bar exchanges between drums and alto, Davis and Byard come in too soon.

"It's still a thirty-two-bar tune, gentlemen. We gotta go from the blowing top again. Back to four before B."

The control room gallery breaks up at the ingenious insertion of a phrase from "Slaughter on Tenth Avenue" in a harmonic nook where it couldn't have been expected to fit. Much of Woods's trenchant quoting is subliminal; pointed allusions rather than complete phrases. Take eight, with cries and hollers from Woods's saxophone and unearthly soloing by Byard, concludes on a sustained chord. No one in the studio can hear the applause in the booth.

"All right, people, don't get too excited," Schlitten says. He's smiling.

Three tries at an insert, and "The Last Page" is in the can.

Woods's head arrangement of "Willow Weep for Me" begins with the rhythm section playing the introductory pattern used by Miles Davis for "All Blues." The plan is to continue the figure through the alto solo, but Woods finds it too monotonous. Take one is cut short. There are superior solos on take two from Woods, Byard, and Davis, but the leader is interested in supplemental harmonic ideas and goes to the piano to suggst some chords. The third take opens faster, with Davis adding vibrato and Dawson slapping the brushes on his snare drum just enough to impart a happy dance feeling. Woods responds with a sunny solo that is in sharp contrast to the rather brooding statement of the previous take. He introduces a phrase from "Drum Boogie," chromaticizing it outrageously. Davis solos with an abandon that causes a sharp collective intake of breath in the control room. Byard has a brilliant solo full of Tatum fragments. The piano sweeps under Woods as he re-enters for a final chorus packed with modulations, piping high notes, and gut-rumbling low tones.

"Okay," Woods tells the control room, "we'll bring in a brass section to put a chord on the end."

While the others are listening to "Willow," Dawson is on the phone to the Aladdin Delicatessen: "Cheese on rye . . . no sesame seeds in the rye."

"Perhaps you'd prefer avocado seeds," suggests an eavesdropper.

"Yes, with hot sauce," Dawson grins, and he goes into a monologue full of such gustatory items from old Slim Gaillard recordings as mosquito knees, hippopotamus lips, and reety pooties. The next order of business is "The Summer Knows," the theme from the motion picture *Summer of '42*. After a quick rundown, the machines are started and the quartet records a perfect take. But Schlitten is afraid he has heard electronic clicks. While the source of the clicks is being sought, Woods is gratefully receiving a shoulder massage from a lady in the audience.

"Aha," Schlitten says with a mixture of triumph and annoyance, "there they are. My engineer thought I was psychotic. He only heard it the fourth time. I heard the first three. He thought I was nuts." Goodman says he thinks he has the problem licked. Massaged and relaxed, Woods suggests the next take be a little slower.

"I presume it'll get better," he tells Schlitten.

"Oh, I know it will."

It gets better, but the click is back. Cut. The next take is even slower, and the one after slower yet, saturated with feeling and concluding in an alto cadenza climaxed by a series of low notes that sound as if Woods has suddenly switched to baritone sax. There is no discussion. It is a classic ballad performance.

The time is 5:35. The session is scheduled to end at 6:00. Two tunes to go. Woods calls "Airegin," by Sonny Rollins. It is recorded twice. There is little to choose between the versions. Both are superb, with heated solos from all hands.

"One of these is all right with me," Woods says to Schlitten.

"It doesn't matter," Byard volunteers. "He'll release it all eventually."

It is 5:46. The final piece is Wayne Shorter's "Nefertiti." Everyone is familiar with it, so the runthrough is brief. The first attempt is incomplete. Take two is blues-drenched and funky and has a stimulating tag ending with more of Woods's low-register slaptonguing.

"Throw him a fish," the saxophonist exhorts as he listens to the playback.

Byard has gone. Dawson calls for a cab to LaGuardia Airport so he can catch the next shuttle to Boston. Davis wipes the lion's head and packs his bass. Schlitten is making notes. Goodman slumps in his chair, staring at the needles and dials. The control room clique is congratulating Woods on an unusually successful record date. He thanks them, smiling a bit wryly, as if he knows something they don't. Then his horn is into its case and he's into his mackinaw and headed for the door, leaving an announcement:

"I'm gonna go get me a pear."

Love for Sale

1980

In 1977 an energetic Texas petroleum geologist named Max Christensen, who also owns the Midland Cubs baseball team, rounded up twenty-two sponsors, got them to put up a thousand dollars apiece, and founded the Midland Jazz Association. Its primary activity was holding a jazz party. The party's geneology runs back to 1963, when Colorado millionaire Dick Gibson threw his first annual jazz soirée in Aspen. Gibson's idea spread, and in the early seventies a few well-heeled cognoscenti in Odessa established a jazz party. Scottsdale, Arizona, and Pine Bluff, Arkansas, parties followed, and small private jazz festivals began to pop up all over the country.

Christensen wanted to hear more extended performances than those allowed by the tightly packed, get-'em-on, get-'em-off, three-day Colorado schedule. So each fall, the Midland Jazz Classic runs six days, with a couple of dozen musicians instead of half a hundred. Attendance is by invitation, and ticket sales stop at four hundred. Those who attend, including the founders, pay one hundred dollars per person for five nights and one afternoon of music, sit at reserved tables, and buy their own drinks. The musicians are given room and board and are paid about eight hundred dollars for the week, considerably less than many of them would be earning in the studios of Los Angeles and New York. They do it for love.

For the 1979 Classic, the musicians were Milt Hinton, Jack

Lesberg, and Michael Moore, bass; Johnny Mince, Abe Most, Bob
Wilber, Al Cohn, and Zoot Sims, reeds; Jackie Williams, Gus
Johnson, and Mousie Alexander, drums; Cal Collins, guitar; Dick
Hyman, Dave McKenna, and Ralph Sutton, piano; Urbie Green, Al
Grey, and Bill Watrous, trombone; Ruby Braff and Pee Wee Erwin,
cornet; Joe Wilder, trumpet; Terry Gibbs, vibes; and Carol Sloane,
vocals.

Although the audience contained a sprinkling of people in their
twenties and thirties, most were middle-aged or older, as are most
of the musicians. It was fascinating and unexpected during a notably intense "I Got Rhythm" to see so many members of the Welk
generation popping, snapping, nodding, and tapping in absolute
and accurate observance of the beat. Conversations with some of
the retirees who frequent the jazz party circuit disclosed their encyclopedic knowledge of the history of the music and an informed
appreciation of individual styles. I overheard a Sunday morning
lobby conversation between an octogenarian and cornetist Pee Wee
Erwin in which the elderly man delineated the fine points of Bix
Beiderbecke's phrasing, referring to Beiderbecke's solos by song title
and record label. Several of the fans seemed equally informed not
only about the music of the twenties and thirties but also about
Miles Davis, Freddie Hubbard, and other representatives of new
styles.

Christensen calls upon Jack Lesberg, the bassist whose varied
past includes lengthy stays with Louis Armstrong and with the New
York City Symphony under Leonard Bernstein, to be his musical director. Lesberg assigns the combinations of musicians and lets the
players decide on their own material. Often, the results are un-
orthodox. One night, Dick Hyman unveiled a series of chamber arrangements of Irving Berlin songs for a quintet that included Wilber
and Erwin. "All Alone by the Telephone" was done in the style of
gospel music. "Soft Lights and Sweet Music" was introduced by
Hyman as "not soft and sweet, but loud and hot." It culminated in a
series of drum/bass exchanges between Jackie Williams and Milt
Hinton in which they began trading four-bar phrases and worked
down to trading single bars. At their lickety-split tempo, it might

have gone mashed potatoes, but it remained crisp and very funny. Hyman's tribute to Fats Waller in the same piece was just one instance of his uncanny assimilation of the styles of the major pianists from James P. Johnson to Cecil Taylor. The high point of the set was a gorgeous cadenza by Erwin at the end of "How Deep Is the Ocean." At sixty-six, Erwin is short, stout, bespectacled, and looks like your friendly neighborhood hardware dealer. He is probably the most underrated trumpeter of his generation. His fame as a Benny Goodman and Tommy Dorsey sideman dissolved in years of studio work, and it wasn't until he started as a regular on the party circuit and a member of the New York Jazz Repertory Company that jazz listeners again started paying serious attention to him.

In a later set, after Erwin and Zoot Sims had led the ensemble in a blistering conclusion to "I Want to Be Happy," they got a standing ovation and stood grinning at each other like schoolboys who had just won special awards for rambunctiousness. Sims's tone has darkened over the years to the point that his sound is no longer like that of his inspiration, Lester Young. The same is true of Sims's tenor alter ego, Al Cohn. But their easy swing remains in the Young-Count Basie tradition, and it is so flexible a tradition that no matter who they play with, they fit. Sims was perfect in his soft, abstract obligatos behind Carol Sloane, and he was perfect in the Dixieland treatment of "Just a Closer Walk with Thee" with Erwin, Johnny Mince, and Al Grey.

Cohn, heavily in demand for his composing and arranging talents, played relatively little between 1960 and 1974. I remember encountering him in 1973 when he was orchestrating the Broadway hit "Raisin" during its Washington breaking-in period. The money was good, he said, but the work was hard and gave him few of the satisfactions of playing jazz. Now Cohn accepts a few major television writing jobs each year and concentrates on his horn. He has never played with more intensity, conviction, or lyricism. It seems to me in Midland that, chorus for chorus, Cohn was examining the innermost possibilities of the music with more consistent profundity than any other player. A lingering image is that of Cohn looking over Terry Gibbs's shoulder during the vibraharpist's brilliant solo

on "After You've Gone," studying the keyboard as intently as a
Talmudic scholar searching for revelations, then launching into his
own solo as if he'd found them.

Johnny Mince's gutty baritone sax was an unexpected pleasure in
Midland, and his deep, woody sound in the low register of the clarinet on "St. Louis Blues" was a highlight of the performance. Mince,
Erwin, and Sims were superb, but Grey won the crowd with a classic, plunger-muted, trombone exposition of the verse.

Grey is one of the few trombonists to have mastered the plunger
method virtually invented by Tricky Sam Nanton of Duke Ellington's
band, and he uses it with lightning speed and unfailing humor. In
matters of technique he is at least matched by Bill Watrous and
Urbie Green, both of whom play with such fluidity that the listener
may suddenly realize as he hears their solos that he has been taking
the impossible for granted. Watrous is more likely to be overtly
showy than Green, who can play with dazzling speed at low volume. Both are thought of as bebop or post-bop players, but both
demonstrated, in a "Fidgety Feet" that approached careless abandon that the spirit of traditional jazz is with them. Green, tightly
muted, ripped off a series of whoops and hollers that had the other
musicians raising their eyebrows.

Christensen, the Midland impresario, refuses to categorize his approach to music, and he gets no argument from the musicians he at-
tracts. Though it is safe to say that they are all in a wide mainstream
of jazz, it would be foolish to try to find pigeonholes for them. Ruby
Braff's every chorus is in some way a tribute to Louis Armstrong,
but that can be said of most cornet or trumpet players of Braff's
generation, and his work contains allusions to Roy Eldridge and
Dizzy Gillespie as well. He is, to borrow Duke Ellington's phrase,
beyond category. To hear Braff in a variety of settings over two days
was to be again impressed with the breadth he shares with musicians like Cohn and Sims and, indeed, with most of the players at
Midland. Braff's smoothness, harmonic daring, and control were
nowhere more apparent than in his duets with Hyman at the organ.
The pairing was inspired. On "Chloe," Braff combined elements of
Armstrong and Gillespie into a solo that could be annotated and
studied as a kind of capsule history of jazz trumpet. In another set,

trading phrases with Cohn and Gibbs, he split one four-bar phrase evenly between quotes from Armstrong and the bebop trumpeter Fats Navarro.

Joe Wilder, a trumpeter whose studio obligations have kept him off the streets for twenty-five years, is famous among his peers for a tone so lustrous that he has been engaged to play as few as four bars because only his sound would fulfill the demands of the arrangement. But Wilder is also a first-class improviser. If his soloing can sometimes seem too controlled, too smooth, he can surprise you with explosive quotes like the snatches of "Moose the Mooche" woven into his solo on "Exactly Like You" and with his plunger work on "Cotton Tail," in which he evoked Cootie Williams's days of glory with Duke Ellington. In the same set, Bob Wilber's alto saxophone on "Passion Flower" was as close to the sound and spirit of the late Johnny Hodges as could be imagined. Wilber displayed an enormous knowledge of the styles of the saxophone giants and an ability to incorporate them into his playing, whether imitating Hodges on "Passion Flower," transposing to alto sax the famous Ben Webster tenor sax solo on "Cotton Tail," or mixing aspects of Hodges and Charlie Parker in a stimulating chorus on "Take the 'A' Train." When he was a teenager, Wilber recorded with Sidney Bechet, the founding father of jazz soprano saxophone. For too long he was unfairly considered an aging wunderkind. But in recent years he has been increasingly impressive for his artistic range and depth of feeling. Wilber's playing has taken on a quality described by one of his biggest fans at the Midland Classic as "testicular."

The rhythm sections contained various combinations of Hinton, Lesberg, and Moore on bass; McKenna, Hyman, and Sutton at the piano; drummers Johnson, Williams, and Alexander; and guitarist Collins. The sections were smooth and powerful, swinging with a uniformly light touch that is a hallmark of the best professionals. That is, there was no bashing, regardless of the demands of tempo or the level of enthusiasm. The three drummers are masters of wire brushes; not all good drummers are. There were also laudable solos from all the rhythm section players, but not to single out McKenna and Collins would be too democratic.

While Hyman is able to play like virtually every major jazz pian-

ist he has ever heard, and Sutton is an inspired graduate student
of the Fats Waller school, McKenna is an original. Using elements
of everyone from Waller and Art Tatum to Lennie Tristano, Bud
Powell, and Bill Evans, McKenna has forged a style based on rolling
vigor in the left hand and a melding of single-note lines with orchestral voicings in the right. He loves harmonic adventuring and
frequently has elements of stride and bebop going at the same time,
blending them into an idiom identifiable only as McKenna. A typical McKenna gambit: during a steaming solo on "Things Ain't
What They Used to Be," he came out of a chorus of shouting stride
piano that would have had Waller beaming, and moved seamlessly
and logically into an interpolation of Horace Silver's hip post-bop
anthem "Room 608."

Cal Collins is a forty-six-year-old Indianan who spent twenty-five
years playing nondescript jobs in the Midwest, was discovered by
Jack Sheldon and Benny Goodman, and is astounding everyone
who hears him. He calls himself a "rural type." The roots of his
style go back to the Southwestern tradition best exemplified by
Charlie Christian. Collins performed luminously every night in
Midland. But his apogee came during an "I Got Rhythm" in which
Mince, Braff, Sims, Watrous, and Sutton had each cranked up the
intensity of the swing one more notch. Then Collins blew in, riffing
behind his own solo, playing duets with himself, turning the time
every way but loose and finally executing little rhythmic jokes that
reduced everyone on the stand, including himself, to belly laughs. It
was one of the funniest moments I have ever witnessed, and it had
absolute musical validity at a fever pitch of swing.

Collins was a part of the Terry Gibbs group that created another
moment of high excitement. The occasion was Gibbs's salute to
Benny Goodman, with Abe Most as Goodman, Hyman as Teddy
Wilson, Gibbs as Lionel Hampton, and Collins as Charlie Christian. Drummer Jackie Williams and bassist Milt Hinton, experienced arsonists, joined Collins's rhythm guitar to help build a fire
under Gibbs on "Air Mail Special." The fastest of vibists, Gibbs has
never been known to need a fire to get hot. But the additional energy inspired him to a series of choruses so intensely swinging that

Gibbs looked momentarily astonished at what he had wrought. In the same set, Hinton, who is sixty-nine, looks forty-nine, and plays as if he were twenty-nine, was featured in a beautiful solo on "These Foolish Things." A few moments later, on "It's Only a Paper Moon," the virtuoso bassist Michael Moore and the virtuoso trombonist Watrous traded four-bar phrases, each echoing the other's ideas while adding new ones in a way that amounted to a collaborative solo.

Carol Sloane is one of the few major singers associated with jazz who is almost unknown to the public at large. She has rarely recorded. Little had been heard from her since the sixties until 1975, when she returned to New York after an extended stay in North Carolina. Miss Sloane is one of the few younger singers who has listened to and understands Mildred Bailey. She incorporates Bailey's lyrical purity into a style that also recognizes the tainted sweetness and enthusiasm for life of the young Billie Holiday and the not quite blasé sophistication of Lee Wiley. Miss Sloane had to go easy in Midland because she was recovering from laryngitis, but her clear voice, impeccable diction, musicianly phrasing, and confident swing were intact despite the reduced volume. Accompanied by Braff's cornet one night and Sims's tenor the next, she performed memorably, the horns providing obligatos so successful it seems imperative that she do an album with them. Her Ellington medley culminated in "I Got It Bad and That Ain't Good," and Miss Sloane sang the rarely heard verse with such quiet intensity that there was a collective gasp of recognition from the audience when she began the chorus. Sims's solo was an example of perfect ballad playing, and the intertwined voices of the woman and the saxophone on the final chorus produced a supremely beautiful moment.

For the most part, the players at Midland knew each other well. Their styles were compatible. Although Max Christensen says he and his friends are interested in rotating musicians from year to year "to keep the Classic fresh," it seems unlikely that they will go outside the mainstream in search of freshness. They know something about music, and they know what they like. Certainly, no revolutionary music was heard, no trails were blazed. It would be interesting to throw Sonny Rollins, Freddie Hubbard, or some members of the avant-garde into the mix to see what they would stimulate. But, aside from critics' unsolicited suggestions, there is no reason the Midland Jazz Association should do that. It's their party, and the music they are getting is fresh because it is timeless.

Listener's Journal

1976

Washington, D.C., May 25: The formulized, bass-heavy disco records have the customers at Clyde's drinking and dancing in a frenzy. People are shouting at each other across tables, certainly not my favorite conversational style, but the Clyde's regulars seem to be loving it. As the years go by, I notice, enough gets to be enough increasingly sooner, and my companions and I are quickly out of Clyde's fashionable door and onto a drizzly, fashionable, Georgetown sidewalk. There is a federal law that the word Georgetown must be preceded by the word fashionable.

Down the street, around the corner, in an alley (of course), is Blues Alley. And in Blues Alley tonight is Kai Winding, who immediately sets straight the matter of pronunciation by introducing himself as *Kai* (rhymes with sky). It used to be *Kai* (rhymes with play). Otherwise they would have had to call that famous two-trombone group *Kai and Jai Jai* (rhymes with sky-sky). The name must have been *Kai* in the beginning; that certainly sounds more Danish. But somewhere along the line it became Anglicized, leading to a certain amount of confusion among the less hip. There was that celebrated marquee announcement outside the Seattle Civic Auditorium: "Tonight . . . one time only . . . Stan Kenton and his Orchestra, Featuring the Lovely Kai Winding."

Looking distinguished, if not lovely, in his gray business suit,

Winding arrives on the stand after a short set by the house rhythm section, pianist John Phillips, bassist Billy Taylor, Jr., and drummer Bill Reichenbach. They have been turning in some pleasant playing generally in the manner of the Red Garland Trio, circa 1957. Winding does some pieces from his *Danish Blue* album, also pleasant. If jazz musicians must perform pop material, they can do worse than "You Are the Sunshine of My Life." Winding finds interesting things to do with Stevie Wonder's changes. "Robbins' Nest" moves along nicely, amiable if not particularly inspired music. Then, on a medium blues, Winding finds a groove. The intensity begins to grow, and the room noise begins to decrease proportionately. At first Kai is cooking alone, but the power of his swing begins to lift the rhythm section. After a couple of choruses, they have reached his level. The performance and the remainder of the set are memorable. It is an impressive instance of a superb soloist's ability to take a good rhythm section and make it better. Winding *is* lovely.

New York City, May 26: The neighborhood around Stryker's Pub at 86th and Columbus . . . never a Georgetown . . . is not as fashionable as it once was. Nor is the trumpet player inside this long, narrow, dark little club. There was a time, twenty years ago, when he was as fashionable as any jazz trumpet player ever has been. He won all the polls, his records sold extremely well, and he achieved considerable popularity as a singer. But ten or fifteen years packed with the most damaging kinds of personal problems kept Chet Baker off the scene and out of most listeners' minds, so that when he resurfaced in New York in 1973 for an engagement at the Half Note, it seemed he had been resurrected. The playing was a bit shaky and uncertain at first, but as the 1970s moved along, Baker built up his chops and his confidence. It wasn't long before he could summon up the tonal qualities of his trademark recording, "My Funny Valentine," and sometimes he approached the fleetness of "Bea's Flat" and "Love Next." The singing had acquired a new quality, innocence tempered with experience, the phrasing even more musicianly than in the old days.

Tonight, Baker is in his Upper Manhattan headquarters, having arrived late and preoccupied. He is saying no more than is necessary to make the rhythm section acquainted with his intentions. If one of those intentions is to swing, the rhythm section is disappointing. The bassist, once noted for his swing and crisp sound, is having terrible time and intonation problems. The drummer who is sitting in doesn't play badly. He does play obtrusively, which is the wrong way to play for this leader, and Chet's dark mood becomes black. The other horn is a flutist whose work is nondescript. Pianist Hal Galper, cheerful but apprehensive, plays some good, workmanlike solos, admirable under the circumstances.

Despite all this mediocrity, Baker manages some impressive passages. But none of his solos could be described as successful. His vocals could be; he is singing beautifully. At the end of the bar, three feet from Baker, a group of young businessmen applauds and cheers wildly at the end of each piece. During the performances, however, the men discuss the day's events, loudly. Having had enough, Baker gets up, turns his horn on them as if it were a weapon and lets them have the melody of "I'm Old Fashioned" right in the their faces, loudly. Then he plays his best chorus of the evening, angrily. At the end of the set, he apologizes, the loudmouths apologize, the tensions seem to be alleviated. But the rhythm section doesn't improve. The bass player is deteriorating before our very ears, and it becomes necessary to leave, quickly.

One of my companions grew up listening to Chet Baker, modeled his own playing and singing on Baker's, and departed from jazz to become an immensely successful pop performer. He is saddened by what he has witnessed, as we all are. The cab ride to midtown is full of speculation about why a major artist finds it necessary to work with inadequate sidemen. The guesses range from managerial to financial to psychological and make us even glummer. A disappointing evening.

New York City, May 27: Don Schlitten has invited me to drop in on one of his Xanadu recording sessions at RCA's studio B. He offers no hint about who he's taping. It comes as a considerable surprise to find that the leader is Sam Most, who has been at the top of the jazz missing-in-action list since the 1950s. On guitar is the reclusive Tal Farlow, persuaded by Schlitten to come out of the

Jersey swamps to a record studio for the first time since 1969. The rhythm section . . . guaranteed to make anyone come out of the swamps . . . is Duke Jordan, piano; Sam Jones, bass; and Billy Higgins, drums. Most has been lost in the anonymity of Los Angeles studios and Las Vegas hotels for several years. His flute and clarinet playing have lost none of their individual characteristics, however, and the listener is reminded that after Most and Buddy DeFranco there haven't been any impressive bop clarinet players since Stan Hasselgard. Sam is cool and adroit on both instruments today, and he has some joyous clarinet choruses on "Poor Butterfly." Farlow seems to be experiencing a crisis of confidence in the early hours of the session. His ideas are good, but he isn't quite jibing with the rhythm section. Part of the fascination with Farlow's playing is that he plays close to the edge of the time. That requires a delicate rhythmic balance he is having difficulty achieving. But as he settles in, Farlow begins to sound more and more like the dazzling, daring guitarist who blew so many minds in the forties and fifties.

Jordan has the control room audience enthralled. He is hot this afternoon, every solo a gem of conception and of pianistic touch. There are numerous retakes, but none of them is because of Duke. Jones and Higgins are as one in terms of time; it is doubtful that any bassist and drummer have a finer understanding. Strolling into the control room after a take of "The More I See You" on which he has played a gorgeous solo that had heads shaking, Jordan asks, "Was that all right?"

Everyone breaks up. Duke doesn't know why.

New York City, May 28: Hopper's is a jazz club new to Greenwich Village since I left New York for San Antonio fifteen months ago. It is spacious, with an open floor plan, good food, simple but elegant natural wood decor, some splendid chandeliers and, tonight, Jimmy Rowles and Richard "Groove" Holmes. Holmes, his full-power organ, his trio, and his vocalist are installed in a large room behind the substantial and impressive bar. The windows between the back bar and the dining room are closed, but Holmes's battering ram music can be clearly heard. Conversation is possible, however, and Rowles comes to the table for a chat. As uninhibited, witty, and earthy a storyteller as he is a pianist, he entertains us with jokes, one-liners, and commentaries on music and life. He has been infatuated with stride piano lately, Jimmy says, and is finding ways of putting stride into the most unlikely tunes. He promises to let us hear him stride through "All the Things You Are," even if it means getting fired. He doesn't seem seriously concerned about being dismissed.

The piano is in the front room of Hopper's, surrounded on three sides by tables where the customers may have drinks and light suppers. Rowles's audience tonight is sprinkled with musicians including Paul Desmond, Al Haig, Milt Jackson, and Gene Gammage, and he plays to them. The music is complex, fascinating, often hilarious. Nobody knows as many obscure tunes as Jimmy. The Nelson Eddie medley, à la Fats Waller, has everybody falling out. You haven't heard "Sweetheart" until you've heard Rowles stride it. Musicians' mouths are falling open all over the place as Jimmy works quotes from Stravinksy's "Ebony Concerto" into "Here's That Rainy Day." Across the table, Desmond is responding to Rowles's free-associating improvisations with chuckles and grins of suspended belief. Jimmy should be recorded in this free and easy setting.

He doesn't play "All the Things You Are" as stride. On the other hand, he doesn't get fired.

Bradley's, a couple of long blocks east of Hopper's, is packed at midnight. Cedar Walton is at the spinet, which doesn't sound too bad, for a spinet. Sam Jones is Cedar's partner. Their nearly constant companion, Billy Higgins, is sitting in. There isn't room for a full set of anything but teeth, so Higgins is playing a snare drum with brushes. One snare drum, and he's swinging his fanny off. Walton's recent successes with his RCA fusion records have brought him a certain amount of popular attention, and you might think he'd work some of his pop music into this gig. But what we get tonight is uncompromising, straight-ahead bebop, with some side trips into modality. The crowd is a listening one, for the most part, and the conversation level is held low. Walton's music, out of Bud Powell, has long since taken on depth, polish, and style that make

Cedar a distinctively personal and immediately identifiable pianist. Tonight he's having fun playing for a roomful of congenial listeners, most of whom hang in until closing time. Jones is amazing. Don Schlitten calls him the best bass player in New York today. He may well be right.

New York City, May 29: John Snyder of Horizon Records is playing me tapes of the Dave Brubeck Quartet reunion tour concerts. The repertoire and the sound are pretty much as they were in 1967, when the group broke up. Can it really have been eight-and-a-half years since this was a working band? Everyone's loose, and Desmond has some brilliant playing on "Take Five" and "Don't Worry 'bout Me." Joe Morello and Eugene Wright seem to have found the old groove. Brubeck is happy with the tapes of the Ann Arbor concert, Snyder says. An album is in preparation.

San Antonio, May 30: The big music news here is a hassle over whether Willie Nelson will be allowed to hold his annual Fourth of July picnic in Gonzales. The top record in South Texas is Jody Miller's "Ashes of Love."

Zoot Sims

Zoot Sims was one of a group of tenor saxophonists born in the mid-1920s whose early professional experience came in big bands and who idolized Lester Young. The basic jazz skills of most of these reedmen were developed by the time they had reached their early twenties. But their styles flowered in the bebop atmosphere in which jazz matured so dramatically following World War II.

Charlie Parker, who had been shaped by Young's example in his own formative period in the late 1930s, became the second great influence on this talented collection of tenor men. They melded Parker's complex harmonic discoveries with Young's sound (light, dry, sunny) and rhythm (powerful currents of swing beneath a laconic surface). In addition to Sims, some of the most accomplished members of this school of tenor saxophone were Al Cohn, Stan Getz, Paul Quinichette, Allen Eager, Brew Moore, Herbie Steward, Bill Perkins, Bob Cooper, Richie Kamuca, Dave Van Kreidt, Bill Holman, Phil Urso, and Don Lanphere. Some, particularly Quinichette and Moore, were made up of much larger components of Young than of Parker. It is safe to say that none of them could have become the artist he became if there had been no Lester Young.

Except for Quinichette, all of the players mentioned were white. A number of critics and musicologists have had sociological and psychological field days trying to explain why. Whatever the reasons, the fact is that most black tenor men who came up at the same time as our corps of white Lester Young disciples leaned more toward the overtly muscular work of Coleman Hawkins, Ben Webster, and Chu Berry than toward Young. In the analysis of jazz styles, however, the matter of influences is seldom clear-cut; Young was unquestionably a formative element in the playing of such black artists of the tough tenor school as Gene Ammons, Dexter Gordon, and Sonny Stitt. And the gruff, often raucous Ben Webster was an early and lasting hero of Sims, long tabbed as one of Young's stylistic progeny.

Among those generally considered major Young disciples, Cohn, Getz, and Sims achieved the most fame, initially because of their membership in Woody Herman's Second Herd (1947–49), the famous Four Brothers band, so called because of its saxophone section of three tenors and a baritone. The recording of "Four Brothers" featured Getz, Sims, Herbie Steward, and baritone saxophonist Serge Chaloff. Al Cohn, who had written arrangements for the band, replaced Steward in 1948.

Cohn's formidable abilities as a tenor soloist were equaled and to a large degree obscured by his talents for composing and arranging. Only in recent years has he concentrated on playing and made a wide jazz public fully aware of his gifts as an improviser.

Getz, one of the most lyrical and technically endowed hard-swinging tenor men of any stylistic school, was a darling of audiences years before his hit records of "Desafinado" and "The Girl from Ipanema" made his a household name in the early 1960s.

Sims had neither a top-forty record nor mass box office appeal. But almost from the beginning of his career, he had the unreserved admiration of virtually all jazz artists, whatever their generation or musical persuasion. Over the years, his following among listeners steadily grew. Musicians and aficionados alike recognized the basic human qualities of honesty and warmth that Sims projected in his playing without in any way diluting musical values or contriving to find an acceptable style. Complex in his creativity, as any great improviser incorporating the skills of jazz must be, Sims nonetheless was a kind and simple man whose deep feeling was manifest in his artistry.

The following pieces, one a tribute written shortly after he died, the other a review of a live performance, may offer some insights into the work and character of an artist of great appeal.

1985

Zoot Sims died March 23 at the age of fifty-nine. He was the most dependable and consistent of tenor saxophonists. Never dull, never predictable, he symbolized the spirit of jazz. A performance by Zoot carried two guarantees: it would swing, and it would have surprises. He was always on the brink of the next surprise and looking forward to it.

He required no start-up time. Zoot Sims was that rarity, a musician who was capable of swinging from the first note, and his swing was irresistible. He could generate it with superior rhythm sections, with inferior rhythm sections, and without rhythm sections.

He loved to play. I remember a 1955 Seattle concert by a touring group of jazz stars and the jam session afterward, a gathering of big-name players and the cream of local musicians in a little hall near the University of Washington. Zoot staked out a low stool near the piano and played until three in the morning, long after George Shearing, Chet Baker, Toots Thielemans, and the other visiting jazzmen had bailed out. It was just Sims and a rhythm section headed by pianist Paul Neves. Finally, as the rhythm players were packing up to leave, Zoot closed his eyes, rested his head against the wall, and kept on swinging as hard by himself as he had with piano, bass, and drums. It's an indelible image.

Years ago I was on a committee that put together the first New Orleans Jazz Festival. When deliberations began on the all-star group we wanted as a house band, Willis Conover of the Voice of America said, "Well, we'll have to have Zoot, of course," and looked around the table as we all nodded. Then we went on to pick the rest of the players.

Back in the sixties, during a two-week engagement at a New Orleans club called Economy Hall, Zoot found himself with two-thirds of a rhythm section when his bass player took ill. The only reasonably competent bassist available locally was far below Zoot's level and knew it. "Don't worry about it," Zoot told him. "Do what you can do. We'll get along fine." The bassist did what he could, but the first couple of nights were rough for him. Zoot was swinging magnificently while carrying his timorous bass player and adjusting his own improvisation to help the pianist provide simple harmonic guidelines. By the end of the first week the bassist was adequate. Zoot could have called New York for a replacement. Instead, he continued to bring along the New Orleans substitute. Night by night, the improvement was audible. When the engagement ended, the man was a considerably better bass player. And he idolized Zoot Sims.

John Haley Sims was born in California to parents who were vaudevillians. Young Jack was at first the drummer, then the clarinetist in the family band. When he joined Kenny Baker's band as a fifteen-year-old tenor saxophonist, each of the music stands was embellished with a nonsense word. The one he sat behind said "Zoot." That became his name.

Much has been made of Lester Young's influence on Zoot, and rightfully; he revered Young. But Ben Webster was his original inspiration. In 1944, at the age of nineteen, after having worked in four big bands, including Benny Goodman's, Sims replaced Webster in Sid Catlett's quartet. Webster remained a lifelong passion. One evening in the early seventies when Zoot, his wife Louise, and guitarist Jim Hall and his wife were visiting, I asked if anyone would like to hear a record. "All Too Soon," Zoot said without hesitation. We listened to Duke Ellington's 1940 masterpiece, with its regal Webster solo, three times. Zoot asked for a fourth hearing. "I'll never get enough of it. Every time I hear it, it's like the first time," he said.

Zoot married Louise Choo in 1970. To the casual observer it might have seemed an unusual pairing, the itinerant tenor player and the charming, sophisticated assistant to Clifton Daniel, managing editor of The New York Times. But it was one of the most graceful and affectionate of marriages, full of regard, appreciation, and laughter. A couple of years ago in San Francisco, where they had taken an apartment during Zoot's engagement at Keystone Korner, I picked them up for dinner. When I pulled up in front of the building, Zoot, his trench coat collar turned up against the foggy chill and the bill of his plaid car cap low over his eyes, was laughing at something Louise was saying. Then he spoke and she laughed, and as they entered the car they continued chatting and laughing, like the best friends they were. That was at a time when the medical news was not good for either of them and Zoot seemed frail, his Joseph Cotten good looks edged in gauntness. It was typical of their relationship that in the most uncertain of times they brought out the best in one another.

One bone-chilling December day years ago my wife and I went to Yankee Stadium with the Simses and baritone saxophonist Pepper Adams to watch the New York Giants get buried alternately by snow flurries and the Baltimore Colts defense. We could hear but not see the band hired by the Giants' management to entertain the fans and inspire the team. The clarinetist, Adams said, was either Benny Goodman or Sol Yaged, Goodman's greatest imitator. Benny may have been legendary for his thrift, Zoot observed, but he was too rich to need an outdoor gig in this kind of weather. It had to be Sol. Knowing how closely Zoot had worked with Goodman over the years, I had a hunch his ear alone could have led him to that conclusion. Sims apparently never had any of the extraordinary problems of abuse suffered by so many musicians who worked with the notoriously difficult Goodman, beyond simply having to put up with him. Goodman first hired him when Zoot was a teenager and often called him for reunion appearances long after Zoot was a star. Sims allowed as how he and Benny never talked much and that might have been the secret.

Back at Zoot and Louise's midtown apartment, unfrozen and fed, we played Ping-Pong, a game at which Zoot excelled with the same timing and deceptive relaxation that he brought to music. He also liked wood carving and skillfully created birds and other forms from driftwood. He was a major league gardener, and when he and Louise finally gave up the apartment to live full-time at their place in West Nyack, New York, he got into heavy-duty landscaping. Frequently during our get-togethers, Louise and I discussed music or the news business while Zoot and my wife exchanged accumulated wisdom about soil pH factors and peat moss.

In the mid-seventies Norman Granz began recording Zoot extensively, and there is now a series of fifteen Sims albums on Granz's Pablo label. They are all at least very good, and most of them are excellent. A sampler called *The Best of Zoot Sims* contains representative tracks. One of the most recent releases, *Quietly There: Zoot Sims Plays Johnny Mandel* (Pablo 2310–903), is among the best recordings in his forty-four-year career as a professional musician.

Primarily a tenor saxophonist, Sims was also respected for his work on alto sax and, in recent years, on soprano. Arnie Astrup, a Danish saxophonist and critic, may have summed up the feelings of many musicians and listeners when he said, "I hate the soprano saxophone. It is a clown isntrument. They should be burned, all. But when Zoot plays it, I like it."

One of the Pablo albums, *Zoot Sims: Soprano Sax* (Pablo 2310– 770), is devoted entirely to the instrument. He played it with such passion, involvement, and straightforward swing that I can't imagine anyone's not liking it.

As for his alto work, *Zoot Sims Plays Four Altos* (reissued on Impulse 29060) is one of the most admired saxophone records, not only for Sims's creativity and his accomplishment of overdubbing four alto parts but also for the ingenious compositions and arrangements by George Handy. Zoot's alto work is also outstanding on *The Big Stampede* (Biograph BLP-12064), a recording with his superb 1956 band, which included pianist John Williams and trumpeter Jerry Lloyd, two excellent, nearly forgotten musicians.

Zootcase (Prestige P–24061) is a two-album reissue of recordings made from 1950 through 1954. Among them is the memorable session with "Morning Fun," "Zootcase," "Tangerine," and the original recording of "The Red Door," which became a staple developed by Sims and his fellow tenor saxophonist Al Cohn. Besides the tenors, the band was made up of trombonist Kai Winding and the formidable rhythm section of pianist George Wallington, bassist Percy Heath, and drummer Art Blakey. This one belongs in any basic collection.

As the seventies ended, Zoot was stricken with health problems. The worst, a liver malady, prompted strong medical advice that he stop drinking. He did, after an initial de-escalation from Scotch to white wine, and his condition improved to the point that he was working nearly as often as before his illness. But then Zoot's medical troubles began to come in waves, requiring a lot of surgery. Cancer was discovered. The treatment was arduous. Nonetheless, he worked frequently and managed to keep his spirits up.

Last fall, while playing a jazz cruise in the Caribbean, he celebrated his birthday aboard ship. Mel Torme sang "Happy Birthday," then, as Leonard Feather reported it in the Los Angeles Times, Zoot addressed his well-wishers. "I'm fifty-nine today," he said, "but I have the body of a fifty-seven-year-old man."

That brand of durable low-key humor resulted in stories like the one about Zoot's ride with Al Cohn and record producer Jack Lewis in New York. Cohn was driving. Lewis was in the front passenger seat, Sims in the back. The conversation went like this:

"Hey, Jack, you have a glass eye, right?"

"Yeah."

Silence.

"Al, you have a glass eye, right?"

"Yeah."

Silence.

More silence.

"You guys keep both eyes on the road."

A few weeks before Zoot died, I ran into Cohn, who had been his closest musical associate since the two were members of Woody Herman's Four Brothers saxophone section in 1948 and 1949. Cohn and Sims were one of the most celebrated tenor sax teams in the history of jazz. Their collaborations were extraordinarily satisfying, leading the late Paul Desmond to observe that hearing Al and Zoot at the old Half Note in Lower Manhattan was "like going to get your back scratched."

Zoot and Al had just played a week at the Blue Note in New York. Al told me that although Zoot tired easily, his playing sounded as if he were at the peak of health. "I don't know where it comes from," Al said, "but he's doing it the way he wants to, and his doctors say it's the best thing." By then Zoot had been taken off chemotherapy, which wasn't working. His blood cells were not regenerating, and plans for further surgery were cancelled. No one who knew Zoot was surprised when he died. Everyone who knew him or his music felt a terrible loss.

The consolation is that there are dozens, probably hundreds, of albums with Zoot. Many are long out of print, but they pop up in bargain bins at record stores. When you see one, buy it. He is one of the few artists I can unreservedly recommend. You may not like the context, but you are almost certain to like Zoot.

1970

Zoot Sims/The Dukes of Dixieland, Economy Hall, New Orleans
Personnel: Sims, tenor saxophone; Dave Frishberg, piano; Chuck Badie, bass; Harold White, drums.

Dukes: Frank Assunto, trumpet, flugelhorn, vocals; Charlie Borneman, trombone; Harold Cooper, clarinet; Don Ewell, piano; Rudy Aikels, bass; Freddie Kohlman, drums.

The original Economy Hall was on Ursuline Street, and the bands that played it included King Oliver's and Buddy Petit's. Like such other celebrated jazz emporiums as Thom's Roadhouse and Funky Butt Hall, it was a place for dancing as well as listening and drinking. The new Economy Hall in the sumptuous Royal Sonesta Hotel on Bourbon Street was opened last summer as a successor in all regards. There are problems to be overcome, including poor acoustics and a lack of promotion. But given its location, a name policy, and a hotel management sympathetic to jazz, the room should flourish.

Sims arrived in town all but unheralded to share the stand with the house band, the Dukes of Dixieland. The word spread, and by the engagement Sims was filling the room. On all but the most turbulent up-tempo pieces the band attracted dancers without sacrificing the music. The tacit understanding seems to be that the bands will play jazz, and if you consider that jazz is music to dance to, please do. But don't ask for "Tuxedo Junction."

On the evening under consideration, Sims opened with Fats Waller's "Jitterbug Waltz" taken at a medium-up clip and swinging relentlessly from the first phrase. His long solo was full of splendid flutters, swoops, and shouts. Frishberg evoked the stride era in a couple of opening choruses, then settled down to develop some of the rhythmic possibilities of 3/4, building and releasing tension, turning the time around and making a judicious use of space. All with a finely honed humor. Why isn't there a Frishberg trio LP?*

Badie, a New Orleans bassist called in after the engagement was underway, had relaxed considerably during the run and turned in a loose, walking solo with none of the time-lag problems that plagued him earlier.

"My Old Flame" had the dance floor packed. The hallmark of Sims's ballad style is a remarkably unsentimental romanticism composed of warmth with detachment and humor, passion without bathos, lyricism, and an artless swing arising from total confidence and relaxation. Frishberg was a listening accompanist, responding to Sims's ideas as well as supplying the appropriate harmonic inspiration.

"Watch What Happens," done as a bossa nova, coaxed one middle-aged couple—big, blond people—onto the floor. The rhythm was strange to them, but they were determined to find a step to fit it, and they went through changes. Sims had one half-opened eye on them. They tried a new combination. Nothing. Sims went into his second chorus. They discarded their conventional steps, let go of one another and started experimenting with variations on the fox trot. Sims leaned into the solo, and they hit upon what looked like a Mexican hat dance without a hat. The audience applauded. Sims returned full concentration to his solo for three more choruses. The piece ended, and Sims honored his collaborators with a half bow. Lovely moment.

The rhythm section hit a perfect groove on "Red Door," and Sims poured out chorus after stomping chorus. He used a favorite

* By the late 1980s, there were several, and Frishberg had a successful career as a singer and songwriter as well.

device, repetition of a phrase, capped by the slightest hesitation, then a plunge back into the solo with furious improvisation and no discernible clichés. Frishberg, who moves on the bench like a dancer, worked his variations on "San" into a vigorous solo, his right hand making lightning raids on the upper register. Sims and White exchanged choruses, the drummer nearly matching Sims's energy.

"Willow Weep for Me" brought out more of Sims's ballad magic, and the dancers. "Pernod 806" was a 16-bar piece harmonically like "Doxy" and "Hurry on Down" and taken way, way up. Badie had tempo problems, but Sims didn't seem to notice. He roared through the familiar changes, his tone taking on a darker quality, the music intensifying with each chorus so that when he ended his solo several minutes later, the effect was like the release of a head of steam.

"It Had to Be You" incorporated an easy kind of swing, and Sims was closer to Lester Young than he had been all night. Frishberg employed tremolo to amusing effect. The set closed with Al Cohn's "Zootcase," a loping blues line from the early fifties that Sims uses as his ending theme.

The warmth of the audience toward Sims was impressive, as was his toward them.

Dukes of Dixieland

The Dukes of Dixieland can be classified as a Dixieland band because of repertoire and reputation rather than style. Leader Assunto's phrasing and tone are closer to Fats Navarro than to Bunk Johnson. He is our leading Dixiebop trumpet player. When Kohlman and Assunto trade fours on "Sweet Georgia Brown," it sounds more like New York in 1947 than New Orleans in 1925 or the forties revival.

Bassist Aikels is greatly responsible for the contemporary sound of the band. His choice of notes in the ensembles reflects his thorough schooling and his experience with modern groups, and he is a melodically inventive soloist.

On Waller's "Keepin' out of Mischief Now," Assunto set the contemplative mood in an opening out-of-tempo chorus, unaccompanied, which was followed by an ensemble exercise in dynamics, then a lacy Walleresque solo by Ewell. Harold Cooper, a small, quiet man, does the difficult clarinet things easily. His rideout with Assunto had the intensity of a Sidney Bechet-Tommy Ladnier duet.

On "When the Saints Go Marching In," (which doesn't have to be a drag) Cooper went into the superfalsetto range of the clarinet, impeccably in tune, and played phrases that would have seemed corny if they hadn't been so flawlessly rendered. He was poking fun at the "Saints," but what could have been heard as contempt was

transformed into genuine, if broad, humor. Sims, calling Cooper
the Maynard Ferguson of the clarinet, correctly pegged him as "a
bitch."

Assunto played flugelhorn on Lennon and McCartney's "Here,
There and Everywhere" with concern for the considerable melodic
values of the piece. In the second chorus he offered slight embellishments, with an attractive vibrato. Over six weeks, I have heard him
play the tune perhaps a dozen times; it's always close to the melody,
it's never the same twice, and it's always lovely. Assunto's work
takes on softer outlines when he's playing flugelhorn. Unlike many
of the players who pick up the bigger horn, he uses it to express a
different emotional range of his music—and not only on ballads.

"Royal Garden Blues" gave Ewell an opportunity to stride, which
he does with a soft touch and great authority. *Man Here Plays Fine
Piano,* one of his album titles declared years ago, and nothing has
changed. Assunto's choruses were reminiscent of the lyricism of
Kenny Dorham. Aikel walked the band to a driving ensemble close.

Borneman's trombone was blowsy in the Kid Ory tradition on
pieces like "Bourbon Street Parade," but his solo in "Georgia on
My Mind" was understated and tasty. Assunto sang—well—and
played a lovely flugelhorn solo. Ewell had a masterly chorus on
"Georgia," creating a melody the rival of the original. The audience
didn't applaud, but Assunto did.

On "Bill Bailey," Ewell quoted "Singing in the Rain," and Assunto wrapped up the piece with ringing phrases out of Louis
Armstrong.

Kohlman's drum feature was "Sleep," and the long solo had con-
tinuity and thematic development. He made good use of his time in
the spotlight, but Kohlman was most impressive behind the band,
driving the ensembles and booting the soloists along. His time is impeccable, and the success of this latest edition of the Dukes is due in
great measure to Kohlman, one of the most inspirational drummers
New Orleans has produced.

But Assunto is the leader and guiding force of the band, an excellent player, a good singer, a witty master of ceremonies and, with
his modish new wardrobe and hair style, an imposing stage pres-

ence. Assunto has weathered the difficult period following the death of his brother Fred and the end of the Dukes as a family enterprise and built one of the finest small bands in jazz, categories aside.

Frank Assunto died in February 1974 following a short illness. The name "The Dukes of Dixieland" became the legal property of promoters outside the Assunto family.

Gerry Mulligan

Some musicians, once they move past their salad days and establish careers as identifiable stylists, rarely leave the confines of their own groups or, if they do, seldom mingle in performances with players outside their own styles or eras. There are many sensible, even laudable, reasons for such isolation. Some are purely artistic. Some are commercial. Others have to do with preservation of image, which is usually another manifestation of salability. Still others concern sheer preservation of physical and psychic energy.

But there have always been in jazz a few artists at the pinnacle of their profession, admired by their peers, flexible in outlook, quickly adaptable to a variety of circumstances, who love to play in virtually any musical setting of quality. They include Benny Carter, Mary Lou Williams, Dizzy Gillespie, Roy Eldridge, Chick Corea, Charlie Haden, Sonny Stitt, Paul Gonsalves, and Zoot Sims. Charlie Parker was likely to show up on any bandstand, sit in, and enjoy himself hugely, regardless of what kind of music was being played. But among major jazz artists, it may be that no one has sat in more often with bands playing in a greater range of styles than has Gerry Mulligan.

Mulligan, master baritone saxophonist, small group innovator, one of the premier arrangers, is at home in every jazz idiom with the possible exception of the most outré elements of the avant-garde. He was born in New York City in 1927. His early arranging experience came when he was a teenager in Philadelphia; he was nineteen when Gene Krupa's big band recorded several of his arrangements, among them "Disc Jockey Jump." He wrote for and played with Miles Davis, Elliot Lawrence, and Claude Thornhill, then moved to California in 1952. There, he debuted a pianoless quartet with *trumpeter Chet Baker as the other horn. That unconventional band achieved popularity with astonishing speed and although it wasn't together long, it brought lasting fame to both Mulligan and Baker. Indeed, no doubt to Mulligan's frustration, it is still the group most people think of when they hear his name, despite his many distinguished achievements since the early 1950s.*

Gerry Mulligan/Chet Baker:
Carnegie Hall Concert

1974

Backstage, there was enough tension to make things fairly interesting. A near fist fight. A domestic hassle. A financial crisis. I wish I could tell you all the gossip. But you came to hear music, and I have to face all those people again. So let's play it safe and take the non-libelous semi-documentary approach.

(Carnegie Hall, New York City, November 24, 1974.)

Producer Don Friedman (not the pianist) had tried for months, even years, to reunite several giants of the West Coast jazz of the 1950s. Some of them had been reluctant to the point of intractability. Others had been less reluctant, and they include Chet Baker and Gerry Mulligan. Why all this greater and lesser reluctance, you may ask. Because creative musicians tend to think about what they're doing and what they're going to do rather than what they've done. The idea of assembling to play their golden oldies usually elicits the enthusiasm you might have had from Picasso if you'd suggested he re-enter his blue period.

On the other hand, Mulligan and Baker hadn't played together in ten years, and it was intriguing to wonder whether the old magic still worked. Besides, the money was okay and there seemed to be an audience. So why not? It is conceivable that Picasso would have been willing to paint some blue period updates, as opposed to copies. No one really expected to hear Gerry and Chet do their classic recorded solos note for note. Well, someone out there probably did, but the capacity audience was wide open to the updating of every tune, and to the new pieces.

"What'll we do first?," Mulligan wondered aloud on stage.

"'Line for Lyons'?," Chet suggested.

"Lazy."

"It's something to warm up on."

Some warmup.

Chet is inclined to worry more than Gerry. After Baker's set with his quintet, he confided to Mulligan backstage:

"I didn't feel comfortable."

"You're not supposed to feel comfortable," Mulligan grinned.

That seemed to make Baker more comfortable. But he said he was feeling the pressure of playing Carnegie Hall.

"It's like recording with strings. You can't help feeling all that weight. I'd just as soon be playing at Stryker's Pub."

The discomfort wasn't audible.

Chet stood behind the curtain, hands in pockets, locked into Mulligan's solo on "For an Unfinished Woman" as if he were trying to absorb what Gerry had been up to for a decade.

This was the first recording of Mulligan's "A Song for Strayhorn." One of Gerry's loveliest ballads, it's a remembrance of the man who was Duke Ellington's inseparable musical companion until Billy's death in 1967. Congratulated by the backstage coterie on the beauty of the composition and the performance, Mulligan was asked why he had been keeping "Strayhorn" under wraps.

"I always like to save a few surprises," he said.

Mulligan thrives and capitalizes on surprises. At half time he and Bob James, the pianist, reviewed missed cues.

"We came to the A-flat 7th and I said 'Whaaaaat?' but it worked out beautifully," Mulligan laughed. "Why worry? We'll always recover."

"In 'Unfinished Woman,'" James said, "I just kept at that little figure and, whaddaya know, we had four-part harmony going."

"It was lovely," Gerry assured him.

"Of course, little goofs can be edited out later. They can be isolated," James offered.

"Well, I suppose so, but it really came out very nicely."

At the bar, a moderately shabby man offered to buy Mulligan a drink. Someone else paid for it. The would-be host, who had been praising Gerry as the paragon of baritone players, rose to a crescendo of indignation and obscenity, loudly denouncing Mulligan as a woeful musician who wasn't fit to trim Harry Carney's reeds. "Boy, that's the last time I won't let him buy me a drink," said Mulligan, retreating.

For Gerry's set, the basic rhythm section of Ron Carter on bass, drummer Harvey Mason, and James was expanded to include vibraharpist and percussionist Dave Samuels and John Scofield, a young guitarist with romantic leanings and an inclination toward relaxed, understated swing in his melodic lines. He is one of the few younger guitarists who seems to be exploring the style of Jim Hall, possibly because he is one of the few temperamentally and technically equipped to do so.

The amended rhythm team stayed on for the Baker-Mulligan set and added new colors to the basic sound of the Mulligan Quartet that featured Baker and became a sensation in 1952. "Line for Lyons" and "My Funny Valentine" were staples of the original quartet. For the nostalgic, there is abundant evocativeness in "Valentine," a piece Chet owns in all but copyright. As for Mulligan, he has simply never played better than in the past three or four years, and his unfailingly energizing presence is beautifully represented here.

The music Gerry, Chet, and friends played in this auspicious reunion takes care of that intriguing question; Indeed, the old magic still works.

Chet Baker

Baker was born in Oklahoma but lived in Glendale, California, from the ages of ten to sixteen, when he joined the Army and played in the 298th Army Band in Berlin. In 1948, at the end of his two-year hitch, he studied harmony and theory at El Camino College. In 1950 he re-enlisted so he could play in the famous Army band at the Presidio in San Francisco, and in off-duty hours took part in jam sessions in San Francisco clubs, including Bop City. But after being transferred to a post in the Arizona desert, he went over the hill. Eventually, he gave himself up in San Francisco and, following observation in a psychiatric clinic, was discharged.

There followed a period of odd musical jobs in Los Angeles. Then in 1952 he joined a crowd of trumpet players at an audition being held by Charlie Parker, who was in the market for a front-line partner for a series of West Coast engagements. After hearing Baker, Parker announced that the audition was over, and the unknown found himself working for the most idolized musician of the post-war era. Later that year he joined Gerry Mulligan's quartet, made his first records, began winning polls, and set out on a career filled with exhilarating highs and dreadful lows.

Despite the inevitable downgrading by critics and peers when a young artist achieves a great deal in a short time, there is early musical evidence in the form of bootleg tapes made of the Parker-Baker band that Baker's work in the very early 1950s crackled with energy and was quite unlike any other trumpeter's. His closest associates, Mulligan and pianist Russ Freeman, have spoken of the awe they felt when Baker was at his most inspired. Baker, himself awe-struck at Parker's approval, has said, "When Bird went east he told Dizzy and Miles, 'You better look out, there's a little white cat out on the west coast who's gonna eat you up.'"

The following passages about Chet Baker are from liner notes written for two of his albums.

1974

In 1953, upon the success of his best-selling recording of "My Funny Valentine" with the Gerry Mulligan Quartet, Chet Baker became an instant star. He began winning polls here and abroad with rhythmic regularity for five years. His "Valentine" solo was soft and lyrical. Lyricism seemed to be Baker's stock in trade, although he was capable of playing crackling bop lines of great intricacy and inventiveness.

And he sang. He sang with . . . well, let Rex Reed describe it . . . "an innocent sweetness that made girls fall right out of their saddle oxfords." Before he had time to digest the fact of his sudden celebrity as a trumpet soloist, Chet found himself winning polls as a vocalist. In one, he was tied with Nat Cole. From obscurity to status among the jazz public as a more popular trumpet player than Louis Armstrong, Dizzy Gillespie, and Miles Davis, and as a singer the equal of Nat Cole. All in the space of slightly more than a year. Enough to turn the head of the shy young son of an Oklahoma cowboy guitarist. Or send him off the deep end. But the deep end was a few years away, and Baker kept turning out best-selling albums, most of which were also critical successes. He became a leader. He toured Europe. He made a movie. He went off the deep end.

Chet says he "got sick" in 1957. What made him sick was heroin. He battled it, without much success. He made records, some of them among his best. He played clubs and concerts. But narcotics detectives were usually in the house. Baker was harassed out of one European nation after another, then back home again for more harassment. In 1968, he'd had enough. He began methadone treatment. For two years, he didn't play.

This is Chet's first major recording since the night in San Francisco in 1968 when five junkies relieved him of his dope money and his teeth and made him decide he'd have to give up heroin or die.

"Believe me," Chet explains, "when a trumpet player has had his teeth pulled, it is a comeback."

Baker says that with the lack of self-pity that is as characteristic as the absence of hyperbole when he evaluates his artistry, past and present.

Of those early triumphs in the polls, he says "I never really believed in that, and I never really believed that I deserved it. As far as my playing now, I believe I have progressed conceptually, which is the important thing. At the time I won the polls, my style was very lyrical, a style the average person could listen to and understand without being overwhelmed with technique. I can still play that way, very cool, few notes, lots of empty spaces. I can also play very fly, very hard. I believe I play ten times better now than I did then. And I don't want to lose people, I want them to understand what I play on my horn."

1977

In 1938, five months before he died so tragically young, Thomas Wolfe went to Purdue University to make a speech in which he summed up his life. Recalling the publication and overwhelming success of his first novel, *Look Homeward, Angel,* Wolfe discussed with frankness the things he had not known in 1929.

. . . I did not know that for a man who wants to continue with the creative life, to keep on growing and developing, this cheerful idea of happy establishment, of continuing now as one has started, is nothing but a delusion and a snare. I did not know that if a man really has in him the desire and the capacity to create, the power of further growth and further development, there can be no such thing as an easy road. I did not know that so far from having found out about writing, I had really found out almost nothing . . . I made a first and simple utterance; but I did not know that each succeeding one would not only be . . . more difficult than the last, but would be completely different, that with each new effort would come new desperation, the new, and old, sense of having to begin from the beginning all over again; of being face to face again with the old naked facts of self and work; of realizing again that there is no help anywhere save the help and strength that one can find within himself."

Wolfe's encapsulation of the challenge and agony of artistic growth is as timeless as are his books. There are few mature creative artists who haven't reached the conclusions drawn in that paragraph of insight and honesty. And there is no jazz artist alive who parallels Wolfe's experience of struggle and growth more exactly than does Chet Baker.

The barest outline of Baker's career . . . the early success, the decline and crash, the self-doubts, the discipline and control of his comeback . . . is a synopsis of the process Wolfe described at Purdue.

Born in 1929, the year of Wolfe's first triumph, Baker achieved his early acclaim in 1952 when his solo on the Gerry Mulligan Quartet recording of "My Funny Valentine" made the record a best seller and young trumpeter an overnight star. His acceptance included popular and critical response unusual for a new jazz artist, and it continued more or less unabated for five years. Then Baker began a thirteen-year contest with heroin which heroin nearly won. But after one climactic drug ordeal that could have cost him his life and left him with dental damage that might have ended the career of someone less determined, Baker faced Wolfe's "new desperation, the new, and old, sense of having to begin from the beginning all over again; of being face to face again with the old naked facts of self and work; of realizing again that there is no help anywhere save the help and strength that one can find within himself."

He kicked the habit. He imposed upon himself the pain and frustration of adapting his embouchure to the new configuration of his teeth and lips. Having overcome those obstacles, he began to move into a new and deeper phase of development as a creative musician.

In no other field of expression has the artist less chance of privately refining the creative process than in jazz. The nature of the work is public. Every experiment, every advancement, every set-back is for all to hear. Baker's return to active playing caused something of a stir in New York in 1973. His work was uneven, but there were stretches of brilliance. In club dates he was often hampered by unworthy rhythm sections, and he is not one of those soloists who plunges ahead impervious to the slings and arrows of bad time and wrong chords. But if you heard Baker often through his renaissance period of the 1970s, you were aware that in spite of occasional aimlessness, his expression was deepening, that within himself he was finding a new profoundness. There was a burnish and a passion that, for all his fleetness and lyricism, Baker had not demonstrated during his days of early fame. Having developed his robust yet wistful romanticism even further, he achieves one of the most expressive solos of his career in the album at hand on Bud Powell's "Un Poco Loco." In fact, lifted and inspired by some of the best young players of the day, and by Don Sebesky's stimulating settings of the music, Baker's performance throughout this collection shows him to be at a new level of growth.

The implications of Sebesky's song title inspired by Wolfe's novel and of the novel itself are full of meaning for Baker. It is probably best expressed by Wolfe in a long letter to a friend, a letter written about his book but, typically, never mailed. In it, Wolfe listed all the things to which you can't return, from family to dreams. And he concluded that ". . . although you can't go home again, the home of every one of us is in the future: there is no other way."

For Chet Baker, renewed and rededicated as an artist, there is no need to try to go home again; the future is full of challenge and promise.

After 1977, Baker roamed the world, occasionally maintaining his own band but more often appearing with local rhythm sections, and recording copiously. As it had been for twenty-five years, his level of performance was inconsistent, but at its best his playing still had the ability to go directly to a listener's emotions in a way attained by few artists in any medium.

Many people close to Baker believe that in his final years he sometimes succumbed to his old nemesis, heroin, and that it may have been involved in his puzzling death. Baker died on a tour of Europe, in the early morning darkness of May 13, 1988, in a fall from a second story hotel window in Amsterdam.

Art Pepper

Among the leading alto saxophonists of his generation, Art Pepper shared with Paul Desmond and Lee Konitz the distinction of not being a Charlie Parker imitator. Although Parker's inescapable influence had its effect on Pepper's work, his strongest early influence was the tenor saxophonist Zoot Sims. Sims was two months younger than Pepper but even more precocious, having become a professional at fifteen, and Pepper studied his playing at jam sessions and gigs in the Los Angeles area, where both men were born in 1925. Later in the 1940s, when bebop broke through, Pepper was to absorb the harmonic syntax developed by Parker and his colleagues. Two decades after, he incorporated some of the unbridled methods of John Coltrane's later work. But even when Pepper had consolidated his highly personal style and taken it through several evolutionary steps, his playing carried intimations of the Sims warmth and relaxation.

Pepper's musicianship was always admired, although in evaluating his playing critics and peers were a bit baffled by his unclassifiability. In the arts, what cannot be pigeon-holed is frequently regarded warily. Since his death in 1982, Pepper's work, like Paul Desmond's, has been increasingly recognized by musicians and critics for its power and universality. It seems inevitable that regard for Pepper's music will continue to grow and that, when ultimately inconsequential considerations of sociology and fashion recede, he will be remembered as one of the important soloists of his generation. Happily, as the following pieces indicate, the process of recognition began before his death.

Art Pepper: *Living Legend*
Contemporary S7633
Spotlight Review

1976

Art Pepper, alto saxophone; Hampton Hawes, piano; Charlie Haden, bass; Shelly Manne, drums.

"Ophelia"; "Here's that Rainy Day"; "What Laurie Likes"; "Mr. Yohe"; "Lost Life"; "Samba Mom-Mom."

Except for a couple of solos on a Buddy Rich album, this is the first record date for Art Pepper since November of 1960, when he did "Intensity" for Contemporary. Through reissues and through the force of his originality of conception, he has been remembered during those fifteen years as a major player. His records of the 1950s sound fresh and adventuresome, as this new one will fifteen years from now, for Pepper is perennially a fresh and adventurous player, surveying new developments and selecting from them what works within his style. On this album, the title of which must be an embarrassment to Pepper despite its accuracy, there are touches of John Coltrane and Ornette Coleman as well as the firm foundation of Parker that has always undergirded his improvisation.

Pepper's difficulties are well known; they plagued an enormous number of jazzmen of his generation. Like Hampton Hawes, his colleague here, he spent years in prisons on narcotics convictions. Like Hawes, he has overcome the monster and emerged from the struggle a strengthened person and a deeper artist. Successes like theirs console us to some degree for the bitter losses of the Charlie Parkers, Wardell Grays, Fats Navarros, and Serge Chaloffs. Aside from the free aspects of Pepper's playing today, the listener will hear an emotional concentration, a cry—sometimes a sob and sometimes a joyous shout—that comes from the wisdom of experience.

In that sense, this is autobiographical music, a testament of the artist's life.

In 1957, Pepper made the celebrated LP called *Art Pepper Meets the Rhythm Section*, with Red Garland, Paul Chambers, and Philly Joe Jones of the Miles Davis Quintet. It was the best rhythm section of the day. If Hawes, Haden, and Manne worked together regularly, they could quickly develop the same reputation in the seventies. Pepper's meeting with them is just as impressive as the get-togethers with the Davis rhythm sections of 1957 and 1960. On the blues called "Mr. Yohe," the section builds such a powerful swing that by the thirteenth of his fifteen choruses, Pepper has been propelled to an intensity that for a few bars becomes nearly unbearable. It is a cathartic listening experience. Pepper's melodic and lyrical qualities are frequently mentioned. He is also a formidable rhythmic player. Following the piano chorus on "Yohe," when the swing has diminished to a merely sensational level, Pepper and Manne play a three-chorus duet, throwing the time back and forth like a ball and never losing the pulse. No drummer does this better than Manne; remember the ten-inch LP of duets he and Russ Freeman made in 1954?

"Samba Mom-Mom" is really more West Indian calypso than samba, packed with the lunging, dancing rhythmic movement that Sonny Rollins likes to play around with. Lee Morgan was another master of it. Pepper is definitely in the same league. This is a happy, even ecstatic, performance, with some stunning Birdlike passages from Art, including a delightful turnaround on "Billie's Bounce." During an exchange of fours, Hawes and Pepper feed off each other's ideas in an amazingly logical cooperative effort at building a solo. Hawes solos on electric piano, with a succession of bell-like phrases. With one of the most finely developed senses of keyboard touch, Hawes is able to avoid the muddy sound so many pianists bring to the electric instrument. Manne's short solo is musical and entirely successful.

Pepper's penchant for going outside is evident on "Ophelia." What seems to be a late-period Coltrane influence is detectable here, and Pepper has the musicianship and mature judgment to keep it from using him, as it has so many musicians who try to incorporate free playing into their styles. The overtones are Middle Eastern and moody, although the piece is fairly bright in tempo. "Lost Life" has a brooding, Moorish atmosphere, with a blues cast and a minor feeling. Pepper makes dazzling, remarkably clean and fast runs without compromising the thoughtful mood of the performance. He is a virtuoso but not an exhibitionist.

"Here's That Rainy Day" and "What Laurie Likes" display opposite sides of Pepper's personality. The ballad is sheer beauty, with a moving chorus by Pepper, his sound deep and burnished, his long-tone duet with Haden at the end a sonic wonder. "What Laurie Likes," obviously, is to have a hell of a good time. This is rhythm and blues, with Shelly playing the kind of drums he did on "Big Girl" in the 1950s and Art spinning out genuine soul music, good to hear after all the manufactured funk we keep getting from soloists backed by strings, French horns, voices, and synthesizers. Hawes has an ingeniously constructed solo on electric piano, and there's a marvelous round of four-bar exchanges.

Little has been said about Haden's contribution. He does little soloing, although he is superb when he does solo. He's primarily in a supporting role and, as always, he offers precisely the kind of support that's called for, with that added element of inspiration that makes him one of the great bassists. Haden's tone and his placement of notes make him unique. He has never been better recorded than he is on this album.

Pepper's generation produced a bounty of superior alto players, a number of whom are still extremely productive. They include the two Sonnys, Criss and Stitt; Phil Woods, Paul Desmond, Lee Konitz, and James Moody. For a long while, it seemed that Pepper's career had ended. With this record, he has clearly announced that he is back and playing better than ever. In the minds of serious listeners, Art Pepper was never really away, but it is satisfying to know he is well, happy, and again creating important music.

Art Pepper's Last Chorus

1982

Art Pepper had been quiet and a little sad all evening. But he grinned at the irony of posing for the Polaroid photographer in the Bourbon Street Jail. San Quentin was on his mind. He and his wife, Laurie, were in New Orleans on a book-plugging tour, and everywhere they went he was asked about the five years he had spent in prison on a narcotics conviction. What had evolved into his autobiography, *Straight Life* (Schirmer Books, 1979), began as a series of cathartic tape recordings in which Pepper told Laurie everything he could recall about his unremittingly broken life. His memory was comprehensive, and he spared himself and his readers nothing.

Pepper's merchant seaman father was twenty-nine and his mother was fifteen when they were married. He was rarely at home after Pepper was born, and she was often drunk. Pepper learned to play the clarinet at nine, the alto saxophone at twelve. At seventeen, he had played in the bands of Gus Arnheim and Benny Carter and was working with Stan Kenton. After two years in the Army, he freelanced around Los Angeles, then rejoined Kenton in 1947. His reputation as a brilliant and original saxophonist became established.

By 1950, when he was twenty-five, Pepper was a veteran of the military, big bands, alcohol, pills, and pot. That was the year he became addicted to heroin. He was first sent to jail on a narcotics conviction in 1953. From then until 1966 he spent more time in prison than out. After a short period of rehabilitation, during which he played with Buddy Rich's band, Pepper reached the depths. Sick almost literally unto death, in 1969 he checked himself into Synanon. There he met Laurie, who, along with methadone maintenance, proved to be therapy and salvation. He resumed playing and recording, and he regarded himself with wary realism. "I'm a junkie. And that's what I will die as—a junkie."

His account of the hell of his struggle with heroin puts into miraculous relief the beauty of his artistic achievement. From a childhood of rejection and neglect, Pepper had taken into manhood the only trustworthy and stable element he was to know in his first fifty years, his music. Not until he met Laurie did he have another reliable anchor.

Pepper's expressiveness on alto saxophone had deepened and broadened, and his recordings after 1976 had been acclaimed as his finest. Finally lauded worldwide as a master soloist, he was, in his cautious way, basking in the recognition and the star treatment. At dinner, between waves of his customary reticence, Pepper allowed that his playing was at a keen edge he had been seeking for years. He said that at last he was often able to accept his performances. It's a nice memory of Art Pepper. At a sparkling table under the old ceiling fans at Arnaud's with the woman who helped him gain control of his life, he was content and smiling.

In June, he died shortly after suffering a stroke as he sat at their breakfast table chatting with Laurie. He was fifty-six.

Modern Jazz Quartet

The big band Dizzy Gillespie formed in 1946 was one of the most powerful and exciting in the history of jazz. Its brass and reed sections were given arrangements that demanded heavy expenditures of energy. The horn players were young and full of stamina, but they were not superhuman. Gillespie knew that to preserve them, relief had to be provided.

So the rhythm section performed, often for long stretches, while in the background embouchures recovered from the grueling charts put together by Gillespie, Gil Fuller, George Russell, and John Lewis. The rhythm section consisted of pianist Lewis, bassist Ray Brown, vibraharpist Milt Jackson, and drummer Kenny Clarke. Clarke was the drummer who, in the late 1930s, freed the bass drum from its strict 4/4 function, using it for accents, and showed the way to the rhythmic changes that in part led to the evolution of bebop.

The section functioned as a band within the Gillespie band, and a close musical and personal bond was created among its members, particularly between Jackson and Lewis. The four men eventually went their own ways. But in August, 1951 they reassembled as the Milt Jackson Quartet for a record date on Gillespie's short-lived Dee Gee label. The resulting four pieces and others recorded the next month and in the spring of 1952 have been reissued in The First Q (Savoy 1106). In them, there is magnificent music made by four empathetic, and very strong, individualists.

Later, John Lewis's abilities for composition and organization, and his conception of a group identity, led inevitably to his becoming the band's musical director. Many of the ideas germinating since the Gillespie big band days and expressed in the Dee Gee recordings took on more formal shape as the quartet worked them out *and intensively rehearsed Lewis's sketches and arrangements. Lewis's credentials included work not only with Gillespie but with Charlie Parker, the other bebop horn genius. He had also accompanied Lester Young and was one of the driving conceptual forces behind the Miles Davis "Birth of the Cool" band. One of the most distinctive blues soloists in the modern idiom, he combined his impeccable jazz background with a deep feeling for the forms of European music.*

When the Modern Jazz Quartet was officially launched by that name in 1952, Brown had been replaced by Percy Heath, a less compelling bassist but one whose capacity for growth became quickly and startlingly apparent. The MJQ became a full-time unit in 1954. When Clarke left in 1955, the drum chair was filled by Connie Kay, a young veteran of Lester Young's combo. Lewis, Jackson, Heath, and Kay have been the stable personnel of the Modern Jazz Quartet ever since.

Creating a quartet setting that would encompass both Jackson, one of the most unrestrainedly earthy soloists in jazz, and Lewis's preoccupation with formalism presented a challenge brilliantly met. Although Lewis was to be accused of bridling Jackson, recorded evidence clearly shows that the vibraharpist functions most effectively in an organized context. It is often assumed that Lewis imposed tightly arranged structures on the quartet, but many of the "arrangements" are meldings of written material, variable patterns growing out of the members' collective experience, and spontaneous creation. The fact is that among listeners to the MJQ, only experienced jazz musicians are likely to know what is written and what is improvised, and many of them have been fooled often enough to be amazed at what seems to be the group's extrasensory perception.

In the early days of the quartet, Lewis said his vision for the group grew out of the essence of the Count Basie band of the thirties and forties, ensemble playing that sounded like "the spontaneous playing of ideas which were the personal expression of each member of the band rather than the arrangers or composers." The MJQ has achieved that difficult goal.

In 1974, largely because Milt Jackson wanted to strike out on his

*own, the Modern Jazz Quartet disbanded. Each of its members in-
volved himself in an assortment of successful pursuits. In 1981, they
reunited temporarily for a tour of Japan. But they found such satisfaction in working together again, and the reaction and demand
among audiences were so overwhelming that reunions, tours, club
dates, and recordings became more and more frequent. By the approach of the 1990s, the Modern Jazz Quartet could once more be
considered virtually a permanent entity.*

Modern Jazz Quartet/Paul Desmond

Town Hall, New York City, December 25 1971

The MJQ decked Town Hall with a notably robust holiday spirit
Christmas night. Desmond's participation as guest artist was more
than Yuletide ornamentation. Floppy hats, beards, and leather gar-
ments embellished the house, which was full. At least a third of the
audience was between eighteen and twenty-five. Since none of the
five musicians is under forty and there is no rock mystique sur-
rounding them, the clear conclusion is that the young people came
to hear some uncompromised and uncompromising jazz music.
That's what they heard.

Applause greeted the opening notes of a superb performance of
"Django," that classic piece of Lewisania in which the quartet has
discovered greater meaning year by year. With this band, there are
often visual clues on stage to support the aural evidence that the
group is having a particularly good night. Sudden smiles. Amused
glances. Raised eyebrows. That sort of thing started about a chorus
and a half into "Django" and continued through the last notes of
the encore.

The MJQ played three Christmas songs, converting "News of the Day" (We Wish You a Merry Christmas) into an ingenious calypso excursion during which Heath generated an amiable, lunging forward motion. "England's Carol" (God Rest Ye Merry, Gentlemen) and "The Twelve Days of Christmas" have been featured by the quartet for many years; they were offered with the old charm and renewed vitality that marks all of the MJQ's recent work.

Four relatively recent Lewis compositions, "Visitor from Venus," "Visitor from Mars," "Plastic Dreams," and "Dancing" opened extended solo space for Lewis and Jackson. Both were in top form, Lewis never wittier, more subtle, nor inventive, Jackson swinging relentlessly and chewing up the changes. Electronic assistance from a tape loop, filling the hall with appropriately eerie effects, was judiciously used on "Mars."

Heath was extremely strong all evening, his tone in the upper register frequently reminiscent of the dry, full-bodied sound for which Oscar Pettiford was so admired. He and Kay work together uncannily, increasing in intensity or loosening up behind a soloist as if by ESP. Kay may be the living archetype of the listening drummer. When a soloist is ready to take a new direction, he somehow knows whence and is there to lend appropriate support. In that regard and others, he is a latterday Sid Catlett: the drummer as accompanist and catalyst rather than crashing ego. His cymbal work is as functional as it is innovative. Each of the triangles, bell trees, and exotic chimes adorning his drum set plays a well defined and integral role in the quartet's performances.

Jackson doesn't make a practice of quoting, but at the beginning of his lovely solo on Tim Hardin's "Misty Roses," he pulled the neat harmonic trick of working in a snatch of "To a Wild Rose." Jackson's "Monterey Rose" was greeted by applause at the outset, and he responded with a great solo.

Desmond has recorded frequently with Heath and copiously with Kay. When he walked on stage their faces lit up in proprietary grins. Lewis also seemed to be anticipating the occasion, crouching over the keyboard, hands at the ready. Jackson looked vaguely skeptical, but that expression is chronic. Desmond's incomparably clear alto sound inspired applause that lasted through the first several bars of

"Greensleeves." Although there was a certain stiffness in the performance, it quickly became obvious that Lewis, Heath, and Kay are
an ideal rhythm section for Desmond. By the time he hit the bridge
of the second tune, "You Go to My Head," things had relaxed considerably and stayed relaxed through eight more pieces about which
the only criticism is that the soloists played too few choruses.

Desmond's celebrated propensity to quote was in check for the
evening, with exceptions; he managed to work in one of his favorite
melodies from "Petrouchka," and there was a line from the Gerry
Mulligan songbook. Mostly, however, he just dug in, relishing
Lewis's firm, suggestive comping and the buoying support of all that
power in reserve built up by Heath and Kay. "Valeria" was a haunt-
ing, enigmatic Lewis piece worthy of further exploration. Desmond
and Jackson were outstanding on it and on "La Paloma Azul,"
which followed. Desmond was at the peak of his lyricism on the
Mexican folk song, which is so attractive harmonically that it is sur-
prising more jazz players haven't adopted it.

Now the concert took on the aspects of a well-controlled jam session. There were good solos all 'round on "East of the Sun," and
a splendid exchange of fours between Jackson and Desmond, the
two working together to build what amounted to a tandem solo. It
could profitably have continued for at least a chorus or two. The
melody of "Jesus Christ Superstar" (that's right) was used to launch
the quintet into stimulating counterpoint; the improvisation was
not connected with the changes of the tune, an excellent decision.
Back to familiar ground with a ballad both the MJQ and Desmond
have recorded, "Here's That Rainy Day." Fine solos again, with
honors going to Jackson.

Then came the piece that should have lasted forever, a blues,
"Bags' Groove." Desmond applied long lines and that remarkable
sense of when to change pace and came up with his most interesting
solo of the night, swinging hard. When his solo had ended, there
wasn't an immobile foot in the house. Jackson and Lewis maintained the intensity through their solos. When the audience applauded for an encore, it was more of that they wanted.

But they got (what else?) "Take Five." 5/4 time is not a staple of the MJQ, but they were relaxed with it. After all these years, Desmond, of course, is as comfortable in 5/4 as in smoking jacket, slippers, and Eames chair. "Take Five" worked very well, partly as nostalgia, partly as a curiosity because of the combination of players, mostly as first-rate music. That can be said for the entire concert. There is no guarantee that unusual combinations of master jazz artists will work. But this was a perfect alignment of talent, tastes, and temperaments among five peers. The concert was an authentic event, a happy prelude to the quartet's twentieth anniversary and further evidence that Desmond is one of the most original and inventive saxophonists in jazz today. If it wasn't recorded, someone should get Desmond and the MJQ into a studio without delay. The Modern Jazz Quintet should be preserved for listeners to come.

A full decade later it turned out that the Desmond portion of the concert had been recorded. It was released in 1982 as Paul Desmond with the Modern Jazz Quartet *on Finesse FW 37487.*

Duke Ellington

Since Duke Ellington's death in 1974, record companies have issued a more or less steady flow of Ellington music never available during his lifetime. It includes live location recordings made at dances, which over the years provided the bulk of his band's employment. There are studio sessions taped at Ellington's expense and added to what he called "the stockpile." And there are concert recordings including some of the maestro's landmark musical occasions. The following pieces discuss a few of these posthumous discoveries.

Duke's Carnegie Ball

1978

For years the recordings of Duke Ellington's enormously important Carnegie Hall concerts of the forties have been available only from bootleg producers and distributors. Characteristically, the pirates have operated high on opportunism and low on quality. Now, for the first time, the 1943, 1944, 1946, and 1947 concerts are available virtually intact in four attractively produced and informative albums. The sound quality is all that modern technology and engineering sensitivity could make of acetate test pressings never intended for commercial release. The music, particularly in the 1943 and 1944 concerts, is among the glories of Ellingtonia.

In the Prestige three-record album of the 1943 concert "Black, Brown, and Beige," Ellington's ambitious "Tone Parallel to the History of the American Negro" is given its first full-length release. For more than three-quarters of an hour, Ellington and his musicians explore the composer's nonpareil world of melodies, rhythmic vitality, and tonal colors. Many of the melodies, notably the incomparable "Come Sunday," are familiar after more than three decades of Ellington reprises and adaptations by thousands of other musicians. But not until now could the mass of Ellington fans hear the maestro's longest work as a whole. It is not in the form of a symphony, but it has scope and variety reminiscent of the best symphonic composers. "Black, Brown, and Beige" is not a perfect work. Rather than effectively developing variations on themes, Ellington in spots settled for repetition. Recognizing that flaw, he pared down the piece for later performances. But, whatever its shortcomings, it is a phenomenally successful work. The richness of Ellington's scoring, the perfection of the band's performance, and the excellence of the soloists make this one of the supreme moments in American music. Alto saxophonist Johnny Hodges's introduction of the "Come Sunday" melody is thrilling—there's no other word for it. His performance is at once peaceful and passionate, joyous and pastoral, an inspired reading of a melody so perfect Schubert would have been envious.

The remaining two LPs of the 1943 concert are made up primarily of staples in the Ellington book. "Ko Ko," one of Ellington's masterpieces, suffers slightly because Junior Raglin's bass playing is inferior to that of the pioneering Jimmy Blanton on the original 1940 recording, and the bass part is more than rhythmically functional; it is in the fabric of the composition. Tenor saxophonist Ben Webster's patented solo on "Cotton Tail" is typically fleet and rugged, but the ensemble is slightly disjointed. The band cooks with vigorous precision on "Rockin' in Rhythm." Other highlights are Hodges's creamy exposition of "Day Dream," Lawrence Brown's amazing playing on his perennial trombone specialty, "Rose of the Rio Grande," and the intriguing "Blue Belles of Harlem," which Ellington seldom dusted off in his later years.

In the 1944 concert, "Black, Brown, and Beige" has undergone about fifteen minutes of cuts. Some critics feel nothing was lost in the reduction. Today, with the complete version available, the argument is merely academic. Al Sears has taken Webster's saxophone chair and although Sears is an adequate replacement, no one could have matched Webster's blend of muscle and tenderness. Vocalist Betty Roché is gone, and none of her successors was to achieve her musicianly grasp of the requirements of "The Blues"; but then, after she left Ellington, neither was Roché. Ellington's alter ego, Billy Strayhorn, begins to be strongly heard in the cool, almost boppish voicings of "The Perfume Suite," which showcases gorgeous Ellington piano. Sonny Greer's idiosyncratic drumming is replaced by that of Hillard Brown, who is workmanlike but relatively colorless. Rex Stewart's antic cornet was replaced in this band by the powerful trumpet stratospherics of Cat Anderson, who was to remain with the Ellington band for the next thirty years.

In 1946, Ellington took his first two-bass orchestra into Carnegie, with Al Lucas and the fiery bop trailblazer Oscar Pettiford. Here, "Black, Brown, and Beige" is an eighteen-minute echo of its former self, still vital but without many of the riches of 1943. Familiarity with the material allows the band to handle it with a kind of relaxed élan that borders on downright looseness. "Tone Group," a new composition, reaches its peak with "Jam-a-ditti," an orchestrated jam session. "Diminuendo in Blue" is polite compared with its show-stopping performances of 1939 and 1956; the latter, when it was paired with "Crescendo in Blue," was the emotional high point of all Newport Jazz Festivals.

The 1947 concert presented a number of compositions far too rarely played by the orchestra in years since. They include Strayhorn's "Snibor," Mercer Ellington's "Blue Serge," and "East St. Louis Toodle-oo," a not so grizzled survivor of Ellington's so-called "jungle period" of the late twenties and early thirties. The concert also presented Johnny Hodges in a series of pieces associated with his and Ellington's small band recordings. Items like "Junior Hop" and "Squatty Roo" are the essence of the magic Hodges and Ellington created in their small group collaborations. "Trumpets No End" is a slight elaboration on the "Blue Skies" arrangement heard two years earlier at Carnegie. "Clothed Woman" and "New York City Blues" (which is not a blues) are unique Ellington pieces more or less forgotten by Duke in the fifties, sixties, and seventies. In 1947 came the premiere of the "Liberian Suite," which was neither a suite nor prime Ellington. It did include two first-rate melodies in "I Love the Sunrise" and "Dance Number 3." By this time the orchestra was no longer the incredible collective instrument it had been in the early forties. Nonetheless, it was the expressive outlet for the most gifted composer of the day and therefore an ensemble of major importance. Difficult times were ahead for Ellington, with the big-band era nearly ended. He was to have excellent bands again, and he would again write extremely valuable works. But there was never to be another period in which he equaled the achievements that grew out of the felicitous marriage in 1943 of his best orchestra and his most inspired artistry.

Ellington Carnegie Hall Concerts are contained on Prestige albums P–34004, P–24073, P–24074 and P–24075.

1984/1986

The all-stars in *Duke Ellington All-Star Road Band* (Doctor Jazz W2X39137) were not guest soloists but working members of Ellington's orchestra in 1957. The occasion of the recording was a dance in Carrolltown, Pennsylvania, one of hundreds or, more likely, thousands, of one-night stands by Ellington and his men. Twenty-seven years later the music is being released for the first time; recorded in superb early stereo with a judicious balance of separation and depth, it is delightful to hear.

Occasionally the Ellington band fell victim to languor, but on this June evening its special brand of slightly cynical but good-natured oh-what-the-hell professionalism took over and a classy performance ensued. The musicians were relaxed and happy, playing with a loose togetherness born of long association. Ellington was wry in his short addresses to the audience: "Ladies and gentlemen, I would like to remind you that the bar will close at one o'clock tonight. We regret to tell you that we will be here a half hour later." He was generous in his compliments to the soloists. He was enthusiastic at the keyboard, allowing himself three choruses of "Mood Indigo" despite a piano that had long been a stranger to tuners. Johnny Hodges, a paragon among alto saxophonists, was featured on four numbers and captured at the height of his expressiveness. Trumpeter Clark Terry presented his redefinition of a stock item in the Ellington repertoire "Perdido," filling it with whorls and skitters.

Shorty Baker, a unique and largely unheralded trumpet stylist, had a gleaming solo on "Star Dust." Harry Carney, Paul Gonsalves, and Russell Procope stepped out of the reed section for characteristically solid statements. Drummer Sam Woodyard manned the engine room with his customary authority; there is no doubt as to who kept the time straight in this band. The ensembles were played with punch and verve.

The recording captures the special feel of a road date. It's not milestone Ellington but just another night of high-level performance. For those who caught the Ellington band on the road, the recording is an unexpected reminder of that talented and warmly responsive group of artists.

The best of Ellington's small band recordings are exquisite miniatures, reductions of his big band orchestration to a kind of concentrate of his musical thinking. The success of the small group dates was achieved through his unprecedented ability to spontaneously create ideas, meld his musical notions with those of his sidemen, and unite their talents, often with little formal preparation for a recording. The amount of actual writing, in the sense of putting pen to paper, was minimal. Ellington in the studio in the creative act was more akin to a fine motion picture director than a composer in the classical sense or even in the pre-Ellington jazz sense. Frequently under the titular leadership of star sidemen like Hodges, Stewart, and clarinetist Barney Bigard, these sessions for seven-piece bands in the late thirties and early forties produced such masterpieces as "Clouds in My Heart," "Pyramid," and "Good Queen Bess." To the list add "Where's the Music?," recorded in 1957 but now issued for the first time on *Happy Reunion* (Doctor Jazz FW 400300). To mention Ellington's voicing of the horns that makes four sound like more, his ingenious adaptation of a venerable riff figure, his sagacious but restrained application of churchy harmonies, his nostalgic main melody, is merely to offer a list of ingredients. It is impossible to describe the brilliance with which those elements are combined in the ensemble passages and in support of superb improvisations by Clark Terry and clarinetist Jimmy Hamilton. The result is exemplary of the distilled wisdom and craftsmanship of a master musician.

The three other septet pieces on the album are successful performances based on familiar material. They have fetching solos by Terry and Hodges. The rest of the album consists of a 1958 quartet date featuring tenor saxophonist Paul Gonsalves. It includes an exhilirating seven-minute ride by Gonsalves on "The Wailing Interval," a section of "Diminuendo and Crescendo in Blue." In it he at least equals the passion of his famous 1956 Newport Jazz Festival performance. But it is the remarkable "Where's the Music?" that makes the belated issue of these sessions an occasion worth celebrating.

More "new" Ellington material includes a 1964 concert recorded in Sweden, the band playing a dance in Chicago the same year and, incredibly, the 1932 band in stereo. *Harlem* (Pablo Live 2308–245) finds the Ellingtonians in top shape in Stockholm and contains a notable version of the title piece, which is a towering achievement among the composer's longer works. Trumpeter Cootie Williams, two years back in the band after a twenty-two-year absence, is at his gruff, outrageous best in "Harlem," "Caravan," and the blues portrait "Tutti for Cootie."

If the band was to be admired for its crispness and precision in the Swedish venture, the engagement a couple of months later at the Holiday Ballroom in Chicago highlighted another aspect. *Duke Ellington All-Star Road Band, Volume 2* (Doctor Jazz W2X40012), is a study in the insouciance that endeared this edition of the band to so many. The event was a dance in friendly, familiar territory, and pleasing the dancers was the primary task. They were having fun, so Ellington and the band responded in kind, and if getting a little tight made things a little too loose, the worst that could ensue was that the boss would punish you by repeated solo calls. That happened to Johnny Hodges near the end of the evening, from the sound of things, and when his customarily flawless alto saxophone lines developed a few tiny cracks, the result was not embarrassment but general amusement. Throughout the two-record set, the listener hears laughter, joshing, wry asides, cheerleading, and an occasional ad hoc choir made up of a few hip customers plus whoever in the band didn't have a horn to his lips. He also hears and senses how Ellington's inimitable style as a leader centered on the authority and sensitivity with which he used the piano to drive and direct the band. Except for a few rare items ("Silk Lace," "Guitar Amour," "Timon of Athens"), the selections are from the standard Ellington repertoire. No trails are blazed. What you get is a good evening's work by a band unlike any other, paying the bills with a dance job and enjoying it.

There's not enough space here to tell the whole story of Ellington's 1932 stereo recordings. Briefly, RCA Victor engineers used two complete recordings setups to make simultaneous master discs of the same performances. Why, no one knows. The microphone placement resulted in a stereo recording, with one track on each master cutter. All of that took place more than twenty years before technology allowed the commercial reality of stereophonic sound. In 1981 two collectors named Brad Kay and Steve Lasker began the detective work that three years later brought together the two tracks from issued and unissued pressings of the two Ellington medleys. In 1985 the reunited sonic halves were released in stereo on *Reflections in Ellington* (Everybody's 30050).

The result is not only a separation and a depth that were obviously impossible in monaural recordings but also a fuller realization of the qualities of Ellington's music during an important transitional period, after the band had left the Cotton Club and was refining its approach. The stereo medleys include marvelous solos by trumpeters Arthur Whetsol and Cootie Williams, clarinetist Barney Bigard, trombonist "Tricky Sam" Nanton, and Ellington, whose seldom-heard stride piano capabilities are fully and impressively aired in "Lots o' Fingers."

Apart from the two stereo medleys, *Reflections in Ellington* is monaural and consists of high-quality radio broadcasts from 1940, the year of Ellington's greatest band and no doubt the peak of his writing genius. The pieces include "Harlem Air Shaft," "All Too Soon," "Riding on a Blue Note" and "Boy Meets Horn." The verve of the soloists and the ensembles is on a par with that of the RCA Victor recordings and the famous Fargo, North Dakota, air checks. There is almost no chance of finding this album in any but the most specialized record store. It may be ordered from Marlor Productions, P.O. Box 156, Hicksville, New York 11802.

In *Duke Ellington and His Orchestra Featuring Paul Gonsalves* (Fantasy F–9636), Ellington used his redoubtable tenor man as the only soloist on all eight pieces. A good idea, and Gonsalves made it work gloriously. This is also new material from the vault. It was recorded in 1962 and emerged, lusty and full-blown, in late 1984.

Reviews from
"Jazz Review"

In the second half of the 1960s I worked at WDSU-TV in New Orleans as anchorman of the six and ten o'clock newscasts, frequently traveling to North Louisiana, Alabama, and Mississippi to report on civil rights developments for that station and NBC News. I also did several radio newscasts each day. Between the early and late evening television newscasts, I broadcast a radio discussion and call-in program on current events and policy issues which once a week was also produced for television. In addition, from 1966 to late 1970 I wrote, produced, and broadcast on WDSU-FM and WDSU-AM a program called "Jazz Review," which commented on new recordings. The following short pieces are reviews or portions of reviews from "Jazz Review." Song titles and timings indicate records played.

Lester Young

1966

The difficulties of talking about—or even of annotating—the solos of the great tenor saxophonist Lester Young are more frustrating than those concerning lesser musicians. His solos can be written out, of course, including the phrasing. But his emphasis, his bending of notes, his tone—in short his individuality—defy capture. Some writers have tried to get around these musicological limitations by conjuring up poetic images. Whitney Balliet, the *New Yorker* writer, who excels at this sort of thing, calls Lester's tone "wheaty" and his general approach "the sunny drybones school of tenor playing."

If you're familiar with Young, "wheaty" seems a pretty fair descriptive word for his sound, and "sunny drybones" has a wonderful sound of its own. But if you've never heard the man Billie Holiday named The President, and someone tells you his tone is wheaty, you're not going to have a useable clue to his sound, much less to his style. This being radio, we can provide a few clues and—better yet—irrefutable evidence.

What Lester Young brought to jazz in the thirties was a lighter, more subtle and legato tenor saxophone style than that of Coleman Hawkins and his disciples. Pres swung hard, but he slid across the beat in a way that has often been described as "floating." Bar lines for Lester Young were minor obstacles to be leaped at a single bound, not the brick walls many improvisers were hitting head-on before picking themselves up to continue. That rhythmic freedom Pres found gave him more uninterrupted room in which to construct long, flowing, logical ideas. He was the first horn to consistently stretch out in the modern sense of rhythmic relaxation. Here is a perfect example from an album called *Pres at His Very Best* (Emarcy MGE 26010), which is a collection of his Keynote recordings of the forties.

"Lester Leaps Again" 4:27
"Destination K.C." 4:54

The Kansas City Seven, with Lester Young, Count Basie at the piano, Freddie Green on guitar, drummer Jo Jones, Dickie Wells playing trombone, Buck Clayton on trumpet, and bassist Rodney Richardson. Now, from an earlier Keynote date, "Sometimes I'm Happy," with an eight-bar phrase at the end that stands after twenty-three years as a perfect piece of melodic improvisation.

"Sometimes I'm Happy" 3:07

That eight bars of music is one of the most memorized, and imitated, in jazz. It has been repeated thousands of times, not only by the army of tenor saxophonists who created themselves in the image of Lester Young, but by players of every instrument and by dozens of arrangers and composers. That day in 1943, Pres didn't know he was erecting a monument. Lester Young on tenor; Sid Catlett, drums; Johnny Guarnieri, piano; Slam Stewart, bass. It's Lester from his classic period, in an indispensable collection reissued on Emarcy, *Pres At His Very Best,* MGE 26010. I recommend the monaural version rather than the electronically reprocessed stereo because the sound is cleaner.

Gene Ammons

1967

Whenever the tenor saxophonist Gene Ammons's name comes up or when I listen to one of his records, I remember a night in the summer of 1962 when Sonny Rollins and his quartet were playing on the South side of Chicago at a wonderful listening emporium called McKie's. I was fortunate enough to be there during two sets when Ammons sat in as Rollins's guest.

The band Rollins had at the time was his best to date, with the guitarist Jim Hall and Rollins practicing a kind of rhythmic and harmonic sorcery I've never heard before or since.* I had heard Rollins, Hall, bassist Bob Cranshaw, and drummer Walter Perkins six or seven months earlier at the Jazz Gallery in New York, shortly after the band was formed. It was interesting but uneven. Now the quartet members were completely at ease with one another and

---

* In 1986, from the vantage point of nearly a quarter of a century, it was still, plainly, Rollins's best band.

willing to take outrageous chances, which ninety percent of the time they got away with. Rollins at his best employs a self-conscious but thoroughly engaging and witty sense of humor for which Jim Hall is the perfect foil. Rollins hasn't found a suitable replacement since he and Hall parted company.

Into this atmosphere of virtuosity and tongue-in-cheek hail fellowship came Gene Ammons; good, solid, sincere Gene Ammons, with no known tricks and not a trace of the kindly cynicism that hung in the smoky air of McKie's. And he played with such passion, involvement, swing, and attention to the basics that Rollins's choruses seemed rather effete, a victory no other tenor player I can think of is likely to have achieved. In plainer language, Jug cut Sonny, and cut him decisively, by ignoring the harmonic challenges and the invitations to turn the time inside out, and playing from the heart. It was a listening experience and a lesson I'll never forget, and I compare any Ammons performance to his playing that night. It is a strong recommendation to say of his new album, *Boss Soul*, (Prestige 7445) that his playing approaches the level I heard at McKie's.

It was recorded in the early sixties but released by Prestige only a few months ago as part of a policy of gradually issuing the Ammons material on hand to keep his name alive until he can rejoin the society that persists in refusing to recognize his narcotics addiction as an illness and not a crime.** Arthur Taylor is the drummer throughout. Walter Bishop, Jr., and Art Davis play piano and bass on half the album. But the pieces with pianist Patti Bown and the redoubtable bassist George Duvivier are superior. Miss Bown is a lyrical, sensitive, powerful, gifted, nearly ignored pianist. She has been playing at least this well since 1954, when I heard her in Seattle before she left for New York. Her solo on, of all things, "Song of the Islands," is delightful. Ammons demonstrates on this piece how to be inventive without departing far from the melody, a difficult art.

** Ammons worked productively after being released from prison in 1969. He died of bone cancer in August, 1974.

Frank Sinatra/
Antonio Carlos Jobim

1967

When an album has given me as much pleasure as the encounter between Antonio Carlos Jobim and Frank Sinatra, I have to tell you about it and play some of it for you.

I don't think we can be accused of stretching the definition of jazz by including Sinatra in "Jazz Review"; there has been no satisfactory definition of jazz. Certainly, Sinatra in the bossa nova context has more to do with jazz than some of the performers disc jockeys pass off as jazz artists. Della Reese, for an example; the Four Freshmen for another. If we called this program "Music Review" it would eliminate the need for this kind of explaining. Without our cultural need for psychological dependence on categories, we could play Sidney Bechet, The Beatles, Chopin, Sinatra, Leadbelly, Archie Shepp, and Flatt and Scruggs one after another without thinking about what kind of music it was. Truer words were never spoken than the truism attributed to both Igor Stravinsky and Woody Herman: There are only two kinds of music, good and bad.

This album has only one kind.

Sinatra's sadness and Jobim's are of the same quality, rueful but not tearful. It's the phrasing that kills most American singers who tackle a Jobim tune. They tackle it. Sinatra holds its hand. He sings the word "cool," and it means cool. Lou Rawls assaults the girl from Ipanema. Sinatra wants her. Andy Williams, how insensitive. Sinatra, how sensitive.

"How Insensitive" 3:15

"Dindi" 3:25

"The Girl from Ipanema" 3:00

"If You Never Come to Me" 2:10

The album is called *Francis Albert Sinatra and Antonio Carlos Jobim*. It's on the Reprise label, number 1021. The impeccable, loose bossa nova drums are by Dom-Um Romao.

Charles Lloyd

1968

Three or four years ago the tenor saxophonist Charles Lloyd made an album for Columbia called *Of Course, Of Course.* It was lyrical, harmonically subtle, well-paced, and vital. It wears well on repeated hearings. On it, Lloyd seemed to have begun to find his own voice after several years of thrashing around in John Coltrane's bag.

Shortly after *Of Course, Of Course,* Lloyd formed a new quartet with Keith Jarrett, a brilliant, erratic pianist; drummer Jack De-Johnette; and bassist Ron McClure. Their first Atlantic album, *Dream Weaver,* was disappointing after *Of Course, Of Course.* It had its moments of hard swinging jazz with a New Thing bias, and although Lloyd's tenor work seemed rather aimless in spots, the performances had a stimulating balance between cohesiveness and freedom.

The album recorded live at Monterey, which followed, offered disturbing evidence of deterioration. Lloyd and DeJohnette seemed to be aping the methods of Coltrane without understanding Coltrane's aims. Lloyd is a good saxophonist, not a great one. What he was beginning on *Of Course, Of Course,* discipline and a discovery of his identity, had gone by the wayside. He sounded self-indulgent and amateurish. Jarrett is a formidable pianist with great stores of technique. He seemed largely content on the Monterey album to pluck the strings and attack the keyboard in clusters, not clusters of chords but of raw sound.

The next two, and most recent, LPs by Lloyd for Atlantic, *Love In* (Atlantic 1481) and *Journey Within* (Atlantic 1493), were recorded at Fillmore Auditorium in San Francisco, the cathedral and Carnegie Hall of the flower children. Apparently the youngsters who idolize Lloyd hear a kinship with the music of the Beatles, the Rolling Stones, the Doors, the Mothers of Invention and other rock groups that have contributed so much to the music of the sixties.

If so, the kids are being deceived. What Lloyd's quartet is doing on these two albums is an evocation of Coltrane's music, and a pale one indeed. The use of two chords and montuna-like Latin rhythmic structures was done more effectively by Shorty Rogers, not to mention Rene Touzet, fifteen years ago. Lloyd's blues playing sounds weak and out of tune on a thing called "Memphis Greens." As for Lloyd's band being the first psychedelic jazz group, as the liner notes of *Love In* quote a ballroom owner, the implication is that they have absorbed or that they reflect the whacked-out trends of these hippy times. That could be. But they don't seem to me to reflect much of the best in either jazz or popular music.

"Tribal Dance" 10:03

There are times on the *Love In* and *Journey Within* albums when the music rises above the level of what you just heard. Jarrett's piano solos on "Sunday Morning" and "Love Number 3" are excellent, although on the latter he sounds like Jaki Byard gone slightly batty. Lloyd's flute work is occasionally attractive. But "Tribal Dance" is all too typical of the melodic and harmonic sterility of the band and of the static rhythm figures Lloyd frequently chooses to use.

Ornette Coleman

1966

I think it's safe to assume that most people, even most jazz listeners, are not familiar with the music of Ornette Coleman. You may have heard about the controversy that has ripped through music the past six years because of Coleman's startling style and his influence on other players.

Ornette Coleman plays alto saxophone, self-taught, and he recently took a couple of years off to teach himself violin and trumpet as well. In the wake of his debut in the late fifties, there erupted a string of nonsense—played, written, and spoken—which has continued and become more absurd. One school of critics proclaimed that he had rejuvenated jazz and given it new direction. Another school said he was destroying jazz singlehandedly and that there was no hope for further good times in music. LeRoi Jones, Archie Shepp, and a few dozen others in New York have decided that Coleman is a prophet of black supremacy. Coleman himself has been notably reticent on that point.

I think enough time has passed to make it clear that Ornette Coleman is neither genius nor fraud, merely a pretty fair alto player who has his own vision. I was going to say, who hears a different drummer. But, as you will hear momentarily, Coleman's drummer, Charles Moffett, is a basic, sort of old-timey drummer working in the avant-garde. And I assume that's what Coleman wants, because in many ways he himself is a basic, old-timey player. He has freed himself from some restrictions of harmony and bar lines, but I don't think he's done it because of some desperate need to escape from formal restrictions.

Coleman is a naive, brilliant musician whose jazz sense is as instinctive as it is learned, who has the blues in his bones and who is an extremely powerful, rhythmic player. He is a man in whose name some of the most outrageous and fraudulent cults have sprung up. Coleman doesn't deserve most of his self-appointed disciples. Nor does he deserve the burden of exaggerated praise that has proclaimed him some sort of messiah.

He is interesting to hear. How much lasting musical value there is in his playing, I just don't know. I've been listening to him for five years, and I have often received tremendous emotional charges from his solos. I'll continue listening.

At any rate, here's Ornette Coleman in his first recording in three years, with Charles Moffett on drums and David Izenson on bass. This was recorded at the Golden Circle, a club in Stockholm. It's called "Dee Dee."

"Dee Dee" 9:10

If you're unfamiliar with Ornette Coleman, this is a good record

to begin with. If you have followed his career, it gives you an idea
what he's been up to since 1962. Ornette Coleman *Live at the
Golden Circle* (Blue Note 84224).

George Russell

1966

*This piece boils down the main points made in a retrospective of
Russell's music that occupied most of "Jazz Review" for five weeks.*

Over the next few programs we're going to consider the recorded
work of George Russell, not only because his music is interesting,
absorbing, listening, but because of his influence on the development of jazz in the sixties. Russell's impact, I believe, is more profound and widespread than is generally recognized, even by many
musicians. It may well develop that he is having as great an effect on
the course of jazz as any composer or arranger at work today, as
important as that of such imitated innovators as John Coltrane and
Ornette Coleman.

Russell believes that jazz must develop on its own terms, from
within. He believes that to borrow the concepts of classical music
and force jazz into the mold of the classical tradition results in
something perhaps interesting, perhaps Third Stream music, but
not jazz. Faced with this conviction that jazz musicians must look
to jazz for their means of growth, Russell set about creating a
framework within which to work. In 1953 he completed his Lydian
Concept of Tonal Organization. The system is built on what he calls
pan-tonality, bypassing the atonal ground covered by modern classical composers and making great use of chromaticism. Russell ex-

plains that pan-tonality allows the writer and the improviser to retain the scale-based nature of the folk music in which jazz has its roots, yet have the freedom of being in a number of tonalities at once. Hence, pan-tonality.

That's a brief and far from complete summary of Russell's theory, on which he worked for ten years. It's all in his book, *The Lydian Chromatic Concept for Jazz Improvisation*, published by Concept Publishing Company.

Freedom within restrictions, however broad.

Discipline.

Improvising Russell's way demands great technical skill. Listening to his recordings, one is struck by the virtuoso nature of the players. Some of them are Bill Evans, Don Ellis, Dave Baker, John Coltrane, Art Farmer, Eric Dolphy, Steve Swallow, Bob Brookmeyer. Evans is the featured soloist in Russell's 1959 Decca recording called *Jazz in the Space Age*, the most thorough application of Russell's theories to a large band. All that talk about concepts and theories and pan-tonality and chromaticism may have led you to expect something dry and formidable. On the contrary, there's a sense of fun and airiness in the music. The humor is subtle and, I should add, more evident after several hearings.

The piece called "The Lydiot" is a good choice to introduce Russell's music. The opening sound is made by Russell running beads over a set of tuned drums. Bill Evans is the first piano soloist, Paul Bley the second.

"The Lydiot" 10:05

To give you an idea of the authenticity and effectiveness of Russell's writing, the first minute or so of this next piece is free improvisation by Evans and Bley. The remainder of the performance by the two pianists is entirely written, but in its verve, swing, phrasing, and placement of accents sounds entirely improvised. At the time of the recording in 1959, Russell said this was his most ambitious piece of music.

"Chromatic Universe," Part 2 3:32

"All about Rosie" is a piece in three movements based on a song game called "Rosie, Little Rosie," which Russell says is played by Alabama Negro children. In this work, commissioned in 1957 by

Brandeis University, you'll hear the same personal approach to voicings and tonality we heard in Russell's *Jazz in the Space Age*. Here, too, there are effective use of repetition, variations on the simple motif of the childrens' song and freedom achieved by the polytonal nature of Russell's Lydian Concept; a poignant feeling of liberation.

The version of the piece we'll hear includes in the third movement one of the strongest, most compelling Bill Evans piano solos on record, a performance that helped boost Evans into prominence at a time when, except to New York musicians and a limited public, he was just another piano player.

"All about Rosie" 10:35

In 1960, Russell returned to the application of his Lydian Concept to a small band. There was a series of albums on Riverside and one LP on Decca. Those recordings are something in the nature of living textbooks of the new jazz, as important reference works for theory and composition as the records of John Coltrane and Ornette Coleman are for free improvisation. Russell's pan-tonal theory works as well for a sextet as for an eighteen-piece orchestra, and the music has the same urgency, logic, and abrasive humor. Here's a composition of Russell's arranged in that astringent way of his for the exploratory group he had in the spring of 1961. The soloists: Eric Dolphy, bass clarinet; Don Ellis, trumpet; Dave Baker, trombone; Steve Swallow, bass. Russell is the pianist.

"Thoughts" 5:26

Now, here is Russell's first recorded composition, "Cubano Be, Cubano Bop," by the Dizzy Gillespie band in December of 1947. You'll notice some of the same elements we've heard in Russell's later writing, the tight, almost tense, voicings, melodic lines interwoven across the trumpet, trombone, and reed sections, dynamics for coloration and, always, the pulse that makes Russell's music unquestionably jazz.

"Cubano Be" 2:24
"Cubano Bop" 3:05

We'll wind up our George Russell retrospective with the concluding portions of his suite called *New York, New York*. This work of

Russell's is more than a superior big band recording by a master orchestrator. It is also a fair summation of what had happened in jazz in the middle and late fifties. In 1959 there was a good deal of thought being given to the directions jazz would take and strong indications that one important departure would be along the path of freedom.

Russell was an invaluable guide along that path, providing the player a means of achieving greater freedom of expression without falling into licentiousness. The means was his Lydian Concept of Tonal Organization. It gave the improviser a theoretical base from which to play with fewer harmonic restrictions than in be bop. Even musicians who have never studied the theory have been influenced by it because it is a spirit that has moved through the music. In the close community of jazz musicians, new ideas spread rapidly. So, in a tangible sense, this was one of the first recordings of the so-called New Thing. It is a good demonstration of Russell's theory. But, theories aside, it is delightful music. The soloists here are part of the importance of this music as a link between the fifties and sixties. All of them—Bob Brookmeyer, Bill Evans, Art Farmer, John Coltrane, Phil Woods—were interesting young players. In a short time, they would be among the most influential soloists in jazz.

"New York, New York," side 2 23:10

(Russell's *New York, New York* and *Jazz in the Space Age* are reissued on a double album on the MCA label, 2 MCA 4017. "All about Rosie" was issued on *Outstanding Jazz Compositions of the 20th Century* Columbia C2L–31. "Thoughts" is from *Ezz-thetics*, Fantasy OJC-070, "Cubano Be, Cubano Bop" is on *Dizziest*, RCA Bluebird.)

Roswell Rudd

1966

Much of what disturbs me about the New Thing is rooted in the insistence of many of its players and advocates that to fully appreciate "their" music one must accept it without reservations and, preferably, exclusively. Since I'm unwilling to chuck Ellington, Mingus, Parker, Armstrong, Evans, Wilson, Young and Teagarden as irrelevant, perhaps I'm slamming the door on what many of the New Thingers have a disconcerting way of referring to as The Truth.

A number of them profess deep reverence for Ellington, Parker, Armstrong, and company, but to listen to their playing is to search for those influences in vain. On the other hand, there are those who may or may not claim to cherish the past but display it in performance. Albert Ayler is one of the former, Archie Shepp one of the latter. For all his racist nonsense and hate-saying, Shepp plays with little hatred, considerable humor, and much more conventionally than he or his volunteer corps of prophets would probably care to recognize. Shepp's companion, trombonist Roswell Rudd, is even more closely connected to the jazz tradition. The difference is that Rudd enjoys remembering his days with Eddie Condon and Shepp glories in publicly chastising himself for once having appreciated Stan Getz.

Rudd's primary concern seems to be joy. He expresses it in the trombone dialect practiced by Tricky Sam Nanton, Vic Dickenson, Lawrence Brown, Bill Harris, and, recently, Rod Levitt. Here is Rudd's nostalgic performance of "Everywhere," written and first recorded by Bill Harris in 1946 with the Woody Herman First Herd. Rudd gives it all the earmarks of the New Thing. But unlike many performances in that idiom, it has humor and a unifying thread.

"Everywhere" 11:35

The album is uneven, but it has frequent satisfying moments and can be recommended above many recordings from the new avant-garde. Roswell Rudd. *Everywhere*, Impulse number 9126.

Stan Getz/Laurindo Almeida

1967

Stan Getz is a universally acknowledged master of melody. His lyrical ability is so pronounced, his sound so lovely that attention is drawn away from the strength that underlies every phrase he plays. On his new album, *Stan Getz/Laurindo Almeida,* notice how the rhythmic intensity deepens when Getz returns after someone else has soloed.

"Minina Moca" 5:45

This music was recorded in 1963 during the same period as the Getz-João Gilberto album which may be the finest bossa nova music yet recorded. The album is near the level of the one with Gilberto, falls short of it only because the rhythmic fabric tends to loosen when Getz is not playing. Within a bar or two of his reentry on every track the performance is back into the groove he set at the beginning.

Almeida has a reputation as a sort of pre-bossa nova musician and, of course, as a magnificent guitarist, jazz and classical. He made a record in 1955 with Bud Shank which implies much of what Gilberto, Antonio-Carlos Jobim, and some of Almeida's other fellow Brazilians brought to music six or seven years later. His playing on this album is impeccable but less muscular than the occasion seemed to call for. He uses a delayed attack which at times falls just enough behind the beat to damage the rhythmic balance. That is true during his solos, but not when he is comping for Getz.

George Duvivier is the rock-steady bassist, providing a firm foundation for the rhythm section of four Brazilians plus the American drummer Dave Bailey. There is an unidentified pianist on some tracks and he has a judiciously understated and reflective solo on a composition by Getz and Almeida called "Maracatu-Too." Listen to Getz's exuberant whooping on his second solo in "Samba da Sahra" and on "Maracatu-Too," the most successful performance in the album.

"Samba da Sahra" 4:50
"Maracatu-Tu" 4:57
The bossa nova fad is gone, but this beautiful approach to music
has immeasurably enriched jazz and been absorbed by many of its
best players. The album is called *Stan Getz/Laurindo Almeida*
Verve 8665.

Book Reviews

New Orleans Jazz: A Family Album
By Al Rose and Edmond Souchon
Baton Rouge: L.S.U. Press

1969

This is a valuable and entertaining volume for either the specialist in New Orleans jazz or the general reader. But it must be opened with the understanding that its premise is a narrow one, however accurate the information within it and painstaking the research that produced it.

The premise is spelled out in the preface by Mr. Rose and Dr. Souchon: "Both of the authors have long since rejected the myth of the evolution of jazz from its so-called primitive or archaic form to what contemporary critics call modern or progressive. Hence, individuals like the late Lester Young (his experience in the King Oliver Orchestra notwithstanding) and the ebullient Sam Butera, we consider, without discussing their musical merit, to be outside the scope of a book on New Orleans jazz, although both were born in the Crescent City."

Their position on Butera is perhaps defensible, but to exclude Young, one of the handful of universally recognized geniuses jazz has produced, seems merely petulant. Needless to say, with Young ruled out, Eddie Blackwell, Al Belletto, Bill Evans, and others who have either been an important part of or drifted in and out of jazz in New Orleans are not included in this encyclopedic treatment.

The authors say that to be jazz "music must be (a) improvised, (b) played in 2/4 or 4/4 time, and (c) retain a clearly definable melody line." Presumably that includes the fantastic set of variations by Louis Armstrong on "Weatherbird," but not Lester Young's "Sometimes I'm Happy" or "Lady Be Good," in which (to use the authors' definition as a weapon against their definition) he departs only slightly from the melody lines yet creates classic jazz statements that have influenced thousands of musicians all over the world.

Within the restrictive definition of jazz they have adopted, Mr. Rose and Dr. Souchon have created a stunning book packed with biographies and photographs assembled after months and years of research, some of it by way of the Jazz Museum and the Tulane Archives, but much of it simply ferreted out.

Anyone who has attempted to converse with septuagenarian or octogenarian New Orleans jazzmen has often found himself either conducting one-sided exchanges to the accompaniment of a good deal of head scratching and chuckling or being treated to some horrendous fabrications. Jazz players are masters of the put-on, and old-time New Orleans Negro musicians are the undisputed champions. It is something of a testimonial to the patience and chaff-separating ability of the authors that they were able to collate and cross-check what must have been a baffling quantity of information.

In many cases, they correct erroneous impressions. Leon's nickname may have been "Rap," but his last name was spelled with an o: Roppolo. Emmett Hardy, not Louis Armstrong, is credited with having influenced the young Bix Beiderbecke in Davenport, Iowa; Beiderbecke heard Armstrong later in Chicago.

The biographical section is full of objective material about nearly unknown as well as famous jazzmen. It is unlikely that the names of such minor figures as Joe Gibson, Behrman French, and Joe and John Guiffre have been preserved in any other generally available jazz book. When objectivity slips, it is usually to make way for praise. But exceptions to that admirable rule are made for Cap'n John Handy and the late Kid Clayton, both of whom are described as "mainly rhythm and blues type" players limited to the blues. Handy, as a matter of fact, currently makes "Cabaret" his feature number and has always included in his repertoire such 32-bar non-blues popular songs as "Perdido" and "When We Danced at the Mardi Gras." His recent RCA Victor album has a tune far removed from the blues in the 1951 popular song "I Laughed at Love." Handy is fond of material much more sophisticated than the blues and has used it over the years. Clayton worked with Handy and played the same songs. Both can be considered superlative blues players, not "players limited to the blues."

There is a listing of bands and their personnel which makes it possible to settle arguments about who went to Chicago with The Five Southern Jazzers, whether the Jimmy Durante who played piano with the New Orleans Jazz Band in 1918 was *the* Jimmy Durante (he was) and whether Leo Adde, Sr. or Monk Hazel was the drummer with the New Orleans Rhythm Kings (both, at different times).

The section devoted to places associated with jazz will throw many citizens into fits of nostalgia recalling the Alley Cabaret, Brown's Ice Cream Parlor, the Halfway House, and Funky Butt Hall.

But the greatest pleasure of this attractive and lavishly produced book is its collection of photographs, many of them never before published. Some of the highlights: Noon Johnson in tails, smiling into his bazooka; Buddy Petit posing rakishly, hat cocked, stance defiant; Bunk Johnson, the personification of dignity in hightop shoes and coveralls; the pre-beard Al Hirt; De De and Billie Pierce in a beautiful family portrait; the only known photograph of Buddy Bolden; the twenty-five-year-old Jack Laine in his blacksmith costume in 1898 when he was not yet a full-time entrepreneur; and dozens of stiffly posed, self-conscious "action" and look-at-the-birdie shots out of the teens and twenties.

One must admire and value this book for the volume of information it brings the student of jazz history. It will be an important research tool for years.

At the same time, anyone whose definition of jazz includes forms of the music that developed after, say, 1931, will wonder at the narrowness of *A Family Album* and, perhaps, reflect that the book is a document of the rear guard battle waged by many members of the New Orleans jazz establishment to preserve their music and memories. The battle has resulted in such victories as the Jazz Museum and the New Orleans Jazz Club, fine institutions. But it has also driven dozens of fine young modern jazzmen away from their hometown and forced others, who didn't care to leave, out of jazz. It would be to the everlasting credit of the establishment represented by Dr. Souchon, Mr. Rose, and their book if some of the energy and pride that went into the Jazz Museum and Preservation Hall could be directed toward the encouragement and development of young musicians who are the artistic and spiritual heirs of the players whose names and faces fill this lovely book. If New Orleans, twenty years from now, is to be anything but a jazz curiosity recalled in the Rose-Souchon album, that step must be taken.

But this is a grand book, and if the authors want to say that Lester Young was not a jazz artist and Candy Candido is, that is their business.

Brother Ray: Ray Charles's Own Story
By Ray Charles and David Ritz
The Dial Press

1978

The rawness and lack of self-pity in the lyrics of Ray Charles's best songs are reflected in his frank autobiography. *Brother Ray* is the antithesis of the cream-cheese puffery of ninety percent of the "as told to" volumes passed off as the life stories of celebrities. Charles treats the poverty of his youth, his blindness, drug addiction, adultery, sexual practices, fame, and the process of music making with equal objectivity and lack of regret. In his afterword, David Ritz explains Charles's insistence, in long hours of reviewing chapters, on precisely the right word or tone to portray his style or a remembered mood. The right word is frequently a shocking one, and the book is littered with phrases and expressions that make it one of the most explicit nonfiction works of recent years.

Ray Charles began losing his sight when he was five; he was totally blind at seven. It is one of the overpowering facts of his existence, yet he refused to let it overpower him. His mother did not allow his sightlessness to become a handicap in his youth, nor was that ever his inclination. Charles's accommodation to his disability is a constant source of amazement, even in his most depressing experiences, such as a 1952 encounter with a couple of race-baiting Houston policemen.

The hardheadedness that characterized his response to blindness typifies Charles's attitude toward every aspect of his life. Known as a demanding and tightfisted bandleader and businessman, he always follows his instincts, drives, and personal standards; if it seems right or feels good, he does it, and he takes the consequences. Although he quit heroin cold turkey, he makes it clear that he doesn't regret his addiction or the legal difficulties it engendered. He disarmingly admits that he enjoyed his dope highs and refuses to advise others not to use narcotics. When drugs finally became a burden to him in his relations with his family, he quit. He says he needs a lot of sex, so he goes to bed with a lot of women. He supports his illegitimate children and does not write bitterly about the paternity suits against him.

Having been labeled "the genius" early in his career, Charles says that he has never endorsed the title, preferring to be known as Brother Ray. But he synthesized elements of jazz, church music, rhythm and blues, and even country music into a style so fresh, personal, revealing, and influential that the question of his genius may easily be settled by others. There are glimpses here and there in the book of Charles's artistic life. But, as in so many books about musicians, there is no organized treatment of the music-making process, the inner struggles, the aesthetic choices, the artist's musical standards, his development of a style. He generously acknowledges his debts to Nat Cole, Charles Brown, Art Tatum, and a few others, but there is no exploration of the creative means by which Charles brought seemingly disparate elements together and melded them into one of the most powerful expressions in American music.

The sense of honesty in the book seems to be David Ritz's largest

contribution. Through his organization and editing, Ritz paid careful attention to the nuances and eccentricities of Charles's speech
and thought. We can only speculate what dimensions might have
been added to the work if Ritz had instead written a biography of
Charles.

A valuable discography at the back of the book traces Charles's
recorded career from his 1948 home recordings, which are still
available, to his latest album on Atlantic. If the book has the effect
of sending you to your Ray Charles collection for another listen to
his work, you will be doubly rewarded.

Stan Kenton: Artistry in Rhythm
William F. Lee
Creative Press, Los Angeles

The World of Count Basie
Stanley Dance
Charles Scribner's Sons, New York

1982

Dr. Lee's 727-page mélange, part fan letter and part scrapbook, will
be invaluable to researchers into the phenomenon of the late Stan
Kenton and his impact on jazz in the forties, fifties, and sixties. The
scholars will have to sift through masses of anecdotes and hundreds
of press notices from publications as diverse as the Landsdale, Pennsylvania *North Penn Reporter* and the *London Times*. They may
suffer, but they will come away with useful material.

It is questionable whether the general reader, regardless of his de-
votion to Kenton, will have the patience for the task. Between the
covers Dr. Lee has intermingled verbatim reminiscences from Ken-

ton's relatives, friends, and colleagues with four decades of newspaper and magazine articles and reviews. Strung together on a mea-
ger chronological narrative, all of this raw source material is almost
indigestible as continuous reading. As a reference work, however, the volume is important. The in-
dex is comprehensive and accurate. The discography is complete,
although it does not include recording-session personnel, a serious
oversight. There is a personnel listing by instrument, but it is alpha-
betical. It is also astonishing; over the years, 130 trumpet players
worked for Kenton, 72 tenor saxophonists, 32 drummers. The
band was a vast training ground for jazz musicians. Some of the
most accomplished and successful soloists, arrangers, and leaders of
modern jazz were given their first breaks by Stan Kenton. His greatest contribution to music was unquestionably his ability to spot talent and allow it to flourish in the creative environment of his orchestra. Radiating from these pages with an intensity far more
compelling than the aggregate of information is the admiration of
his musicians. Even those who question the value of his musical philosophy are lavish in their praise of Kenton as a leader and father
figure.

What is missing from the book is fulfillment of the true biog-
rapher's duty, to put his subject in perspective. It remains for someone else to assess Kenton's impact on the jazz idiom, to critically
sort out his solid musical accomplishments from his bombast, to in-
vestigate the social and cultural phenomena that surrounded Kenton's astoundingly rapid elevation to popular success in the 1940s.
Dr. Lee's effort will be helpful in the task. In the meantime, except
for the extremely patient and knowledgeable reader, more insight
into Kenton's music will be gained from his recordings than from
this well-intentioned but ungainly work.

Stanley Dance's volume on the protean band leader Count Basie
also consists of reminiscences and previously published material.
But Dance, one of the great authorities on mainstream jazz, uses
logical organization and his own solid evaluations to make the
book readable and to place Basie in perspective.

Dance's passages on the components of the Basie piano style and the evolution of the rhythmic aspects of jazz in Kansas City are helpful in understanding why the band was so unexpectedly successful when it reached New York in 1936. He explains why the rhythm section was the heart of the organization, how Basie's deceptively spare piano style drove the section, and why Basie's wisdom in the selection of tempos accounted in great part for the band's unequaled relaxation and power.

Like Kenton, Basie had an ability to hear greatness in young, relatively unknown players and, like Kenton's, his band was a hothouse for new talent. Foremost among his protégés was Lester Young, the tenor saxophonist who carried jazz improvisation a step beyond Louis Armstrong and Coleman Hawkins. Dance's chapter on Young makes one understand why the saxophonist needed the loose power of Basie's band to support him as he scaled new heights in his development of the jazz solo.

Recollections by articulate Basie associates like bassist Gene Ramey and drummer Gus Johnson recreate the Kansas City musical milieu of the 1930s, one of the yeastiest times and places in the history of American music. Ramey's long narrative gives insights not only into the inner workings of Basie's band in Kansas City but also into the stylistic link between Lester Young and alto saxophonist Charlie Parker. Young and Parker, revolutionaries of successive jazz eras, were two of the most important soloists to emerge from Kansas City.

Basie was able to survive the winds of change that Parker and others blew through jazz in the bebop era. Dance tells how the band was allowed to absorb the principles of bop soloing, but was never permitted to substitute bop's complex rhythmic aspects for the smooth, unified swing that underlies Basie's success. Basie is still at the helm of his band* forty-five years after it left Kansas City, evidence that his belief in his concept of music was amply justified.

A definitive biography of Count Basie is yet to come. Nonetheless, Dance's book is of value in explicating the phenomenon of the Basie band and its importance to the development of American music.

* Count Basie died on April 26, 1984.

To Be or Not to Bop
Dizzy Gillespie with Al Fraser
Doubleday & Co., New York

Diz—or: On Creative Dignity

1980

Nearly forty years ago, Duke Ellington warned Dizzy Gillespie
against letting his music be labeled. Gillespie says he didn't know
why until it was too late. Whether he could have done anything to
prevent the labeling is conjectural. In any event, for better or worse,
the music was labeled, and the label was "bebop."

In one of the great injustices of American culture, formal com-
mentary on bebop lumped the music with the bizarre clothing, cus-
toms, and fads which the press publicized in the 1940s with un-
discriminating and condescending glee. As a result, the popular
impression of the most important revolution in the first half-century
of jazz was that it was the work of a collection of eccentrics in berets
and goatees who shook hands in contortions and played wrong
notes. The leaders of the movement were occasional accomplices in
making bebop seem ludicrous. John Birks "Dizzy" Gillespie, one of
the music's virtuosos and its greatest teacher, recalls with regret
when *Life* magazine cajoled or duped him and Benny Carter into a
photo session.

They made us perform a bebop greeting for them. "Hi-ya, man!" "Bells,
man, where you been?," giving the sign of the flatted fifth, a raised open
hand.

"Eel-ya-da!" We gave a three-fingered sign that we were playing triplets,
ending with an elaborate handshake. That was supposed to be the bebopper's greeting, but there was no such thing in real life. It was just a bunch of
horseplay we went through so they could pretend we were something weird.

Gillespie's propensity to lightheartedness, even comedy, has always belied the seriousness of his musicianship. The meteoric alto

saxophonist Charlie Parker blazed bebop's most glorious solos, and Gillespie's trumpet virtuosity was the only near match for Parker's on saxophone. But Parker's talent, honed to dazzling brilliance by the endless woodshedding of his youth, was largely instinctive. Gillespie, a more complete musician if not a better soloist, built his stunning craftsmanship on the most solid theoretical base ever constructed by a modern jazz musician and probably equaled in jazz only by Duke Ellington.

The greatest virtue of this rambling, repetitious, charming autobiography is that it plainly explains the nature of the bop revolution in which Gillespie was the chief theoretician and leading teacher. Unlike most books by or about musicians, music plays the principal role. Anyone with a reasonably good junior high school music education and a Bugs Bower chord book can sit at the piano and patiently find the chords and chord progressions Gillespie discloses as the evolutionary material that led jazz out of the harmonic restrictions of the swing era.

Using the simple, unadorned harmonies that prevailed until the early forties, it was possible for musicians to coast along, even to "fake it." But when Gillespie, Parker, Thelonious Monk, and others began inverting, substituting, and dividing chords, it became necessary for anyone trying to improvise with these men to know exactly where they were going or fail abjectly. Many failed. A few mastered the demanding techniques and survived. Clearly, by Gillespie's own testimony and that of dozens of other musicians interviewed by co-author Fraser, no jazz player has ever known more precisely how every element of his solos related to the harmonic structures of the music. Some of the most sophisticated musicians of the movement, including Miles Davis and Budd Johnson, speak reverently of Gillespie's willingness to patiently unravel the mysteries of bop's often convoluted harmonies. He seemed to have a vocation to teach, and he went about it as if the future of jazz depended on his ability to make the first- and second-generation boppers understand what they were doing. Colleague after colleague speaks with awe of Gillespie's trailblazing musicianship.

Billy Eckstine on Gillespie circa 1940: "Dizzy worked on chord progressions, things like that, finding different ways of doing things. Finding different progressions, alternate ways of using the musical chords, not just the given things that are in the songs. He would work out the alternates and the prettier themes, different progressions to them, and countermelodies, which he still does."

Trumpeter Duke Garrett: "Before, we trumpets had just been screaming and trying to see who could play the loudest and who could get the highest. Then he came out with an intelligent way of constructing solos on the chord structure of a tune and then delivering it in a way that was not an easy way—it was a way you had to study. And some of us right today have never gotten down to his technique."

Saxophonist and arranger Budd Johnson: "Diz would come in where you were working and sit in with the band. And, like, we'd be jamming. He'd let everybody else play first, and while they were playing he would be telling the piano player, he'd say, 'See, when you get to that chord you make a so-and-so.' And so when it got to be Dizzy's time to play, now, the piano player has learned the new changes, and this cat would get up there and blow the roof off the joint. Just wash everybody away. And everybody would start to say, 'Man, play that behind me.'"

Kenny Clarke, who pioneered bop drumming: "I saw the rhythmic aspect of it, the way he played and the way he would hum the time and things like that. I knew it was avant-garde, ahead of time, so I just fell in with what was going on."

The book is rich in such insights into Gillespie's musical essence, but much of it is transcribed tape interviews full of repetition, half sentences, incomplete thoughts. This volume is known to have been in preparation for at least fifteen years, and this reviewer recalls Gillespie making notes for it as long ago as 1962. Nonetheless, it sometimes has the roughness of a hurried project. Whether through Gillespie's choice of a collaborator or Doubleday's editing process, the volume is a bit of a jumble. However, it will be a gold mine for biographers to come. It is valuable not only for the musical assessments but for Gillespie's recollections of his childhood in Cheraw, South Carolina, the deprivations and poverty that followed the death of his father, and how the discovery of his talent deflected him from the path toward a sharecropping existence into an extraordinarily productive life. Throughout the book, Gillespie is generous in his recognition of the aid and talents of others. His credit to his boyhood music teacher and mentor, Alice V. Wilson, is touching. One cannot help being moved by her description of Gillespie's presenting her to his Carnegie Hall audience. He is expansive in his praise of Parker, Monk, Clarke, Bud Powell, and others in the development of bop. He helps revive recognition of the importance of pianists Billy Kyle and Clyde Hart as transitional figures from swing to bop. He attributes great talent to largely forgotten musicians like trumpeters Bobby Moore and Willie Nelson.

In a recent issue, *down beat* magazine carried an interview with a prominent jazz artist and repertoire director who expounded on the need for musicians to accomodate the requirements and compromises of business if they are to succeed. Gillespie, whose lack of artistic compromise is legendary, has received that advice throughout his career, and his response to those who urged him to sell out in order to reach a wider audience should be required reading for the young musicians being guided by that A&R man:

"We never carried big crowds because jazz is strictly an art form, and so there was always a division between jazz and what other people were doing who were not really participating in a creative art form. Those other things people were doing were not creative; they were pretty, manufactured meaningless tinsel rolling off an assembly line."

The Bass Saxophone
Josef Skvorecky
Alfred A. Knopf, New York

Truth Through the Art of Riff

1979

It is possible, although I have seen no serious defense of the idea, that the recent defections to the United States from the ranks of the Bolshoi Ballet had their inspiration in political ideology. Even fellow members of the Bolshoi company, however much they have attempted to devalue the talents of the defectors, have rather wistfully agreed that the Koslovs and Aleksandr Godunov wished for the opportunity to explore areas of dance forbidden by the Soviet Union. There is little possibility of establishing an underground ballet company to perform avant-garde works late at night in the cellars of Moscow and Kiev, and no chance of sneaking modern dance movements into the traditional repertoires of state-controlled Soviet ballet companies. The thought of some daring performer slipping a few Martha Graham touches in among the prettinesses of "Swan Lake" is alluring but ludicrous. So the Nureyevs, Baryshnikovs, and Godunovs defect.

In literature, painting, and music, the opportunities for defiance are broader. The samizdat is well known, as are the punishments of those who dare to write for it. Defection is once again the answer for a few who are courageous and lucky, or who have accumulated enough international fame to provide a kind of immunity.

Those within repressed societies who wish to absorb the output of banned artists find ways of doing it. Modern paintings hidden away and surreptitiously enjoyed, rumpled samizdat manuscripts passed from hand to hand, phonograph records purchased on the black market, tape recordings endlessly dubbed and redubbed; all of this involves degrees of heroism. Elsewhere* I have written about the strange encounter during World War II between the editor of this journal and a Nazi soldier. Leopold Tyrmand, a Polish forced laborer in Germany, discovered by chance that the soldier was a fellow jazz enthusiast. At considerable risk, they spent a Sunday afternoon in a rowboat in the middle of a river, alternately spelling one another at the oars and the crank of a windup phonograph, listening to the recordings of Benny Goodman.

There are no doubt millions of stories about people putting themselves in peril to enjoy what they seek in art. But to create under circumstances of repression and fear, knowing that detection could mean the end of everything, seems even more daring. That, in part, and on the surface, is Skvorecky's theme in the poignant title story of *The Bass Saxophone* and, more explicitly, in "Red Music," the essay that begins the book. Skvorecky, growing up in occupied Czechoslovakia, was a semi-professional dance band tenor saxophonist consumed by the "forceful vitality," the "explosive creative energy" of jazz. He and his fellow musicians did not think of their beloved jazz as protest music, ". . . but of course, when the lives of individuals and communities are controlled by powers that themselves remain uncontrolled—slavers, czars, fuhrers, first secretaries, marshals, generals and generalissimos, ideologists of dictatorships at either end of the spectrum—then creative energy becomes a protest." Jazz, he says, "was a sharp thorn in the sides of the power-hungry men, from Hitler to Brezhnev, who successively ruled in my native land."

The essay catalogues the ways in which jazz survived in Europe under the Nazis; secret jam sessions with hidden lookouts, phony song titles ("The Wild Bull" for "Tiger Rag," "Evening Song" for "Star Dust"), forbidden reception of short wave broadcasts, band arrangements smuggled in by Wehrmacht officers, swing bands in Buchenwald and Terezin. European repressions of jazz were far worse than American ignorance and neglect of jazz. Merely shunned in the United States, but pursued, bedeviled, and outlawed by the

* see page 49

fascist rulers of Europe, jazz became a recognized cultural force there decades ago, and only now may be achieving high cultural respectability here. It was not the repression that established jazz in European culture, although, strangely, it may have helped to ingrain it. Europeans seem to have grasped the significance of the music almost from the moment of its recognizability as a distinct idiom, as far back as 1919, when Ernest Ansermet, the great Swiss conductor, wrote of Sidney Bechet's "rich inventiveness" and "bold disconcerting freshness."

When the young Skvorecky was discovering Duke Ellington, Jimmy Lunceford, Chick Webb, Andy Kirk, and the Casa Loma band (he and his friends thought Casa Loma was the band leader), appreciation of jazz was an established component of the makeup of many cultured Europeans, from Aldous Huxley to Andre Malraux.

For the narrator of "The Bass Saxophone," life in his little Czech town is dominated on the one hand by the Nazi occupation and on the other by his preoccupation with the fact and lore of jazz, hearing it, playing it, dreaming of half-mythical figures like Armstrong, Ellington, Chick Webb, Eddie Condon, Bix Beiderbecke, and Adrian Rollini. He has never heard Rollini, has never heard a bass saxophone, but he fantasizes Rollini's prowess on this brontosaurus of the reed family. He then unexpectedly catches a glimpse of a bass saxophone, only to discover it belongs to a German band brought in to entertain the Nazi officers. Mesmerized by "a mechanism of strong, silver-plated wires, the gears, the levers like the mechanism of some huge and absolutely nonsensical apparatus, a fantasy of some crazy mixed-up inventor," he risks the ostracism of his townsmen and punishment by the Germans for a chance to inspect the instrument, to try it out and ultimately to substitute in disguise for the mysterious bass saxophonist of the visiting German band. At a grotesquely staged concert, the bass saxophonist appears and demands the restoration of his chair and his instrument. Through a solo of mind-blowing ferocity, power, and daring, he annoys and offends his Nazi audience, which had been enjoying Bavarian oompah music. But for the Czech boy the moment is an epiphany in which the central truth of his life is forged. A fascination with jazz is transformed through revelation into a faith that recognizes only fidelity, purity, and sacrifice. Skvorecky is writing about what he calls "the desperate scream of youth" that will always be inside us when we have been touched with the indelible truth of art.

It is a simple story told with complexity and beauty. Skvorecky's writing has rhythms that seem to grow out of the music he loves; long, lyrical sentences relieved by short interior phrases that punctuate and comment upon the central ideas. While the technique has obvious precedents in modern literature, Skvorecky's application of it is musical even in the book's other story, "Emoke," which is not essentially about music. His musical imagery, however, is always close at hand: ". . . her kitchen too was an island of security where she became an artist, a virtuoso with absolute pitch for tastes and odors, like a violinist can tell a quarter tone and even an eighth, not rationally but intuitively, with a sense that others don't have and can't have."

The author's quick, intensive development of the characters in "The Bass Saxophone" and "Emoke" is consummate, his descriptive writing stunning. The most incidental figures seem fully alive and intimately known after only a few strokes of description. The members of the bizarre, almost hallucinatory German orchestra in "The Bass Saxophone" emerge as clear and stark as the characters in a George Grosz drawing. The few minor usage problems in the book, as in "like" for "as" in the above example, may be errors of translation. One serious mistake, "Charlie Bird" for Charlie Parker, whose nickname was "Bird," should have been caught by the editor.

Skvorecky's upper level themes, the importance of jazz in European culture, the difficulties and possibilities of expression under repression, are impressively developed. But the underlying revelation of the book is in the beauty of the climax of "The Bass Saxophone," the young man's blazing recognition of the truth he must follow. Skvorecky enters the current American literary scene as a purveyor of an unusual classicism of feelings and a masterful communicator of his own message.

Louis Armstrong: An American Genius
James Lincoln Collier
Oxford University Press, New York

1984

Louis Armstrong, in the 1920s, changed music once and for all. Before Armstrong, jazz was interesting, and probably important, folk music. Armstrong, the first great soloist, transformed jazz by dint of his genius. Until now, even the best books about Armstrong have barely risen above the quality of fan magazine evaluations, departing from idolatry only for the obligatory notation that Armstrong's artistry declined after his Hot Five and Hot Seven recordings. Collier identifies Armstrong as "the preeminent musical genius of his era." This major critical biography addresses the subject with the seriousness and thoroughness commanded by a figure of such stature.

Collier is provocative. Without attempting to devalue the Armstrong legend, he uses sociology and psychology to cut away the myth and to disclose substance. With careful research and a flair for the ambience, he evokes the times and places that helped mold Armstrong, the underbelly of New Orleans in the Teens, the gangland nightside of Chicago in the twenties, Harlem after the jazz mainstream swept east to New York. And he understands the nature of Armstrong's genius.

He came, in the end, out of himself; and out of that same source came so much more, as if he were a funnel through which twentieth century music had to pass before it could find its way.

There come at moments in history people who gather into themselves threads around them and weave from them a new pattern. Armstrong was one such person.

Collier's musicology, while not as clinically precise as the benchmark chapter on Armstrong in Gunther Schuller's *Early Jazz*, (Ox-

ford University Press, New York, 1968), is helpful in reaching en-
lightenment on the genius of his inventiveness and the workings of
his imagination. Collier occasionally creates just the right metaphor
to explain an element of Armstrong's music-making process, as in
these lines from the author's description of Armstrong's 1924 solo
on "Shanghai Shuffle" with the Fletcher Henderson band: "For the
first eight bars he plays just one note, repeated some two dozen times.
He is not designing cathedrals here, he is driving in tent pegs."

Equally perceptive and accurate musical analyses are found in the
chapters devoted to evaluation of Armstrong's recorded work. But
Collier's primary contribution to Armstrong scholarship and to a
general understanding of the artist and the man comes from his assessment of the effects on a budding genius of family, environment,
and society. That methodology is likely to bring Collier under attack from some quarters as a ruthless iconoclast. But if his evaluations are occasionally harsh, even insensitive, they offer an additional way of looking at Armstrong's creativity and cannot impair
the artist's monumental achievements.

Armstrong's personality, open but unaggressive and dependent
on powerful father figures, developed in Jane Alley and black Storyville. Those sections were dirty, poor, raw, and libertine in an early-
twentieth-century New Orleans noted for permissiveness and for
the abjectness of poverty among its poorest blacks. Pimping, pros-
titution, beatings, and murder—as well as music—were in the air
that the young Armstrong breathed. It was not the sanitized "Glory
Alley" of the motion picture in which Armstrong appeared forty
years later. Collier emphasizes this largely unrestrained atmosphere
as the background for Armstrong's "open expressiveness" as a performer. His mother was lax but wholly supportive. His father was
absent. To compensate, Armstrong found a succession of tough, au-
thoritarian father figures who protected him, made decisions, and
provided approval during each stage of his development.

But Armstrong's most significant need was for applause. Collier
makes the case that the brilliant trumpeter, virtually the inventor of
true jazz improvisation, deteriorated from his peak artistic form of
the late 1920s largely because of that need. As a singer and a showman, Armstrong was enormously popular with masses who could

not have been less concerned with the purity of his art. Indeed, in a theme Collier develops throughout the book, it is clear that Armstrong thought of himself not as an artist but as an entertainer who played the trumpet, sang "and did a fair amount of comedy." It never entered his mind that he had sold out to commercialism, as purists maintain to this day, but that he was providing what his audiences demanded—simply doing his job.

The attitude was typical of his generation of jazzmen and of the tradition, until the advent of bebop, of jazz as entertainment. Pianist Earl Hines often said that he considered himself first and foremost an entertainer. This was the Earl Hines who collaborated with Armstrong in the 1920s on recordings that set new artistic standards and transfigured American music. Yet Armstrong and Hines thought of themselves not as keepers of the flame, but as audience pleasers. Contrast their self-assessments with the view two generations later of Charlie Parker, perhaps the only jazz soloist other than Lester Young whose achievements approach Armstrong's.

Music is your own experience, your thoughts, your wisdom. If you don't live it, it won't come out of your horn. They teach you there's a boundary line to music. But, man, there's no boundary line to art.

Armstrong discovered early in his career that rooms full of people responded eagerly to his singing and clowning. In Collier's words, "the benefit to Armstrong was to be immense, but the loss to jazz was incalculable." The gain to jazz had also been immense, as Collier recognizes, and he speculates for the reader what the music might have become without Armstrong. But he fails to define it, despite a mighty effort incorporating jazz genealogy and deductive reasoning, concluding that:

In the music of the twentieth century, the presence of Louis Armstrong is simply everywhere, inescapable as the winds, blowing through the front door, seeping in the windows, sliding down the chimney. He is a mountain in the path: you can go over him or around him, but you cannot avoid his effect.

In tracking Armstrong's career from playing for the slow-drag dances of pimps and prostitutes in black Storyville dives, to the

Fletcher Henderson Orchestra, to the glories of the Hot Fives and the discovery of pure improvisation, Collier carefully melds musical and cultural factors. He recognizes that Armstrong's special musical qualities—"a razor sharp attack, a broad terminal vibrato, a rich tone"—were simply among the means of expressing what Armstrong had developed by 1922, "that *sine qua non* of a great artist, an individual voice." He likens the instantly identifiable character of Armstrong's work to that of Dickens, Faulkner, Titian, and Van Gogh. Collier's analogies recall a passage from Fred Robbins's moving eulogy at Armstrong's funeral in 1971:

> He was truly the only one of his kind, a titanic figure of his and our time . . . a Picasso, a Stravinsky, a Casals, a Louis Armstrong.

Yet, after the early 1930s, this titan took to showboating, high-noting, clowning, and singing to please his wider audience. There were moments of the musical brilliance in his final four decades, but his magical presence largely subjugated his protean imagination, his inventiveness, his subtlety. The beauty of Armstrong's tone, which reflected his great soul, could not be diminished, and it frequently carried him through substandard solos. His singing (he literally invented jazz singing) was a part of the "individual voice" that made him a universally loved figure. But by 1934 his development as an innovator was ended. Given his achievements, that hardly constitutes a tragedy. But Collier's treatment of Armstrong's decline has the elements of a tragedy, in the classic sense of a basic flaw leading to a character's downfall.

Based on his stringent assessment of Armstrong's work in his final decades, Collier may feel justified in giving summary treatment to the last twenty years of the artist's life. But during those two decades, it must be recalled, Armstrong led bands that were often joyous and that produced, among other fine moments, the glories of his albums of Fats Waller and W. C. Handy compositions on the Columbia label. Regardless of the level of artistic achievement, however, it was a period in which Armstrong was a dominant and influential figure in American life and around the world. Music aside, that phenomenon justifies extensive documentation and analysis.

But Collier has written an invaluable account and evaluation of Armstrong's life and output up to the 1950s. It is admirable for its sympathetic weighing of Armstrong's achievements and shortcomings against the pressures on a lower-class black man who came out of one of the sinkholes of his society.

Riding on a Blue Note
Gary Giddins
Oxford University Press, New York

1983

Gary Giddins's range is impressive. He is of a generation of jazz critics and reviewers reared in the age of rock, most of whose lack of perspective has resulted in some of the most wrongheaded evaluations since the know-nothing apologists of the Dixieland revival of the 1940s.

The pages of *down beat* are awash in these writers' obeisances to the watery deposits of the fusion movement. But Giddins, Robert Palmer, and Peter Keepnews—almost alone among jazz writers of the rock generation—have rounded themselves into first-rate generalists. Of the three, Giddins is the most compendious in his knowledge. Few, if any, other jazz critics have even listened seriously to The Dominoes, much less traced the performance genealogies of the group's members to such unexpected influences as Eddie Cantor and Al Jolson. His consideration of the question of Bing Crosby's minstrel heritage is intriguing, and he is illuminating on the similarities and differences in the piano styles of Jelly Roll Morton and Professor Longhair. His comments on the symbiotic relationship between Jewish songwriters and black jazz musicians in the first half of this century are thought-provoking.

"The blue note is endemic in jazz, blues, and gospel," he writes, "and has settled in every corner of American music, from Tin Pan Alley to Nashville and from symphonies to New Wave rock. Yet it is invisible in Western musicology; a microtone—a wavery pitch between, say, a third and a flat third—can't be notated." So, using the title of Duke Ellington's "Riding on a Blue Note" as the umbrella for this collection of reviews and essays, Giddins finds the "illusory blue note" linking such disparate artists as Elvis Presley, Cecil Taylor, Bing Crosby, Sonny Rollins, Ethel Waters, and Dutch modernist Willem Breuker. Along the way, he offers useful insights: in the chapter on the singer Bobby Blue Bland, for instance, we find Giddins's perceptions of the difference between expectations of the jazz audience (progress and innovation) and the hunger of the blues audience (satisfaction of the tradition), and of why Bland is a champion at delivering what blues fans want:

He is not an intuitive singer, but a master at employing a cache of techniques for the optimum expression of a song's lyrics . . . he does not take overt chances; to do so might imply that his mastery of the tried and true is less than sufficient.

Giddins is convincing in his explanation of why the music of the iconoclastic Ornette Coleman can be effectively interpreted by other players and why that of the more tradition-oriented Charles Mingus has not been. He is less convincing when he introduces into his jazz pantheon Betty Carter, a singer whose abilities have been obscured in a cloud of mannerisms. And he is occasionally just wrong in some of his assessments. To call the self-renewing and unclassifiable pianist Don Ewell a "thumping stride tickler with few original ideas" evinces his unfamiliarity with the artist's work or, worse, close-mindedness. There are times when Giddins assumes too much knowledge on the part of the reader, as when he describes Frank Sinatra's style as including "Dorsey-like vowels" and fails to mention that Charlie Parker's instrument was the alto saxophone. But his evaluation of the contradictions in Sinatra is perfect: "it's difficult to listen to the singer without hearing the clatter of the man," and his Parker scholarship is based on creative listening. Giddins has discovered that Parker's celebrated opening phrases in his

"Embraceable You" solo are a quote from a deservedly obscure 1930s pop song, "A Table in the Corner." And he claims correctly that the quote is an example of Parker's genius for transcending and improving his musical raw materials. He properly excoriates Warner Brothers Records for ignorance and carelessness in including the wrong takes of several Parker performances in its supposedly definitive reissue of his best work from the old Dial label. He raises penetrating and important questions about the music industry, particularly its commercialization of the brilliant guitarist Wes Montgomery, who became a financial success by using a highly stylized but minor part of his talent.

Giddins sometimes falls short in attempting to match words to his ideas and—like most prose writers—fails to approximate in words the sounds of music, as in this effort to catch the essence of a trumpet style: "The best of the teasers was Harry Edison, whose solos came in three basic flavors: beep beep beep, beep beeeep beep, and b'beem'm b'beep." But he often succeeds in evoking the music: "[Trombonist Jack] Teagarden's lazy time, the casual triplets percolating unexpectedly from his warming Texas blues riffs . . ." Passages like that demonstrate his "professional fan's" appreciation of excellence. His tough review of portions of the 1979 Kool Jazz Festival in New York reveals him as a discerning, occasionally acidulous critic: "(Mel Torme's) arrangement on 'Blues in the Night' was the inspired idea of a mediocre musician—it changed tempo and style every eight measures, and was as arty as designer clothes." "Over the cheering, she finishes the song by sobbing the refrain, an extremely uncharacteristic aesthetic mistake. (Sarah) Vaughan is no more an actress than Joan Sutherland, and her crying is not only musically inept but false to the lyric's irony and her own message of strength."

And Giddins has a flair for physical description; on violinist Joe Venuti, for example: "Venuti was built like a cement mixer. When at rest, his jowls were crepe-paper hangings, and his mouth folded into a quizzical, placid smile. When he laughed he roared, and he talked like an extortionist." In fact, Giddins's style is most engaging in his essays and sketches on individual artists. He is spellbinding in

his recounting of the adventures of Charlie Parker's old sidekick, society bandleader, con artist, and born-again trumpeter Red Rodney.
In his portrait of the late saxophonist Art Pepper he treats the sociology, mythology, and political double binds that sustain and en-
tangle the white jazz musician. The chapter on Dexter Gordon incorporates a brief history of the saxophone in modern jazz and
transmits some of the frustration of a major American artist who
finds more acceptance abroad than at home.

While Giddins has a vision that allows him to place music in so-
cietal and political perspective, he has refrained from polemicizing
from racial or political viewpoints when he writes about jazz. He
stakes out a huge territory, virtually all important American popular music that has developed from blues and jazz roots. This book is
a fragmentary approach to the subject, an indication that Giddens
may be the one eventually to provide a major study of the field. In
the meantime his enthusiasm, intelligence, and ability to entertain
in *Riding on a Blue Note* stimulate the desire to hear and appreciate
the music. No small accomplishment, that.

The Music
Reflections on Jazz and Blues
by Amiri Baraka (LeRoi Jones) and Amina Baraka
William Morrow and Company, Inc., New York

1987

When Amiri Baraka listens to music, he hears things that might escape us if we could not depend upon him to point them out with his
eloquent insistence, indignation, and anger. He hears political op-
pression, capitalist exploitation, racist duplicity, and class struggle.
The beauty in the works of the great jazz masters comes to him
transformed through Marxist-Leninist dialectic into ideology and

sociology. That may seem a grim and joyless route to music appreciation, but Mr. Baraka has been following it for more than a quarter of a century in poetry, plays, essays, reviews, and album liner notes. This collection is made up of work from each of those categories. It has the brilliance of Baraka at his analytical best, with musical and extra-musical considerations in balance, as in his essay on Miles Davis. It also has him at his polemical peak, as in this passage, from a piece about the drummer Max Roach, on commercial exploitation of innovations by the great creative giants of black music.

"And each time, the same corporations that had got over exploiting the African's tragic willingness to sell off pieces of weself" (sic) "to anybody who had the necessary trinketry, these same villains would reappear to scoop out the insides of our hearts and sell them for super profits and then convince us that the scooped-out portions of ourselves existed as such because we had never been whole, never, we had only and always at any time in anybody's history been simply Niggers."

When his spleen is less exercised, Baraka is capable of educating with clarity and a sense of history.

"Jazz incorporates blues, not just as a specific form, but as a cultural insistence, a feeling-matrix, a tonal memory. Blues is the national consciousness of jazz—its truthfulness in a lie world, its insistence that it is itself, its identification as the life expression of a specific people, the African-American nation. So that at its strongest and most intense and indeed most advanced, jazz expresses the highest consciousness of that people itself, combining its own history, as folk form and expression, with its more highly developed industrial environment, North America. Without blues, as interior animation, jazz has no history, no memory. The *funkiness* is the people's lives in North America as slaves, as an oppressed nation, as workers and artists of a particular nationality!"

Baraka is largely correct when he writes that . . . "if the non-African-American who played the music had not played it, it would not change the essential history of African-American music." Yet, that position would be strengthened, not weakened, were he willing to allow more than a crumb of recognition of major white jazzmen.

His attempt to downplay the influence of Bill Evans is made ludicrous by the inconvenient fact that Evans, a white man, was the last great mainstream jazz piano innovator in a line of stylistic development that runs from Earl Hines through Fats Waller, Teddy Wilson and Bud Powell to Evans.

Baraka is helpful in explaining the genealogy of the current jazz avant-garde and why he believes social, cultural, and commercial conditions have always made necessary the creation of the next avant-garde movement. He has insights into the work of such geniuses as Lester Young (. . . "underneath Pres's distance he was very very hot.") and Charlie Parker ("He took it from the quarter note, as the main tongue, to the eighth note . . . The point being to make sense at higher and higher speeds!").

He writes about poetry as a form of speech and music, an understanding that is helpful in dealing with his own poetry, which makes up about half of this book. His poems are full of rhythms and subliminal meanings that cannot possibly be grasped in a silent reading. At its least self-conscious, Baraka's poetry has a surprisingly stateliness, as in the love poem, "For Sylvia or Amina (Ballad Air& Fire)." When it attempts to reproduce musical sounds . . . "uuuudeeeelyah uudeeeelyall/yaboom rabbababab . . ." it encounters difficulties that have plagued poets going back at least as far as Vachel Lindsay. At the beginning of the volume, there is a short selection of poems by Mrs. Baraka.

Baraka evaluates music based on its quotient of authentic funkiness, which he convincingly traces to its source in the blues. It is apparently impossible for him to consider music without passing judgment on its makers' presumed political and racial convictions and intentions. This has produced, inevitably, the fiery anger that is the hallmark of his frequently trenchant criticism.

For the reader who is interested simply in learning about the music and who does not go all the way with Baraka on racism, imperialism, and exploitation, his political message can be a barricade. His answer to this objection is that you can't have all of one without all of the other, "Your aesthetic is created by your deepest politics, whether you are *consciously* making political choices as such or not. In other words, what you think of as 'hip' is essentially a political choice."

Years ago, I heard the great bassist Eugene Wright talking backstage at a Dave Brubeck concert with a group of younger musicians. Art Blakey, Horace Silver, and Sonny Rollins were on their minds, and funky music was under discussion. "Absorb it, feel it," Wright told his admirers. "Then get past that funk thing, man, and *all* of music will open up to you."

Baraka has never been able to get past that funk thing, and he may well believe that a musician like Eugene Wright, by expanding his musical aesthetic to encompass more than the social and political, has sold out to the . . . "corporations that . . . scoop out the insides of our hearts and sell them for super profits." But that is not Eugene Wright's problem. Or mine. Or yours. It is Amiri Baraka's.

A Few of My Favorite Things

1976

Isolating a few recordings, a critic runs the risk of indicating that others don't measure up. But there has been an astounding number of great jazz records, and I could quickly draw up another list of equally valuable performances, many even more obscure than some of these. The records are not discussed in order of preference.

BIJOU: Woody Herman (Columbia). Exquisite in every detail, right down to Dave Tough's tom-tom tag. Ralph Burns's flawless arrangement is effortlessly executed by the First Herd, and trombonist Bill Harris is at the full crest of his mastery and humor. I've listened to "Bijou" at least a thousand times since I first heard it. According to the actuarial tables, I have a fair chance of being able to hear it a thousand more. Hooray.

EBONY CONCERTO: Woody Herman (Columbia Masterworks). Igor Stravinsky was inspired to write this for the First Herd, who played it with a panache the piece has never received since. Woody negotiates the tricky clarinet parts with aplomb. "Ebony Concerto" led me to the rest of Stravinsky, for which I am grateful.

YANKEE NO-HOW: Roswell Rudd (Impulse). This is from Rudd's *Everywhere* album, which leaped out at me from the mass of angry shuckin' that was being heralded in the mid-sixties as the New Thing. Rudd had (and has) taste, humor, and a sense of perspective. He is also a hell of a trombone player and a fine composer. "Yankee No-How" is fun to listen to.

WEATHER BIRD: Louis Armstrong, Earl Hines (Columbia). Mind-blowing music. Two geniuses capable of executing any idea, inspiring one another to one of the most exciting stretches of mutual improvisation ever recorded.

FINGERS: Thad Jones, Mel Lewis (Blue Note). The piece de resistance of the *Consummation* album, this is possibly the quintessential big band exploitation of the "I Got Rhythm" changes, certainly right up there with the Ellington/Webster "Cotton Tail." It has a string of excellent solos, but the performance is climaxed by the sax section's lickitysplit unison chorus. Over the years, this piece has been played so often by the band that the tempo has just about doubled from that of the original, and it would be interesting to hear a new recorded version, just to find out how fast reedmen are capable of moving their fingers.

THEN I'LL BE TIRED OF YOU: The Hi-Los (Columbia). The entire *Hi-Los and All That Jazz* album is a highlight of that remarkable singing group's career, which was too short. But in performing Clare Fischer's sensitive arrangement of "Then I'll Be Tired of You," they outdid themselves. The piece is further enhanced by trumpeter Jack Sheldon's bridge, one of the finest eight-bar solos ever recorded. Why Columbia won't reissue this one should be the subject of a Congressional investigation.

FUNKY BLUES: Charlie Parker (Verve). Bird's "Funky Blues" solo from the *Jam Session No. 2* album was the theme for a radio program of music and criticism I did for several years. The more I heard those two choruses, the more it became evident that the solo was one of Parker's deepest blues statements. It is architecturally perfect, profound, and moving in an extremely happy way.

WORK TIME: Sonny Rollins (Prestige). Rollins was beginning to recognize his full prowess and to channel his remarkable abilities like a world class athlete reaching his peak. The energy and invention in his solo on "There's No Business Like Show Business" would have overwhelmed most rhythm sections, but with Max Roach aboard a fine balance was achieved, and the performance takes on monumental proportions. Roach has an incredible drum solo on "Show Business," and pianist Ray Bryant one of the loveliest solos of his career on "There Are Such Things."

WEST COAST JAZZ: Stan Getz (Verve). This would be one of my favorites if for nothing more than Stan's breathtaking a capella introduction to "Shine." But Getz is hot throughout the album, and his heat and drive are matched by Conte Candoli, one of the most underappreciated trumpeters in jazz. Candoli's fresh approach to "A Night in Tunisia" produces a memorable solo. The rhythm section: Lou Levy, Leroy Vinnegar and Shelly Manne. They were hot too. Cool jazz, indeed.

THIS YEAR'S KISSES: Billie Holiday (Columbia). This is probably not prime Billie. But it has a sunny quality that disappeared from her voice not long after she recorded the piece in 1937. It also has a ravishing Lester Young first chorus. His treatment of the changes in the final four bars may be the reason this record is so indelibly printed on my memory.

KIND OF BLUE: Miles Davis (Columbia). Miles's corner-turning 1959 session, full of ideas that helped point the way to the free playing of the sixties and seventies. A landmark album and a milestone band, with John Coltrane, Bill Evans, Cannonball Adderley, Paul Chambers and Jimmy Cobb. The modal and scalar approach turned out to be tutorial, but there is nothing that sounds theoretical or instructional in the performance. This is unpretentious, simple, and profoundly affecting music.

FREE JAZZ: Ornette Coleman (Atlantic). I'm still listening to this one with a sense of adventure and anticipation. The double quartet idea was fraught with so many possibilities for failure that the success of the event is overwhelming nearly sixteen years later. It would have been easy for virtuoso players like bassists Charlie Haden and Scott LaFaro, drummers Ed Blackwell and Billy Higgins, trumpeters Freddie Hubbard and Don Cherry, Coleman and fellow alto saxophonist Eric Dolphy, to cancel one another out, or at least to muddy the music with one-upsmanship. Instead, as repeated hearings make dramatically clear, there is an order and a resiliency to this collective improvisation that any composer would be proud to have written into his symphony. A remarkable achievement, one which stands unapproached in modern jazz. It encouraged legions of would-be free players to try the same thing. Virtually all of them failed. But that's their problem. *Free Jazz* is a must for any serious listener.

LADY BE GOOD: Gerry Mulligan Quartet with Lee Konitz (Pacific Jazz). This is the alternate take that was included in the *Jazz West Coast* sampler in 1955. It is a brief, incendiary performance, one minute and fifty seconds long. Konitz's solo is stunning in its logic and energy, so superior that it puts Mulligan's and Chet Baker's very good statements in the shade. A gem.

INTRODUCING GUS MANCUSO: (Fantasy). Introducing who? Gus Mancuso plays at least a half-dozen instruments well. He was featured on baritone horn on this album, recorded in 1956. He brought such fire, humor, and technique to a cumbersome instrument that it seemed he was in a fair position to become a sort of Sonny Rollins of the baritone; his conception was not unlike Rollins in terms of ideas, attack, and phrasing. For whatever reasons, certainly including the limiting musical atmosphere of Las Vegas, where he later settled, Mancuso never became well known. But on this album, done with a variety of groups in the Los Angeles-San Francisco orbit, he showed that he had it all together and was ready. "Goody Goody" is one of the most aggressively happy performances of the 1950s, with chorus after chorus of brilliant blowing. A bonus is the drumming of Cal Tjader. Yes, drumming. Tjader is a personal and inspirational drummer, and in 1956 he was willing to set aside the vibes and back Mancuso, who was a sort of protégé of his.

DON'T LET IT BOTHER YOU: Fats Waller (RCA). A great instance of Fats's ability to convert a ridiculously bathetic popular song into a joyous jazz performance.

TENNESSEE FIREBIRD: Gary Burton (RCA). You had to act quickly to catch this one; RCA pulled it about two minutes after it was released in 1967. This was vibist Burton's amalgamation of jazz and country, complete with Nashville musicians like Charlie McCoy and the Osborne brothers. The combination worked, and it was worth the price of the album (when you could buy the album) to hear Roy Haynes kicking the kickers along on the title tune. This was fusion music ahead of its time.

KO-KO: Duke Ellington (RCA). Perfection from the 1940 Ellington band.

BRUBECK AND RUSHING: Dave Brubeck and Jimmy Rushing (Columbia). It is possible that working with Rushing brought out the Basie in Brubeck. At any rate, on this album we began to detect the single-line simplicity that Dave had been hiding under a bushel of Brahmsian chords and Bartokian clusters. The quartet accompanied Jimmy to perfection; Brubeck is one of the finest accompanists around, but that fact has somehow escaped general acknowledgement. Paul Desmond has some marvelous solos on this one and Gene Wright and Joe Morello seem to know instinctively what Rushing needs. Mr. Five By Five responds with a set of brilliant, relaxed vocals. Among latterday recordings, this ranks with *The You and Me That Used to Be* (RCA).

JUST ABOUT EVERYTHING: Bob Dorough (Focus). Dorough is apparently too rarified a taste for the general public, although his "Multiplication Rock" music is a hit with pre-schoolers, who know honesty, simplicity, and direct emotion when they hear it, even if it's good for them. The title song here is an ingeniously constructed Dorough original with good lyrics. The album has the best version of Bob Dylan's "Don't Think Twice" since the one Waylon Jennings did for A&M, also in the mid-sixties. It also has a unique reading of Hoagy Carmichael's "Baltimore Oriole." *Just about Everything* is a superb vocal album. Naturally, it was discontinued almost as soon as it was released.

CRAZY RHYTHM: Coleman Hawkins (French *Swing*, reissued on Prestige). This may be Hawk's masterpiece, "Body and Soul" notwithstanding. Recorded in a Paris all-star session with Benny Carter and Django Reinhardt in 1937, "Crazy Rhythm" has two blistering Hawkins choruses in which he builds steadily in intensity and inventiveness to the point where even his amazing solo on "Honeysuckle Rose" from the same date takes a back seat.

A LOVE SUPREME: John Coltrane (Impulse). Coltrane at his most passionate in the post "Giant Steps," pre-mumbojumbo period. This was a religious experience for Trane, and it has the joy and exaltation of religious discovery. The classic Coltrane quartet, with McCoy Tyner, Jimmy Garrison, and Elvin Jones, at its roiling best.

INDEX